Derrida's *Voice and Phenomenon*

Edinburgh Philosophical Guides Series

Titles in the series include:

Kant's *Critique of Pure Reason*
Douglas Burnham with Harvey Young

Derrida's *Of Grammatology*
Arthur Bradley

Heidegger's *Being and Time*
William Large

Plato's *Republic*
D. J. Sheppard

Spinoza's *Ethics*
Beth Lord

Descartes' *Meditations on First Philosophy*
Kurt Brandhorst

Nietzsche's *Thus Spoke Zarathustra*
Douglas Burnham and Martin Jesinghausen

Deleuze's *Difference and Repetition*
Henry Somers-Hall

Foucault's *History of Sexuality Volume I, The Will to Knowledge*
Mark Kelly

Kant's *Groundwork of the Metaphysics of Morals*
John Callanan

Derrida's *Voice and Phenomenon*
Vernon W. Cisney

Visit the Edinburgh Philosophical Guides Series website at
www.euppublishing.com/series/edpg

© Vernon W. Cisney, 2014

Edinburgh University Press Ltd
The Tun – Holyrood Road
12(2f) Jackson's Entry
Edinburgh EH8 8PJ
www.euppublishing.com

Typeset in 11/13pt Monotype Baskerville by
Servis Filmsetting Ltd, Stockport, Cheshire,
and printed and bound in Great Britain by
CPI Group (UK) Ltd, Croydon CR0 4YY

A CIP record for this book is available from the British Library

ISBN 978 0 7486 4421 6 (hardback)
ISBN 978 0 7486 4420 9 (paperback)
ISBN 978 0 7486 4422 3 (webready PDF)
ISBN 978 0 7486 9564 5 (epub)

Contents

Acknowledgements

First and foremost, words cannot sufficiently express my appreciation for the inspiration and support of my family. To my wife, Jody, who has been with me on this journey from the beginning, who has graciously tolerated seemingly countless late nights of work on my part, and who has tirelessly motivated me when my spirit was exhausted; and to my children, Jacob and Hayley, who can always find ways to melt my heart and make me laugh, even when things are at their craziest, thank you. I love you; you are the reasons why I do what I do.

I would like to also express my deep gratitude to Edinburgh University Press, and more specifically, Carol Macdonald. For taking a chance on me, for demonstrating infinite patience when I asked for deadline extensions, and for supporting my work and being in my corner on this project and others, thank you so much.

In addition, I would like to say thank you to Michael Naas, with whom I spoke about this project in the early stages of its inception, and whose enthusiastic expression of support for the project was an inspiration.

Finally, this book would not have been possible without the help and friendship of Leonard Lawlor. I received my first in-depth exposure to Derrida's thinking in Len's spring 2006 seminar at the University of Memphis, centred on the concept of animality in Derrida's works – it was in this seminar that Derrida got his hooks in me. Len's 2002 book, *Derrida and Husserl: The Basic Problem of Phenomenology*, has been a constant touchstone to me over the years and in the writing of this book. I have no doubt that it was Len's backing of this project from its inception that encouraged Edinburgh University Press to pick it up. He provided feedback on early versions of the manuscript, and has been helpful at every step along the way. I am profoundly grateful to Len for his guidance, his support, and most importantly, for his friendship.

Author's Notes

Here are several points the reader should know when reading this book. They are ordered roughly according to their importance.

1. Throughout this text, the citations concerning the text of *Voice and Phenomenon* will each contain three page references. In the first instance the citation refers to Leonard Lawlor's 2011 translation of Jacques Derrida's *La Voix et le phénomène*, translated as *Voice and Phenomenon: Introduction to the Problem of the Sign in Husserl's Phenomenology*. The second reference cites the corresponding page number in David B. Allison's 1973 translation, *Speech and Phenomena, and Other Essays on Husserl's Theory of Signs*. Finally, the third reference directs the reader to the corresponding reference in the original French text. Thus, a standard citation in the book will look like this: *VP*, p. 19/22/23.

2. The only exceptions to this format of citation for *Voice and Phenomenon* will occur when reference is made to Leonard Lawlor's 'Translator's Introduction' or his 'Notes' to his 2011 translation, which only appear in this 2011 version of the text. A citation of Lawlor's material specifically will include only one page number, and thus will look like this: *VP*, p. xxiv.

3. Citations for any of Derrida's texts will appear within the body of this text itself.

4. Husserl citations will follow one of two formats. In the parts of the book where I am exclusively citing Husserl without the analysis of *Voice and Phenomenon* (such as the Introduction and Chapter 1 of this *Guide*), in-text citations are employed. However, once we get into Derrida's analysis in Chapter 2, the in-text citation, even when it is a quote from Husserl, will cite the relevant page number in *Voice and Phenomenon*, followed by an endnote

that points the reader to the corresponding reference in Husserl's text.

5. All other citations, from all other authors, will be endnoted.

Series Editor's Preface

To us, the principle of this series of books is clear and simple: what readers new to philosophical classics need first and foremost is help with *reading* these key texts. That is to say, help with the often antique or artificial style, the twists and turns of arguments on the page, as well as the vocabulary found in many philosophical works. New readers also need help with those first few daunting and disorienting sections of these books, the point of which are not at all obvious. The books in this series take you through each text step-by-step, explaining complex key terms and difficult passages which help to illustrate the way a philosopher thinks in prose.

We have designed each volume in the series to correspond to the way the texts are actually taught at universities around the world, and have included helpful guidance on writing university-level essays or examination answers. Designed to be read alongside the text, our aim is to enable you to *read* philosophical texts with confidence and perception. This will enable you to make your own judgements on the texts, and on the variety of opinions to be found concerning them. We want you to feel able to join the great dialogue of philosophy, rather than remain a well-informed eavesdropper.

Douglas Burnham

Introduction

Why Read this Book?

This book is a reader's guide to Jacques Derrida's 1967 classic, *Voice and Phenomenon*, and it is designed to serve a couple of functions. First, its purpose is to historically situate Derrida's text within the overall body of Derrida's work specifically, and within the larger context of continental philosophy generally. But more importantly, its aim is to help the neo-phytic reader wade through and make sense of a seminal but immensely difficult text in twentieth-century philosophy.

The difficulty of *Voice and Phenomenon* derives from a number of factors. First, Derrida's thought is, in a manner of speaking, parasitic. It arises out of a profound love for and commitment to the tradition of Western philosophy, along with all the problems this tradition has created and encountered. Thus, Derrida's own thought, while highly original and unique, typically takes the form of extended immersions within the thinkers and texts of that tradition, and his own concepts emerge from them. This means that Derrida presupposes of his readers a deep familiarity with these thinkers and their historical roles in that tradition. For instance, in *Voice and Phenomenon*, Derrida's primary interlocutor is Edmund Husserl, the founder of the school of philosophy known as 'phenomenology', both of which will be discussed further below. So in order to read *Voice and Phenomenon*, one must have at least some familiarity with Edmund Husserl, and with the conceptual framework of the tradi-tion he spawned. A lack in this area makes significantly more difficult any meaningful engagement with Derrida.

Second, *Voice and Phenomenon* is difficult in that Derrida often embraces and explores paradoxical lines of thought in his analyses. This is not for the sake of cleverness, nor does it stem from a rebellious desire to destroy the inherited philosophical canon, as some of his most impassioned critics would argue; quite the contrary, in fact. Much of the thrust of Derrida's argumentation consists in his ongoing demonstration that the philosophical tradition is constituted and defined by its contradictory commitments which, despite their oppositional statuses, are nevertheless both demanded by the language of the texts in which they appear. And his originality comes largely from the fact that, while most other historical commentators would seek to water down or overlook one or the other of these commitments in the name of a presupposed ideological and authorial consistency, Derrida draws out and expands upon both, in the name of fidelity to the language of the text and to the tradition in which the text is situated. Therefore, while a standard work of historical philosophical commentary will seek to demonstrate that a philosopher holds to a specific position, and that therefore any apparent occurrences of claims in support of the opposite position are just that, *apparent*, Derrida's 'deconstructive' (a term yet to be explored) reading will attempt to show that the text of the philosopher does indeed demonstrate a commitment to a specific position, but also, an equally forceful and necessary commitment to its contrary. Thus, while the author might very well wish to be committed to a specific concept or view, at the exclusion of its opposite, the language in which he writes operates with rules of its own, which bind him at the same time to the opposing view, and moreover, that this oppositional element is an essential and constitutive factor in the author's thinking. But this requires that we call into question everything that we have always held to be self-evident regarding authorial intention and the way in which we read a text.

The point in Derrida's analyses is to reveal a differential play of force lying behind the very possibility of meaningfulness generally, and hence all constituted, empirical languages, including the language of our tradition; but this cannot be done successfully without allowing for a certain level of comfort with paradoxical thinking. The twists and turns that Derrida makes through the course of a reading are therefore often quite difficult to follow, and he even creates new concepts in order to *think* these turns (which can thereby augment the difficulty for the uninitiated reader). To this revelatory strategy of analysis that reveals the inherently differential structure of meaning, Derrida gives the controversial name, 'deconstruction'.

Finally, and perhaps most frustratingly for the newcomer, Derrida almost never takes a position himself, at least not in the traditional 'either/or' sense of the term. When we read a philosophical text, we typically want to analyse the arguments and figure out the author's position on any given philosophical question. For instance, which is a more certain ground for knowledge, the mind or the senses? Is the soul immortal or does it die with the body? What ought to be the ground of ethical decisions, their consequences or the intentions behind them? In a standard philosophical text, we want to know the author's *position*, and assess his or her arguments *for* that position, so that we can evaluate whether or not the arguments are valid and sound, and hence whether we have good reason to subscribe to that position also. With very few exceptions, Derrida simply does not write in this way. Typically, when one thinks that Derrida can be pinned down on some point, his line of thought will take an unexpected turn and the would-be position slips away. What Derrida will continue to show throughout the entirety of his work (and *Voice and Phenomenon* is one of the first and finest examples), is that there are fundamental commitments and assumptions hiding behind the ways in which our philosophical questions and binary alternatives are formed in the first place, and hence his work will attempt to revitalise the very act of questioning, and thinking, itself. Thus, like a modern-day Socrates, Derrida is something of a *gadfly*[1] on the back of modernity – unsettling assumptions, posing questions, and never content to rest with any would-be answers that would seek to attenuate the complexity that is an inherent feature of the real world – and because of this point, Derrida's thinking is fecund and exciting, a veritable ocean of possibility. But it can also appear hopelessly frustrating to the first-time reader.

With all this in mind, I shall wherever possible provide the historical and philosophical backgrounds necessary to read *Voice and Phenomenon*. I shall not assume that the reader is familiar with the names and histories of Friedrich Nietzsche, Edmund Husserl, Emmanuel Levinas, phenomenology, Martin Heidegger, différance, trace, supplement, etc. Rather, I shall, at the appropriate times, explicate in a comprehensive yet succinct manner, the essentials that the reader needs to grasp in order to approach Derrida's text (beginning, shortly, with a discussion of Husserl). Moreover, I shall endeavour to comprehensibly explicate the necessities for the various paradoxical concepts that Derrida reveals. Thus, I shall help the reader in figuring out just what Derrida's commitments are, revealing the stakes underlying his project, and thereby providing an overarching trajectory that will guide his work throughout his life. When all is said and done, if the reader will grant a modicum of patience and diligence, he or she will possess the tools necessary not only for understanding *Voice and Phenomenon*, but also, I believe, the backbone of all of Derrida's thought, and along the way, a general introduction to continental philosophy. Let us now briefly address the question of *who* Derrida is, and what he is about.

Life and Works[2]

Jacques Derrida is one of the most important philosophers of the twentieth century, one whose influence continues to extend well into the twenty-first, shattering traditional academic and scholarly boundaries as it disseminates. Derrida is a member of that rare class of philosopher whose works enjoy, for better and for worse, a far-reaching sphere of influence – in the arts, in literary theory, in cinema and in architecture, among other arenas. Both culturally and intellectually, Derrida himself represents a conflux of influences. Jackie, as his parents named him, was born in 1930 into a family of Sephardic[3] Jews in El-Biar, a suburb of Algiers, Algeria's capital city. Algeria is located in North Africa, not far east from where the Gibraltar Strait separates it from the south-western part of Europe, at the intersection of two historically imperial religions, Catholicism and Islam. This, and the long history of oscillating conquests it entails, provides Algeria with a rich mixture of cultural influences. During Derrida's childhood, Algeria was a French province, a result of a period of French conquest stretching from 1830–48, and in 1870, Algerian Jews had been granted full French citizenship. Thus, Derrida's upbringing is an amalgam, informed by aspects of African, Arabic, Christian, Jewish and French culture, along with a dose of American pop culture (the name 'Jackie' was chosen by his parents after American actor, Jackie Coogan; as a young man, Derrida changed his name to 'Jacques' because he thought it sounded more authentically French and more sophisticated). This cultural eclecticism is a fact of which Derrida is later proud, referring to himself as 'the purest of the bastards' (*The Post Card*, p. 84). During World War II, as Algeria fell under the authority of the Vichy government, Derrida faced harsh anti-Semitic aggression, including a year-long exclusion from his lycée.[4] He found solace (as well as an appreciation for the subversive and rebellious side of intellectual life) in the writings of authors such as Albert Camus, André Gide, Jean-Jacques Rousseau and Friedrich Nietzsche.

Philosophically, Derrida's background is no less diffuse. As a young student, Derrida was fascinated by French literature, and was interested in pursuing a career in literary studies. Through a series of chance events, after hearing on the radio that Albert Camus, who hailed from Algeria, had attained international success after attending the École Normale Supérieure (ENS), Derrida set his sights on this prestigious school. The ENS is an extremely competitive, highly selective French college dedicated to the education of professors and educators in France. Alan Schrift writes, 'In the context of philosophy, and the academic world more generally, without question the most important *grande école* is the École Normale Supérieure', adding:

Until the middle of the twentieth century, it was a virtual requirement for academic success in France for one to attend the École Normale Supérieure [. . .] and this was particularly true for academic success in a department of philosophy.[5]

Besides Camus, the ENS had been the academic home to generations of French intellectual giants, among them, Jean Hyppolite, Simone de Beauvoir, Henri Bergson, Jean-Paul Sartre, Georges Canguilhem, Louis Althusser and Maurice Merleau-Ponty. Though it took him three years of study and two tries at the entrance exams to secure a spot, Derrida entered the ENS in 1952, and began his prolonged engagement with Husserlian phenomenology, completing a thesis on Husserl's work in 1954 (*The Problem of Genesis in Husserl's Philosophy*, finally published in 1990), publishing in 1962 his own translation of (and 170-page critical 'Introduction' to) Husserl's late essay, 'The Origin of Geometry', and continuing to publish extensively on Husserl until 1967, when he published *Voice and Phenomenon*.

1967 is a watershed year for Derrida, one in which he published not only *Voice and Phenomenon*, but two other groundbreaking texts that set the stage for the project that would come to be known as deconstruction. One is *Writing and Difference*, which collects together many of Derrida's seminal essays on his contemporaries and influences. Many of these essays had originally been delivered in public throughout the early 1960s (often in the presence of the respected figures whom Derrida was critiquing), and had announced to the academic world that Derrida's star was on the rise. The other text of this period is *Of Grammatology*, where Derrida outlines an account of a 'science' of writing which, more accurately, characterises a deep meditation on the very possibility of science itself (or, the 'scientificity of science'), and on the meaning of truth.

Together these three texts introduced deconstruction to the European cultural and academic scene. Of the three, as we shall argue, *Voice and Phenomenon*, the culmination of nearly two decades spent working closely in the phenomenological tradition, is the most important.

In January 1968, Derrida delivered the now-famous lecture titled, simply, '*Différance*', before the Société française de philosophie (The French Philosophical Society). In this lecture he spells out, in brief programmatic language, the structure of argumentation underlying his textual analyses up to that point. Derridean scholar John Caputo playfully says of this lecture that 'for the most loyal deconstructionists', it 'has a status something like the Sermon on the Mount',[6] and he is right, in the sense that it provides a rare glimpse into the theoretical underpinnings of deconstruction, without a prolonged immersion into a specific text or thinker, and so, serves as a constant touchstone for those wishing to grasp the heart of Derrida's thought. The lecture made clear (if it was not so already), that Derrida had fully emerged, and was now officially a mature philosophical powerhouse. 1972 saw another publication blitz by Derrida. He published a second collection of essays and lectures (which included the '*Différance*' lecture), entitled *Margins of Philosophy*. This text reveals a wider body of influences than *Writing and Difference* had – by this time Derrida is focusing more on the work of Martin Heidegger,[7] and demonstrating a much more explicit connection to Friedrich Nietzsche.[8] In addition, some of the essays contained therein (specifically 'The Ends of Man') reveal a more political undercurrent to Derrida's thinking that will mark the whole of his future work. The other two texts from 1972 are *Dissemination* – which contains, in addition to its titular essay, Derrida's most extended discussion of Plato, 'Plato's Pharmacy' – and *Positions*, a short but very important collection of interviews, in which Derrida answers more pointed questions about the strategies and stakes of the deconstructive project.

After this there was no turning back, as Derrida was catapulted to international fame, attaining a level of media and cultural popularity unknown by most academic philosophers. Throughout this decade, Derrida begins teaching in the United States, intermittently holding positions at Yale, Cornell, Johns Hopkins, The University of California Berkeley and The New School for Social Research in New York, and establishing a lifelong relationship with The University of California Irvine, where Derrida's archives are today housed.

Two significant developments occur in Derrida's life and work during the 1970s. First, Derrida's works, from 1974 through 1980, assume a more playful, literary *style*. Given Derrida's own history and comfort in the literary tradition, this might come as no surprise; what *is* a bit surprising, however, is the extremity of the playfulness with which he writes at this time, which incited some of his most ardent criticisms to date. Second, Derrida's work, in publication and in practice, becomes more directly political, and these two developments are intimately connected by the 1974 publication of *Glas*. This text is significant for a host of reasons. The first is that it is Derrida's *most* explicitly literary work of philosophy. The text is divided into two columns, with the left offering Derrida's most extended critical engagement with the German philosopher Georg W.F. Hegel, and the right column dedicated to a reading of French poet and playwright, Jean Genet. The text of each column that opens the book begins, apparently, mid-sentence, and after the fashion of James Joyce's novel, *Finnegans Wake*, each respective column, at the close of the book, loops back onto its own beginning. Each column contains, at times, extended citations of the respective authors, interspersed with Derrida's remarks and interactions, employing varying fonts and sizes of text, sometimes lacing the comments within margins created *inside* the body of text; and each column is thematically related to the other as it progresses. It demonstrates a multiplicity of authorial perspectives, and is cleverly designed to reveal the contamination of the philosophical with the literary, and the literary with the philosophical. Interestingly, however, at no point does the text feel forced or strained to produce its effect. For these reasons, *Glas* is Derrida's most performatively *pure* demonstration of the act of writing which, throughout his earlier publications, he had been attempting to display from within the texts of his interlocutors. Second, it is in this text that Derrida, through engaging with Hegel on the question of the family, begins to address questions of familial relations and responsibility, as well as institutions such as the nation, the state and marriage. (It is also one of the first places where Derrida begins to explicitly address the philosophy of Karl Marx, which he will later examine more completely in *Specters of Marx*.) Put otherwise, Derrida, in the most literarily 'playful' text in his corpus, begins to shift his thinking, and the capabilities of deconstruction, towards a more explicitly political, so-called 'real-world' arena.

Thus it comes as no surprise that it is also in this very same year (1974) that Derrida begins discussing with friends the idea of forming a group dedicated to the preservation and augmentation of philosophical instruction in the French educational system. With Sarah Kofman, Jean-Luc Nancy and Philippe Lacoue-Labarthe, he organised a preliminary conference, and in 1975, Groupe de recherché sur l'enseignement philosophique (GREPH) was officially established. The focus of the group was to bring together educators at all levels who wished to see the instruction of philosophy expanded, more specifically to the earliest, formative levels of pedagogical instruction, and reciprocally, to fight against increasing administrative and political cuts made to existing positions of philosophical instruction. His involvements with GREPH reveal an activist side to Derrida's philosophical orientation, demonstrating at the same time that deconstruction, contrary to what its detractors might say, is not removed from so-called 'real life', but rather, intervenes and operates wherever institutions hold sway. The same 'deconstructibility' that Derrida demonstrates in textual constructions, he begins to reveal at this time, holds for *all* constructions, political, religious, pedagogical, disciplinary, etc. Derrida's writings from this group involvement are collected in the two-volume *Right to Philosophy*.

Throughout the 1980s Derrida begins to publish more extensively on Heidegger's thought, writing a series of essays and lectures ('Geschlecht' I–IV) on various appearances of difference in Heidegger's philosophy – sexual difference, the difference between the 'natural' and the 'technological', and the difference between 'the animal' and 'man' – and in 1987, Derrida publishes *Of Spirit: Heidegger and the Question*, on the matter of Heidegger's use of the word *Geist* ('spirit'), and how it relates to his affiliation with the Nazi party. Then, in the 1990s, Derrida's work trifurcates into three overlapping spheres – the political, the ethical and the religious.[9] In 1989, at a conference at Cardozo Law School entitled, 'Deconstruction and the Possibility of Justice', Derrida delivers the essay, 'Force of Law: The Mystical Foundation of Authority', in which he makes the startling claim, '*Deconstruction is justice*', and, 'Deconstruction is possible as an experience of the impossible . . .' ('The Force of Law', p. 243). Laws are the essential structural elements of any political or governmental systems; but as Derrida attempts to show over a life's work dedicated to the inherently differential (and hence 'undecidable') nature of meaning, both the laws themselves and the specific applications of these laws are themselves constructions which, by their very definition, are always *deconstructible*; or, put otherwise, *pure justice* as such is unattainable. Therefore, it must forever be sought. Deconstruction, he claims, is thus the insatiable pursuit of 'infinite justice' ('The Force of Law', p. 248).

This notion of 'infinite justice' opens nicely onto the religious concerns in Derrida's later writings, demonstrating the essential overlap of these various spheres, as he will argue in *Specters of Marx* (1993) for a 'messianic' structure of experience, but one without a determinate messiah, one that is not the property of any religion, but a structure of pure openness, to what he calls 'democracy to come'. Pure democracy, like pure justice, is impossible, and therefore, it must be relentlessly sought and is always *to come*. At roughly the same time he publishes *The Gift of Death*, one of his only significant interactions with Søren Kierkegaard[10] and with the biblical story of Abraham. Here he analyses the paradoxical structure intrinsic to the notion of 'responsibility' (that responsibility means *both* speaking in one's own voice *and* answering to the demands of one's society), questions of faith and its relation to madness, and its openness to the *wholly other*. This structure of pure openness informs his later writings on animality, hospitality, cosmopolitanism and forgiveness.[11] Through his final years of life, Derrida continues to publish influential and original works. Among them are *The Work of Mourning* (2001), Derrida's collected individual reflections on the deaths of his contemporaries; *On Cosmopolitanism and Forgiveness* (2001), in which Derrida articulates the aporetic nature of forgiveness (that pure forgiveness can only apply in the case of the unforgivable, because an act that would be forgiv*able* entails an economic equivocation such that the act can somehow be redressed, or made right); *Rogues: Two Essays on Reason* (2003), where Derrida once again engages with the question of law and the exception, linking the responsibility for this questioning within the inheritance of the philosophical tradition; and *The Animal That Therefore I Am* (2006 – published posthumously, but based upon lectures and essays that Derrida delivered and published from 1997–2003), in which he aggressively deconstructs the Western tradition's radical distinction between 'the animal' and humankind (a project first opened up in his 1980s Heidegger 'Geschlecht' essays), while at the same time problematising the activist's desire to proclaim a charter of animal rights. This problematisation is not to *maintain* the specificity of human sovereignty over the animals (and he says we must support the motivation behind the demand for animal rights), but rather, because merely extending the concept of 'rights' to animals does nothing to challenge the notion of 'sovereignty' (the problematic concept at root in the mistreatment of animals) at all. In 2002, Derrida was diagnosed with pancreatic cancer, and he died on 8 October 2004. By way of conclusion, we note that Derrida's thought, from beginning to end, is tied together by a deconstructive reflection on the Western concept of 'sovereignty', a concept of self-identity which posits the unmediated purity of an 'ego', or 'subject', or 'soul' that resides at the core of one's being as *one's lord and master*. This notion of sovereignty, in greater and lesser degrees (psychological, political, ethical, religious, etc.), informs all appearances of the worst violence and injustice. The deconstruction of sovereignty begins with his long study of Husserl, culminating in the 1967 publication of *Voice and Phenomenon*.

Voice and Phenomenon

As we shall demonstrate in Chapter 1, there is not a single aspect of French academic culture that remains untouched by Husserlian phenomenology during the time period that Derrida's thought is maturing. Derrida's engagement with Husserl, however, represents an interesting collision and divergence from the standard bifurcated emphases. While, as Michel Foucault notes,[12] Husserl's reception in France results in two basically distinct streams – one rooted in the subject and one rooted in the scientificity of science (the former resulting in existentialism and the latter largely contributing to the 'movement' known as structuralism) – Derrida's work explicitly brings these two ostensibly distinct lines of interest into communication with each other, problematising each through the lens of the other. As just discussed, Derrida begins working on Husserl in 1949, intensifies his studies when he settles in at the ENS in 1952, and begins writing on Husserl in 1953. He completes a thesis on Husserl in 1954 (*The Problem of Genesis in Husserl's Philosophy*), and in 1962, translates into French Husserl's very late essay, 'The Origin of Geometry', writing a substantial introduction to it. In 1963, he writes a review of Husserl's *Phenomenological Psychology*, and in 1964, he delivers 'Violence and Metaphysics', in which he defends Husserl (and Heidegger) against some of the criticisms made by Emmanuel Levinas (a prominent French phenomenologist) in his work *Totality and Infinity*. In 1965, Derrida writes '"Genesis and Structure" and Phenomenology', also writing in that same year a review of the English translations of Husserl's *The Idea of Phenomenology* and *The Paris Lectures*. In 1966, Derrida writes 'Phenomenology and Metaphysical Closure', a critique of the extent of Husserl's project of the purification of dogmas and presuppositions from metaphysics. And in 1967, he writes 'Form and

Meaning: A Note on the Phenomenology of Language'. Throughout these years Derrida is also working through the texts and writing reviews of prominent Husserl commentators and students such as Eugen Fink, J. N. Mohanty and Robert Sokolowski. In the period between 1954 and 1967, Derrida writes, publishes and speaks far more on Husserl and on the phenomenological tradition, than he does on all other areas and figures combined. This interaction culminates in the publication of *Voice and Phenomenon* in 1967, after which time Derrida will not publish specifically on Husserl again.

The significance of this text should not be underestimated. It is at the same time a closure or completion of Derrida's long engagement with Husserl, a treasure trove of discovery and an opening to the entire future of the project of deconstruction. In it, Derrida brings to a conclusion nearly two decades of research on Husserl's thought, and while he refers to Husserl numerous times throughout the remainder of his life, he does so mostly employing, without revising, the theses he articulates in *Voice and Phenomenon*. At the same time, it is here that he first discovers and puts to work the terms, concepts, structures and strategies that will govern his thought for many years to come: différance, supplementarity, trace, archi-writing and the metaphysics of presence. Of the three 1967 texts, Derrida claims of *Voice and Phenomenon*:

It is perhaps the essay which I like most. Doubtless I could have bound it as a long note to one or the other of the other two works. *Of Grammatology* refers to it and economizes its development. But in a classical philosophical architecture, *Voice and Phenomenon* would come first: in it is posed, at a point which appears juridically decisive for reasons that I cannot explain here, the question of the privilege of the voice and of phonetic writing in their relationship to the entire history of the West, such as this history can be represented by the history of metaphysics, and metaphysics in its most modern, critical, and vigilant form: Husserl's transcendental phenomenology. (*Positions*, pp. 4–5; translation modified)

It is *through* this culminating work on Husserl that Derrida *becomes* Derrida; it is here that he finds his own voice and articulates the project that he will christen with the name 'deconstruction'. Hence we can echo Leonard Lawlor's paraphrase of Derrida, when he writes that '*Voice and Phenomenon* contains "the germinal structure" of Derrida's entire thought' (*VP*, p. xi).

Conclusion

This book is designed to help the reader work through *Voice and Phenomenon* for the first time. Chapter 1 discusses the historical context of *Voice and Phenomenon*, by first discussing the historical significance of Husserl's work itself, as it emerges against the backdrop of the nineteenth-century 'crisis of foundations', and as it forms and informs the entirety of the French tradition in which Derrida comes of age. Moreover, we shall deal in summary fashion with the key elements of Husserl's thinking that will occupy Derrida throughout the text of *Voice and Phenomenon*. Chapter 2 then goes on to offer an exhaustive commentary on the text of *Voice and Phenomenon* itself, beginning with the indication/expression distinction from the first *Logical Investigation* and concluding with the structure of supplementarity that closes out the book. Finally, Chapter 3 offers helpful advice for those wishing to work further on Derrida, both in *Voice and Phenomenon* itself and on the later writings as well. It provides two glossaries – one defining key terms in Husserl and in *Voice and Phenomenon*; and the other explicating some of the more important concepts discussed in the writings from Derrida's later period. In addition, it points the reader to further secondary literature, as well as providing helpful advice for the person faced with the difficult task of *writing* on Derrida for the first time.

Nonetheless, this text remains a *reader's guide*; it is meant to be read alongside *Voice and Phenomenon*, but is not meant to be a substitute for the act of *reading* the text itself. Out of the generation of thinkers who emerged in France in the 1960s (Derrida, Deleuze, Foucault, etc.), none so much as Derrida embraced and emphasised the notion of responsibility. To engage with Derrida's text is to engage with the very meaning of responsibility; we have inherited a tradition – literary, ethical, cultural, metaphysical, philosophical – and it is our responsibility to remain faithful to it. However, as Derrida's reading of Husserl demonstrates, often the most faithful fidelity entails an essential act of infidelity. It is in this spirit that we embark upon our faithfulness to the reading of *Voice and Phenomenon*.

Notes

1. In the *Apology*, Socrates famously declares to his jurors that Athens is a great city which is like a great horse that, because of its size, has become

sluggish; he, Socrates, is the gadfly, sent from the god to annoy the horse just enough to breathe some fight back into it, or in other words, to teach it to care once again for the good of its soul.

2. In writing this section, the following sources have been consulted: Leonard Lawlor, 'Jacques Derrida', *The Stanford Encyclopedia of Philosophy*, Fall 2011edn, Edward N. Zalta (ed.), <http://plato.stanford.edu/archives/fall2011/entries/derrida/> (last accessed 27 November 2013); Benoît Peeters, *Derrida*, trans. Andrew Brown (Cambridge: Polity, 2012); Jason Powell, *Jacques Derrida: A Biography* (London and New York: Continuum, 2006).

3. 'Sephardic' is a term that means 'Spanish', and is applied to descendants of Spanish and Portuguese Jews who lived in the Iberian Peninsula until the Edict of Expulsion, issued by Isabella and Ferdinand, in 1492.

4. A French secondary school.

5. Alan D. Schrift, *Twentieth-Century French Philosophy: Key Themes and Thinkers* (Malden, MA: Blackwell Publishing, 2006), p. 195.

6. John D. Caputo, *The Prayers and Tears of Jacques Derrida: Religion Without Religion* (Bloomington and Indianapolis: Indiana University Press, 1997), p. 2.

7. Heidegger's philosophical contribution will be discussed in a little more detail below, but here we will introduce him by saying that he was a student of Husserl, and, with Husserl, is the most important of the phenomenological thinkers. He rose to prominence in 1927 with the publication of *Being and Time*, a work extending the methodology of phenomenology into more basic questions of the meaning of Being. Heidegger is also quite likely the most controversial philosopher of the twentieth century. In 1933, as Hitler ascended to power, Heidegger quickly jumped in line behind the new regime, and was appointed to the position of Rektor of Freiberg University (the equivalent of a President in the American Academy). His level of identification with the more pernicious elements of Nazi orthodoxy remains a matter of scholarly controversy to this day.

8. Nietzsche is a German philologist from the late nineteenth century, who is *far* more well-known for his work in philosophy than in philology. Born in Röcken in 1844 to a long line of Lutheran ministers, Nietzsche is most famous for: (1) his proclamation that 'God is dead', which is to say, that Western culture, whether it knows it or not, has lost the transcendent absolute as its centre of value; (2) relatedly, the history of the West as one of a progression of nihilism, of life turned against the

living, emphasising the negative, death and self-destruction; (3) his genealogical analysis of the concepts of good and evil, a methodology which is adopted and adapted by Michel Foucault in his archaeological histories of truth systems and genealogical analyses of power structures; (4) his concept of the 'will to power' as the fundamental impulse for expansion, inherent to all life; (5) the *Übermensch* (*Overman*), posited as a *post-human* stage of humanity, having overcome its self-loathing, self-limiting, resentful and self-destructive tendencies; (6) the eternal return, a reassessment of the nature of time; (7) finally, the essential metaphoricity behind all 'truths', which, Nietzsche claims, are in fact *deceptions* which have coalesced and solidified to the point that a culture *forgets* that they were useful *deceptions* to begin with.

9. This is a *bit* of a simplification, as Derrida's work is, all along, concerned with questions in these areas; nevertheless, it is at this time that he makes the concerns explicit, and ties the three together into a series of more straightforwardly linear and argumentative essays and talks.

10. Nineteenth-century Danish religious thinker, who broke sharply with the predominant Hegelian philosophy of his day. Kierkegaard went largely unnoticed as a philosopher during his own life, but was profoundly influential on existentialist thinkers in the early to mid-twentieth century. Derrida frequently speaks fondly of Kierkegaard, but rarely engages closely with his thinking.

11. Many of these topics will be discussed more extensively in the section of Chapter 3, titled 'Aporias: Derrida's Later Concepts'.

12. This will be explored in greater detail in Chapter 1.

1. Historical Context[1]

On Beginning

Approaching *Voice and Phenomenon* for the first time and situating it historically is challenging for a few very important reasons. First, as we said above, Derrida's text itself is immersed in a very close reading of the body of thought of *another* thinker, Edmund Husserl, which means that we must familiarise ourselves with that body of thought as well. But, on top of this, Derrida's *own* reading of Husserl arises within a specific French cultural and academic scene that requires a fair amount of contextualisation. Finally, *Husserl's* thought too is radical, revolutionary and, just like Derrida's, it emerges within a specific period of time, complete with its own sets of crises and concerns. So, in order to genuinely understand *Derrida's* concerns and make sense of *Voice and Phenomenon*, we must situate not only his own milieu, but also that of Husserl as well. These are the aims of this chapter.

The Crisis of Foundations[2]

Strictly speaking, the expression 'crisis of foundations' indicates a specific historical period of crisis in the philosophy of mathematics, coming to articulation in the late nineteenth century and continuing well into the twentieth. However, the mathematical form of this crisis is in point of fact a smaller version of a much larger problem – namely, the articulation of the problem of founding the very possibility of meaning and truth – and it concerns the relationship between philosophy, ethics, logic and the sciences.

There is a long-standing history of crises in the Modern period of philosophy. Descartes' *Meditations on First Philosophy* is philosophy's attempt to right itself as the foundational, unifying discipline, against the backdrop of theological and epistemological scepticism becoming increasingly prevalent in the sixteenth and seventeenth centuries, and in light of the Copernican Revolution, which had inadvertently called into question the authority of the Church (and by proxy the philosophical tradition) on matters cosmological, ontological and epistemological. This project of the reinstatement of philosophy would find its culminating achievement in the philosophy of Georg Wilhelm Friedrich Hegel, who at the outset of the nineteenth century, attempted to formulate a comprehensively rational ontological system encompassing the entire breadth of development in the unfolding of consciousness, in the sciences, in the arts and in culture, in religion, in nature and in history itself, by way of an explication of a strictly logical structure. Hegel's thought attempted to rethink the entire history of history as a systematic process of development, incorporating every significant moment and thinker, every important rejection, opposition and battle, as a necessary part of the overall development. This process of development, opposition and reconciliation is summed up in the word 'dialectic'. Hegel thus sought to make right once and for all what had been called into question in a radically fundamental way in the period up to and including Descartes, once again situating philosophy in its rightful place as the unifying, systematic thought of the whole of Being.

It should come as no surprise that, being philosophy's most systematic edifice yet achieved, Hegelianism also had the farthest distance to fall, and there were many factors that contributed to its undoing over the course of the nineteenth century. Ludwig Feuerbach, a follower of Hegel, sought to purge Hegel's thought of its more spiritual and idealistic elements, and this trend was continued by Karl Marx and Friedrich Engels (also early followers of Hegel). Marx and Engels transformed the dialectic from an idealism to an atheistic materialism, reinterpreting the historical progression of thought as the historical opposition and resolution of class struggle, culminating in the modern industrial revolution, which had created a self-alienated species of humanity, consisting of a bourgeois middle class and a vast disempowered and impoverished working class, all in the service of capitalism, a process, they argued, which was at a historical end. On the religious side, Søren Kierkegaard rejected Hegel for other reasons, though reasons not drastically different from those of some of his atheistic counterparts such as Arthur Schopenhauer. Specifically, Kierkegaard argued that the overwhelmingly abstract systematicity of Hegel's thought ignored or even disallowed what was most important about existence, namely, the irreducible and irreplaceable singularity of the individual (and for Kierkegaard, this related to the individual believer's relationship to God, who, for Kierkegaard was an absolute singularity unencumbered and inassimilable by Hegelian 'Rationality').

In addition to these philosophical cracks in the system, a final blow was delivered once again, as it had been in the early Modern period, from the sciences; this occurred when, in 1859, Charles Darwin published *On the Origin of Species*. Though he died in 1831 (a full twenty-eight years prior to Darwin's explosive text), Hegel's philosophy of nature, though dialectical and progressive, was decidedly anti-evolutionary. While he allowed for a temporal progression of life on earth, and even variations within the specific 'Concept' instantiated in different animals within the same genus (what intelligent design apologists call 'microevolution', for instance, that spiders *evolve* into different species, while nevertheless remaining spiders, etc.), his thought forbade the development of more complex forms from out of simpler forms. A Concept may contain various contingencies with regard to the particulars housed under it, but a Concept does not become a different Concept altogether. Thus, the scientific realisation of Darwinian natural selection threw into a tailspin the absolute systematicity of Hegel's thought, and once again challenged the once seemingly unconquerable authority of philosophy generally.

These cracks in the system, in tandem with the self-alienation of the industrial/technological age as diagnosed by Marx, gave way to an overall cultural sense of the depletion of spirit and of meaning. Friedrich Hölderlin, a nineteenth-century German poet, wrote of the loss of the gods, lamenting that they seem to care little 'whether we live or do not', while Fyodor Dostoevsky, a Russian novelist, embodies this spirit of aimless self-alienation in novels such as *Notes from Underground*, *Crime and Punishment* and *The Brothers Karamazov*. Friedrich Nietzsche summed up this cultural spiritual collapse, and the era of nihilism which he feared accompanied it, with the forceful phrase, 'God is dead'.

In the fields of mathematics as well, there was an overall revolutionary sense of having had the rug pulled out from beneath, and the necessity for re-establishing foundations became all the more urgent. Again, this was a result of a 'perfect storm' of factors. The emergence of non-Euclidean geometry, thanks to advances made in mathematics by Carl Friedrich Gauss, János Bolyai, Bernhard Riemann and Nikolai Lobachevsky; the climaxing controversy over negative numbers (though widely accepted in Asian mathematics since before the common era, Western mathematicians had, by and large, rejected negative numbers as 'absurd' continuing up into the nineteenth century); and finally, the advances in calculus by Karl Weierstrass (who abolished the notion of the infinitesimal by rooting the foundations of differential and integral calculus in number theory), called into question the foundations of number theory itself. Thus, the question 'what is a number?' becomes a pressing one for philosophers at this time, and it is one taken up by Gottlob Frege and by Edmund Husserl, and in convergence with the overall sense of crisis in the sciences and in culture at this time, is the issue that lies at the origins of the historical fragmentation of philosophy into the traditions of what we now call 'analytic' and 'continental' thought.

Frege and Husserl: The Meaning of 'Meaning'[3]

There is a standard 'story' regarding the early interactions between Gottlob Frege and Edmund Husserl. In 1884, Frege published his *The Foundations of Arithmetic*, a tremendous event in the history of philosophy, followed in 1891 by the publication of Husserl's *Philosophy of Arithmetic*. The two philosophers clearly read and responded to each other. Husserl's book contains a substantive critique of Frege, and Husserl sent his text to Frege for remarks, spawning a correspondence between the two. Frege in turn published, in 1894, a critical review of Husserl's book, after which time the two broke communication for fifteen years. As the story goes, the early Husserl espoused a theory that was dangerously close to 'psychologism', a broad term designating any position that holds that some set of non-psychological facts is reducible to laws of psychology. With respect to logic and mathematics, psychologism holds that, as all logical operations (deduction, inference, proof, etc.) are processes of *thought*, taking place within a human mind, then all of logic (and by extension, mathematics as well), is in fact a subspecies of the field of psychology, and is therefore reducible to the empirically observable operations of the mind. In other words, the laws of logic are in fact simply laws regarding the *proper* exercise of reasoning, and since reasoning is a process of thinking, and thought occurs in accordance with the laws of psychology, logical claims tell us more about the speaker's *brain states* than they tell us anything about *a priori*[4] truths. For reasons that may be obvious, such views are widely rejected by philosophers, as they seem to place the operations of mathematics (which since at least the time of Pythagoras has been held to reveal timeless truths) at the mercy of the empirically observable laws of nature. As the anti-psychologistic thinker would argue, the truths of logic and mathematics (the Pythagorean Theorem, for example) are *timelessly* true, meaning that they were true long before there were ever cognising human minds present to be aware of them, and will be true for all of eternity after we are gone. There are, to be sure, logicians and geometers who discovered, at some specific point in history, the *truth* of those *truths*, but this in no way detracts from the fact that when I claim that in any right triangle, the square of the hypotenuse is equivalent to the sum of the squares of the two legs, I am uttering an essential *truth* about a geometrical relation, which is in no way *dependent* upon my own cognition of it.

The early Husserl, so the story goes, was committed to a position dangerously close to psychologism. Frege read Husserl's book, and wrote a scathing critique of it, after which time Husserl repented his naïve psychologism, beginning his 1900–1 *Logical Investigations* with his famous 'Critique of Psychologism', which would become the *definitive* argumentation against psychologism in Europe for a long time to come. Then he was off and running with the phenomenological method, thanks in no small part to the helpful critical insights of Frege. In other words, the continental tradition is deeply indebted to Frege, the founder of the analytic tradition, for righting an egregious wrong in Husserl's thought at the outset, thereby making the foundations of the phenomenological project possible. Such is the story, but like most black and white stories, it masks a reality far more complex.

In *The Foundations of Arithmetic*, Frege proclaims that he has 'kept to three fundamental principles' in the work, two of which are 'always to separate sharply the psychological from the logical, the subjective from the objective' and 'never to lose sight of the distinction between concept and object', claiming that, 'it is a mere illusion to suppose that a concept can be made an object without altering it'.[5] A *concept* for Frege is predicative (meaning that it is a categorial designation that can be applied to multiple objects), while an *object* is a singular thing in the world, which may or may not fall under the concept. It is for this reason that Frege distinguishes yet a third term, 'idea', which is distinct from both concept and object, and applies only to subjective representations. We can see then that when Frege claims that one cannot make a concept into an object without altering it, he means that when a concept becomes an *idea*, represented within a human mind, it is thereby 'corrupted' by the subjective sphere. Here we can already draw a sharp distinction between Frege and Husserl in that from the beginning of his career to the end of his life, Husserl will be interested in the reality that it is only *ever* as an object that a concept is given. In other words, concepts, however objective, ideal or *omni-temporal* they may be, only ever *light up* in the consciousness of a knowing subject. And it is precisely this point that interests Husserl so much. With this distinction in mind, let us look to their respective concepts of 'number' so as to determine the extent to which the early Husserl was and was not close to some form of 'psychologism', as this will highlight a very important point in the interests and motivations of the early Husserl.

For Frege, the concept of 'number' is what he calls a second-order concept, founded upon the 'equinumerosity' of comparable groups. Suppose I have several items in my pocket: coins, a tissue, keys and a pack of mints. If I now ask, 'How many are in my pocket?', the correct answer will be drastically different depending upon *what* precisely we are talking about, whether items generally, or coins, or keys, or mints, etc. The precise *first-order* concept in question – 'keys in my pocket', 'coins in my pocket', etc. – will determine the *number* that here applies. So 'number' is a second-order concept, according to Frege, because it is a concept that is applied according to a more elemental concept. Now, let us look at the *equinumerosity* part of our definition. Suppose I say, 'I have five pennies in my pocket.' What does this mean for Frege? We have asserted, Frege claims, that the concept 'pennies in my pocket' accords with the concept 'five'. This in turn means that the concept 'pennies in my pocket' is equinumerous with the infinitely conceivable set of concepts under which five objects fall; for instance, 'ants on my porch', 'cents in a nickel', 'days in a work week', etc. In other words, that there are five pennies in my pocket means, for Frege, that if we were to compare the set of pennies in my pocket with the set of days in a work week, there is a direct, one-to-one correspondence between the two sets. 'Five' is just the second-order concept extended to all conceivable sets containing five objects.

Husserl strenuously rejects Frege's definition of number, claiming that 'its results are of a type that can only make us wonder how anyone could even provisionally take them to be correct' (*Philosophy of Arithmetic*, p. 128). For Husserl, to cite *equinumerosity* as the constitutive defining element of number is to already invoke a concept of number – it is to say that this set of objects contains the same *number* of objects as these or those other sets. But this just implies that we know *how many* objects those sets have, for we must know the *number* within those sets in order to know whether or not the set of things in question has the *same number*. What is significant about groups of five, Husserl argues, is *not* that they have the *same number* of things, but rather, that they each have a *precise* number, namely, five, of those things. In *Philosophy of Arithmetic*, Husserl argues that to arrive at an authentic concept of number requires that we analyse the intuitive processes by which we come to possess such concepts, and these are obtained by acts of serial enumeration, wherein a group of things presents itself to us as in some sense *related together* and *to be counted together* as opposed to those things present in our field of consciousness which are demarcated *from* those things as *not to be counted*. Let us return to our 'items in my pocket' example. Suppose I were to remove from my pocket its contents (the mints, keys, tissue and coins), and place them on the desktop. Of these items, the pennies in particular *present* themselves *to* me as related in a particular way, and my conscious field then excludes the remaining items for the purpose of enumerating the pennies. Now, what is presented is a *something* **and** a *something* **and**, etc., up to the enumeration of *five* such *somethings*, from which I derive the concept of 'five'. 'Five' then is an *abstraction* (Husserl uses the word 'abstractum') derived from and founded upon my experience of groups of *five* somethings.

It is crucial to understand, however, that the concept I now possess, and which presents itself *to* me, is and always was for Husserl an *objectivity*; that there are *five* pennies is not an arbitrary point, and the subject is not free to see it or number it however he or she chooses. Furthermore, the rules that govern the combination of this group of five pennies from my pocket with the group of *two* pennies on the desk, forming a group of *seven* pennies total, are neither arbitrary nor subjective either. The laws, functions and operations of arithmetic are, in other words, in no way dependent upon or reducible to empirical facts of human psychology. We merely come to *possess* those concepts, Husserl claims, by way of empirical, intuitional acts. In other words, I may come to know what 'two' is by way of an empirical presentation of two *things*, but then, the relation between *two* and *two*, or that the *totality* of two *twos* is and always will be equivalent to *four*, does not depend upon my *representations* at all. We can therefore assert that Husserl is not, even early on in his career, committed to a psychologism of the more pernicious sort outlined above, which *reduces* the laws of logic and mathematics to the laws of psychology.

What, then, do we make of the accepted story, and what, more importantly, of Husserl's own apparent repentance when, in the Foreword to the *Logical Investigations*, he claims, 'As regards my frank critique of the psychologistic logic and epistemology, I have but to recall Goethe's saying: There is nothing to which one is more severe than the errors that one has just abandoned' (*Logical Investigations*, p. 3)? Is there *no* merit at all to the psychologistic charges directed towards the early Husserl, even those that come from Husserl himself only a few years later? This seems unlikely, so let us turn back to what Husserl himself says:

Where one was concerned with questions as to the origin of mathematical presentations, or with the elaboration of those practical methods which are indeed psychologically determined, psychological analyses seemed to me to promote clearness and instruction. But once one had passed from the psychological connections of thinking, to the logical unity of the thought-content (the unity of theory), no true continuity and unity could be established. (*Logical Investigations*, p. 2)

In the *Logical Investigations*, then, Husserl once again points to the empirical *acts* of enumeration, according to which one abstracts the concept of 'number', and even in the passage just cited, he still, in 1900, does not seem to find that account unsatisfactory or unacceptable, nor does he seem to back off from his claims from *Philosophy of Arithmetic*. What he *does* find problematic arises from difficulties which he himself discovers in the later chapters of *Philosophy of Arithmetic*, namely, the *foundation* of the objectivity he seeks and its relationship to the *subjectivity* of the subject.

The first part of *Philosophy of Arithmetic* is titled 'The Authentic Concepts of Multiplicity, Unity, and Whole Number', and Husserl makes an important distinction between *authentic* and *inauthentic* presentation (a distinction that appears only a few times in the two volumes of the *Logical Investigations*, and then only in a drastically modified or critical way). An authentic presentation, according to Husserl in *Philosophy of Arithmetic*, is one given as immediately present to the subject, while an *in*authentic presentation is one that Husserl refers to here as 'symbolic', meaning, given only by way of symbols or indirect representations. An example of an *authentic* presentation, Husserl says, would be when we are actually standing in the presence of a house, looking directly at it, thus having an experience of the house, while an example of a *symbolic* or *inauthentic* presentation would be when a friend is describing the house to us, through which we form images of the house in our mind. For Husserl in *Philosophy of Arithmetic*, it is possible to have authentic presentations of the concepts of 'five', or 'two', or 'three'. This is because consciousness is capable of directly cognising, all at once, that *this particular group* (of pennies, for example), falls under the concept of 'five'; I am capable of recognising, in an intuitional act, the presence of *five* pennies. However, this becomes more difficult the higher up the number scale one ascends. Can I see eighty-seven things *as* eighty-seven things? No; but if not, then how can I ever hope to have an authentic concept of 'eighty-seven'? And for Husserl, the answer is simply, *it is impossible*. But then the question arises, how then is it possible that I can understand what it means when I see the representation of the equation, $53 + 34 = 87$? Not only can I *understand* it, but I can moreover almost immediately recognise that it is *true*. This seems problematic on Husserl's account.

Husserl's claim is that arithmetic operates by way of *symbolic* representations. The numeral '5' is a symbol representing the concept 'five'. For a handful of number concepts (up through, Husserl says, 'twelve'), it is possible for me to have authentic presentations of them. However, the moment I symbolise them with numbers and enter them into an arithmetic operation, they pass into the realm of symbolic representation. And once I have the basic grasp of the rules governing these symbolic operations, I am then capable of calculating sums for as many addends as I like, and in quantities as large as I like. Thus, it is not the case that I have *no* access at all to these concepts. Once I have a basic understanding of the patterns of symbolisation and of the signs that indicate collecting and dividing of groups, I do have the capability of representing the concepts. However, these formulations will always be only *symbolic representations*, and hence *can only ever* be mere *inauthentic* presentations of the concepts towards which they point. This distinction is brought to the fore by Husserl in Chapter X (the beginning of the second part) of *Philosophy of Arithmetic*, and he spends the rest of the book (just over one hundred pages) trying to resolve the difficulties that it raises, more specifically, the methodology by which enumeration, calculation and higher operations of mathematics might be grounded upon the basis of those elemental *authentic* presentations. In the end, none of his results are satisfactory as far as Husserl is concerned: 'The fact that in the overwhelming majority of cases we are restricted to *symbolic number formations* forces us to a rule governed elaboration of the number domain in the form of a *number system . . .*' (*Philosophy of Arithmetic*, p. 299).

The problem, as Husserl will later say in the Foreword to the *Logical Investigations*, is the 'relationship, in particular, between the subjectivity of knowing and the objectivity of the content known' (*Logical Investigations*, p. 2). How does one move from a foundation of *authentically given*, or indubitable elemental concepts, *by way of* a repertoire of symbolic representations and functions, *to* a higher-order knowledge that is also objective and indubitable? In other words, how does thought proceed *from* the subjectively given *to* and *as a foundation of* the objectivity of the objective? This is Husserl's question. In other words, at no point does Husserl suppose that the objective *really just is* subjective (and hence relativistic). The objective nature of mathematics as such is never called into question. (This is why Husserl is never committed to a more pernicious form of psychologism.) What *is* called into question is the way in which, starting from the foundation of subjectivity, one attains the level of the objective. It is this question that Husserl never satisfactorily answers in *Philosophy of Arithmetic*, and Husserl comes to recognise that the problem lies in formulating the question in terms of bridging a presupposed gap between a knowing subject and an object of knowledge by way of mediation or representation. The recognition of this limitation forces Husserl to move away from the *authentic* vs *symbolic* distinction, alluded to above. But in a more general way, *his thought begins to shift towards a non-representational reformulation of the meaning of meaning itself.*

We conclude this section by summing up the origins of the split between the analytic and continental traditions in philosophy. We have discussed the 'crisis of foundations' which begins to arise in the mid-nineteenth century across all disciplines. A convergence of factors – cultural, intellectual, religious, scientific, mathematical, etc. – resulted in immense and rapid advances in knowledge, which simultaneously called into question all of the dominant and traditionally accepted foundational principles, with the overall effect being the general breakdown of orthodoxy across the board. One of the more significant forms of these crises occurs in the mathematical fields which, since Plato, have been understood as exemplars of timeless and eternal truth. Two German philosophers, Gottlob Frege and Edmund Husserl, both sought to provide a rigorous philosophical foundation for mathematics. Frege, from a desire to avoid all forms of relativism, sought, as he said, to rigorously distinguish the subjective from the objective, and the concept from the object, claiming, furthermore, that one cannot make a concept into an object without thereby altering it in some way. The methodology he formulated on the basis of these foundational principles – a methodology of linguistic analysis and a rigourisation of symbolic notation (which made possible revolutionary advances in the fields of logic) – spawned the tradition that would come to be known as the 'analytic' tradition in philosophy, taken up by Bertrand Russell, Ludwig Wittgenstein and subsequently by Rudolf Carnap and Willard Van Orman Quine.

On the other side of this divide lay Husserl. For Husserl, such a radical distinction between subject and object is insufficiently rigorous in that, however *objective* the objectivity of knowledge may be, it is nevertheless the case that that knowledge always arises within the relationality of the intentional act. Husserl, like Descartes and Kant before him, will attempt to situate philosophy as *the* foundational science, foundational in that it provides an apodictic account of meaning, which provides the basis for all other scientific endeavour in all the other fields of study. And he seeks to do so by eliminating all presuppositions, and abolishing the break between thought and object established by Descartes. The philosophical methodology he established was the phenomenological method, and it lies at the origin of the 'continental' tradition in philosophy, taken up by Martin Heidegger, Maurice Merleau-Ponty and Jacques Derrida.

Husserl uses the term 'phenomenology' (a term first employed by Georg W. F. Hegel), to characterise what Husserl understands to be philosophy in its most rigorously scientific form, as the study of the structures of consciousness and the very possibility of meaningfulness generally. In the name of a return to *the things themselves* (*Logical Investigations*, p. 168), he argued that we must *bracket*, or put into suspension, all questions regarding the *actual existence* of a world of objects external to consciousness. Since Descartes,[6] the bane of the philosopher's thought was the epistemological[7] problem of ascertaining and assuring the correspondence of one's *experience* of the world with the *actual nature* of the world. In other words, *given that my experience of the world is filtered through my senses and cognitive faculties, how can I ever be absolutely sure that my experiences accurately reflect the world?* The thrust of Husserl's project consists in his groundbreaking way of addressing this problem. Put briefly, so long as philosophy begins from the presupposition that the subject is ontologically distinct from the world of objects in which it finds itself (what Husserl called 'the natural attitude'), once we have radically divorced thought from being, there is *no way* of ever again bridging that gap.

This is why the Modern period begins with the absolute certainty of Descartes, and ends in the radical scepticism of David Hume a mere 135 years later. If we wish to give to philosophy its proper role of assuring the absolute foundational certainty necessary to ground the other sciences, we must remain purely and completely within the sphere of *immanence*.[8] This means we must *bracket* (not doubt or deny, but suspend) any and all questions as to the *real* existence of the *real* world, keeping our sights set rather upon the relations constituting the intentional[9] acts themselves, and what makes those acts possible and meaningful. Given that this sphere of experience, as Husserl argues, is absolutely certain, and given that *meaningfulness* generally is the basic foundation of all sciences, it is only phenomenology, Husserl argues, that can restore philosophy to its rightful place as the foundational science that it has, since Plato and Aristotle, believed itself to be.

In the next few sections, we will look at some of the important distinctions, problems and discoveries that occupy Husserl throughout the remainder of his life; these concepts will be the ones most central to Derrida's analyses in *Voice and Phenomenon*, but, at the same time, in discussing them, we will be providing an introductory overview of the Husserlian project.

Indication and Expression

The opening chapter of Husserl's First *Logical Investigation* is titled 'Essential Distinctions', and it is therefore appropriate that we should begin by noting an essential distinction in the meaning of the term 'essential' itself. Sometimes when we use the term 'essential', we mean to emphasise the *importance* of the concept in question. For instance, we might say, 'It is absolutely essential that you pay attention to what I'm saying.' This colloquial use of the term 'essential' is founded upon a more technically precise sense, in which what we mean to invoke is the *essence*, or characteristic nature, of the thing in question. Thus, we might say, for example, 'The essential elements of an ethical life are compassion, sensitivity, tolerance and generosity,' by which we mean that these are the *defining* characteristics, and anything else (commands, duties, responsibilities, *rules*, etc.) is founded thereupon. Husserl's use in this opening chapter is playing on both senses of the term, but more specifically it points to the second. In other words, Husserl wants the reader to note a difference *in essence* between the two terms he explicates.

Those two terms are 'indication' and 'expression'. There is an ambiguity, Husserl notes, within the term 'sign'. Oftentimes we treat the words 'sign' and 'expression' as synonyms, when in fact there is another kind of sign, the *indication*. All signs are signs for something; in other words, every sign is a place marker of something meaningful, but the status of this relation takes two different forms. The first is the indicative form. A sign is an *indication* when it points the knower away from the sign itself to something else, which is separate of the sign which serves as its indication. Sometimes this is a deliberate *pointing*, as when a nation flies its flags at half mast in order to indicate a national spirit of solidarity and mourning. Sometimes it is a natural *pointing*, as when we interpret our child's fever to signify that there is something wrong with her body, or when we interpret animal tracks in our vicinity to signify the recent presence of animal activity. In an even more general sense, *any* mark written on a paper is an indication. Whether it is a meaningful word, a meaning*less* word, a word in a foreign language or a child's scribblings, the mark is an *indication* that someone was here and *did this*. Of indications, Husserl claims:

In these we discover as a common circumstance the fact that certain objects or states of affairs *of whose reality someone has actual knowledge* indicate to him *the reality of certain other objects or states of affairs*, in the sense that *his belief in the reality of the one is experienced* (though not at all evidently) *as motivating a belief or surmise in the reality of the other.* (*Logical Investigations*, p. 184)

An indication is a sign that *points to* something else, something whose meaning is distinct from the sign itself.

The expression, Husserl says, is a meaningful sign. Here Husserl sets forth a rigorous definition, isolating strictly the communicatively meaningful sort of sign. Oftentimes, we might refer to someone's facial configuration as an 'expression': 'His face had the oddest expression', for instance. This colloquial use of the term, however, ignores the essential nature of the expression, according to Husserl. Husserl's definition is as follows:

We shall lay down, for provisional intelligibility, that each instance or part of *speech*, as also each sign that is essentially of the same sort, shall count as an expression, whether or not such speech is actually uttered, or addressed with communicative intent to any persons or not. (*Logical Investigations*, p. 187)

The expression is the linguistic sign. In its use, it involves the 'intent to put certain "thoughts" on record expressively, whether for the man himself, in his solitary state, or for others' (*Logical Investigations*, p. 188). An individual's facial configuration may indeed say a great deal about a person's psychological or intentional states. A pinkish or reddish hue to her cheeks may indicate anger or embarrassment; a sudden bout of sweating may indicate nervousness; a sudden onset of pallor may reveal intense shock; etc. But while these signs may tell us something, they do so only by way of *indication*; they *point to* a state of affairs *beyond* themselves. An expression, on the other hand, is a sign that points directly to a sense or meaning.

But this brings us to our next point. In the expressive or communicative act, we *indicate* to the listener or listeners some fact or facts about our internal states. The following configuration of signs, for instance: 'I am very happy to be here today', points all who are hearing or reading that configuration to the internal state of my mind when I uttered the signs. The *literal* sense of the term *ex-pression*, after all, means a *pressing outwardly*. In other words, in the communicative act, I look inwardly to my emotional, psychological or intentional states, and in my desire to make those states known to someone else, I employ various signs, themselves meaningful, and externalise them. I do all of this with the hope that the listener will *hear* and *understand* the signs, and thereby also be made privy to my internal states. The expression serves to *indicate* to my listeners my internal states. Therefore, even in cases where the sign is an *expression*, it is used in an *indicative* way every single time I communicate with someone else. As Husserl says:

If one surveys these interconnections, one sees at once that all expressions in *communicative* speech function as *indications*. They serve the hearer as signs of the 'thoughts' of the speaker, i.e. of his sense-giving inner experiences, as well as of the other inner experiences which are part of his communicative intention. (*Logical Investigations*, p. 189)

To return, however, to the title of the opening chapter, Husserl immediately draws our attention back to the *essential* nature of the expression. If we keep clear the distinction that an expression is a *meaningful* sign, while an indication is a sign that points us from one state of affairs to another, then the fact that expressions are often caught up in their indicative function will be, for Husserl, a merely accidental (that is, a non-essential) characteristic of expressions, deriving from the fact that they oftentimes *go forth* into the world from the mouth of the speaker. If it were possible to examine the expression apart from its *going forth* into the world in its communicative function (as Husserl thinks it is), then it would be possible to isolate the essential nature of the expression. For Husserl, this essential nature is revealed in the use of expressions in the solitariness of the thinking mind. He claims:

when we live in the understanding of a word, it expresses something and the same thing, whether we address it to anyone or not. It seems clear, therefore, that an expression's meaning, and whatever else pertains to it essentially, cannot coincide with its feats of intimation. (*Logical Investigations*, p. 190)

Within the inner monologue of one's own intentional states, the expression does not *communicate*, Husserl says, in the way that it does when we use it in interpersonal relational acts. For instance, suppose I say to myself in my head, 'I mustn't allow myself to get caught up in this.' In this case, I am employing *expressions*, to be sure, but I am *not*, Husserl insists, communicating anything to myself, strictly speaking. Why not? Because the sense of the words is immediately graspable by me, inasmuch as I am the individual experiencing the intentional act itself, at the very moment that I am internally 'verbalising' the experience. So I am not *making known* to myself something that I did not previously know. In the interior monologue, Husserl says, any *indication* would be 'quite purposeless. For the acts in question are themselves experienced by us at that very moment' (*Logical Investigations*, p. 191). Rather, it is as if I imagine myself doing so, but it is nothing more than an imagination or representation.

The Living Present

We should not be surprised to discover that the question of time, and specifically, of the subject's *relation* to time, occupies Husserl's thinking from its very inception. As early as *Philosophy of Arithmetic*, Husserl is already conducting analyses of the consciousness of internal time. Insofar as Husserl is always concerned with the intentional act, and intentional acts always unfold in a temporal relation, or put otherwise, objectivity is always constituted within a subjectivity, and subjectivity is always temporally constituted, the problem of the experience of time must occupy a central place in the phenomenological project. Thus, it comes as no surprise that immediately upon finishing the *Logical Investigations*, Husserl begins explicitly exploring the structure of internal time-consciousness, delivering the now-famous *time-consciousness* lectures in February of 1905; and the question of the subject's relation to time will occupy Husserl's thought for the remainder of his career.

We should begin by saying that Husserl's analyses attempt to lay bare the structure of time as it is constituted within subjectivity, as opposed to what we typically think of as 'real-time' or the moment-to-moment model of time. We frequently think of time as a passage along a represented *line*, where each point of the line represents a discrete and independent moment. The line is capped off at both ends by an arrow which represents infinite passage into the future and into the past. At the centre of the line is a prominently sized point, the now-point, separating future from past. The extension of the line to the left of that point represents all those past *nows* that have been but are no more, while the extension of the line to the right of that centre point represents all the future *nows* which shall be, but have not happened yet. This way of thinking about time, known as the *puncti-linear* model of time, is perfectly suitable inasmuch as it allows us to contextualise the relational occurrences of historical events. At the same time, however, we *falsify* the nature of time if we allow this representational model to serve as *the* way we understand time because in so doing, we treat time as we do space, as though time were somehow *extended* spatially when in fact time is experienced as an altogether different sort of subject matter than space. Thus, it requires a different approach entirely.

To highlight this, let us look at two different ways of thinking about memory. The first way accords with the puncti-linear model of time. If this model is correct, and if the present now-point is the only moment that truly *is*, and if consciousness, strictly speaking, is the perception of what is currently taking place, then consciousness is structurally *limited* to a perception of only what is happening *right now*. But we know that this is not how we experience time. For instance, at the beginning of this very sentence, we typed some words ('For instance'), which you have not forgotten, but which are still *present* in some sense in your mind. If this were *not* the case, you could never meaningfully experience *anything* at all, because all experiences take place within a context: no word is expressed in isolation; a note of a song can only be *heard* in its relation to the other notes; a single frame of a film tells us nothing or too much about its meaning; etc. On the puncti-linear model of time, we have merely perception, which is of the present now-point, and memory, which is the imagined recollection or representation of something that is *no-longer-present*. This is the position of Franz Brentano, Husserl's mentor.

But immediately, further problems become apparent. It seems perfectly reasonable to speak of memory in this manner, as the imagined recollection of a past event, when we are speaking of an event that is somewhat distant in the past. Such an injunction demands that we impart psychological *effort* in order to bring back to consciousness a past event, one that is completely removed from the present situation. But then, this use of the word 'memory' does not seem to apply when we are talking about the reader's act of reading this sentence right now, or of listening to a song, or of watching a scene of a film, as we said above. In order to do any of those things, we rely upon a *type* of memory, but it is not the *forced* recollection of some remote past. If it *were* a forced recollection, we could not truly experience anything either, because in each new *now*, we would be constantly attempting to contextualise by forcibly hanging onto the recent past, in order to contextualise the present. But by that point, of course, the present has again passed, and we would have missed it. Rather, it is a sort of memory that is still, in some sense, living, and attached to the present moment of experience.

For this reason, Husserl will insist, we must think the notion of the 'present' in a thicker, richer way, and he will call this structure the 'living present'. In the living present, the above-referenced type of memory – *recollection*, *reproduction* or *representation* – will be distinguished from what Husserl calls *retention*. Retention is that immediate memory, still pulsing in the present moment. It is a contextualising memory that has not, strictly speaking, ever left consciousness, and is in fact a necessary component of present experiences. Retention, or immediate memory, is what makes possible your hearing a song *as* a song (rather than an unrelated series of notes), or experiencing *anything at all*.

What is the retention a retention *of*? Husserl will derive the retentionality of the retention from a moment he will call the 'primal impression':

The primal impression is something absolutely unmodified, the primal source of all further consciousness and being. Primal impression has as its content that which the word 'now' signifies, insofar as it is taken in the strictest sense. Each new now is the content of a new primal impression. (*Consciousness of Internal Time*, p. 70)

It is the *source-point* in which experience is impressed or stamped.

In addition to primary memory, or retention, the present is always filled with primary expectations as well. For instance, when I enter a room, I sit in the chair without first checking its soundness, because in the very consciousness of sitting down, I *expect* that the chair will support me. Often when opening a door, we lead with our heads and shoulders, nonchalantly tapping the handle as we do so, because we *expect* the door to be unlocked. Oftentimes, these expectations go unnoticed except in cases of rupture (the chair collapses; the door is locked and we bump our heads), but the sheer *fact* of our surprise in such cases indicates that there was an implicit expectation or openness to the future, in the very act of our cognition of the present. This primary expectation, Husserl refers to as *protention*. Thus, Husserl's *living present* consists of the primal impression as the source-point or the nucleus, surrounded by a halo of retention and protention.

The Principle of All Principles

By the time of the publication of the first book of Husserl's *Ideas Pertaining to a Pure Phenomenology and to a Phenomenological Philosophy* (1913), the basic groundwork had already been laid for the establishment of what comes to be known as Husserl's transcendental phenomenology. The *Logical Investigations* had provided an exhaustive account of the structure of intentional and sense-bestowing acts. The *Time-Consciousness* lectures had thoroughly explored the relations of those acts to the subjective constitution of temporality, and Husserl's famous essay, 'Philosophy as Rigorous Science' (1911), had set forth the conditions under which philosophy might claim its rightful place as *the* foundational science, the discipline which offered the highest theoretical standards and which, therefore, could serve as the ultimate foundation upon which the other sciences were to be founded. Specifically, it was, Husserl argued, only in its phenomenological form that philosophy could hope to accomplish this loftiest of goals.

Ideas I thus brought to fruition and set into motion the basic framework of the phenomenological method. Here we find explicated four concepts – the natural attitude, the eidetic and transcendental reductions, and the principle of all principles – which, though implicit in the *Logical Investigations*, are first made explicit by Husserl in the first book of the *Ideas*. The 'natural attitude', we might say, is the non-rigorous, non-philosophically oriented, implicitly accepted *approach* I bring with me to my experience of the world:

I am conscious of a world endlessly spread out in space, endlessly becoming and having endlessly become in time. I am conscious of it: that signifies, above all, that intuitively I find it immediately, that I experience it. By my seeing, touching, hearing, and so forth, and in the different modes of sensuous perception, corporeal physical things with some spatial distribution or other are *simply there for me, 'on hand'* in the literal or figurative sense, whether or not I am particularly heedful of them and busied with them in my considering, thinking, feeling, or willing. (*Ideas*, p. 51)

In other words, as a matter of natural impulse and habit, I find myself in an already-existing, already-constituted, already-meaningful world, consisting of things which are present and on-hand for my cognition. I find myself a subject in a world of objects – houses, cars, other human beings, etc. – which are external to me. Moreover, not only are there objects present for me now, but on the basis of this accessible horizon I am aware of a conceivably infinite domain of being which is inaccessible to me at present. At this moment, for instance, I stand at my desk typing, and I can reverse my conscious regard, without turning my head, to the doorway behind me that opens into the hallway, to the stairs which lead from the hallway into the living room, to the door which leads to the outside world, etc. to the vast world *known* to my memory, the seemingly infinite collection of faces and places that I have encountered in my lifetime. But I can extend my conscious regard even beyond this, to the positing of an infinitely vast cosmos full of objects almost all of which I can never hope to have or have had any experience of at all.

This 'natural attitude' as it applies to space applies in the same way to the infinite span of time. The time that I occupy is but a tiny drop in the ocean of time, against which I can easily project an infinitely extended horizon into both the past and the future. The world, on the natural attitude, was here long before I was, and will be here long after I am gone. Moreover, I find *others* who, like me, find themselves in this same world, for whom (I assume) the world – its objects and time – is the same *objective* world that it is in my case as well, only experienced in different modes than my own experience allows.

This natural attitude is so much a part of who we are and how we *find* the world that we persist in it almost all the time, completely unaware of its governance. Husserl writes:

In my waking consciousness I find myself in this manner at all times, and without ever being able to alter the fact, in relation to the world which remains one and the same, though changing with respect to the composition of its contents. [. . .] Moreover, this world is there for me not only as a world of mere things, but also with the same immediacy as a *world of objects with values, a world of goods, a practical world*. (*Ideas*, p. 53)

Prior to any theorisation, scientific or otherwise, I find myself already in a world. It may be different than I perceive in some ways. My sensory faculties may be limited in number and in scope; they may be impaired for whatever reason; things may *be* otherwise than I understand them. But this just means that the goal of the sciences in the natural attitude is to clarify our perceptions and make sure that we *see* the world correctly:

To cognize 'the' world more comprehensively, more reliably, more perfectly in every respect than naïve experiential cognizance can, to solve all the problems of scientific cognition which offer themselves within the realm of the world, that is the aim of the *sciences belonging to the natural attitude*. (*Ideas*, p. 57)

What is *wrong* with this 'natural attitude'? Well, strictly speaking, the answer is *nothing*. It *just is* how we are and how we find ourselves in the world. Nevertheless, there is an implicit judgement that we almost always make from the starting point of the natural attitude, the judgement that the world *really is*, absent and apart from my cognition of it, the way that I perceive it. The objects *really do* exist, and they *really are* the way they appear; and if I were to suddenly drop out of existence, they would persist, continuing to not only exist, but to exist in just the same manner. This act of judgement, which is not an *essential* element of the natural attitude, makes thematic what was hitherto pre-theoretical; it establishes as the foundation of all the rest of our scientific endeavours a proposition that is not necessarily true, and is in no way measurable or verifiable. For once we have made thematic the proposition that the world is radically distinct from the subjects who cognise it, and that it *really is* thus and so, however much we might struggle, we can never again bridge that insuperable gap between the subject and object.

But we must keep in mind that Husserl wants philosophy to be rigorously scientific. He wants it to be *the* rigorous science *par excellence*, the science upon which all other sciences are to be grounded. Therefore, he seeks to transform the natural attitude: '*Instead of remaining in this attitude, we propose to alter it radically*' (*Ideas*, p. 57). About three centuries prior to Husserl, René Descartes had performed a similar operation. But Descartes' method had been based upon an act of negation, rejecting every concept or principle that can possibly or conceivably be doubted or deceitful. Husserl's alteration, however, is not an act of negation (which would still be a thematic assertion regarding the *true nature* of things). Rather, it is an act of suspension. It does not negate or deny the existence of the world; rather, it brackets it, suspends judgement, with-holds assent to that foundational proposition stated above (*the world really exists apart from my cognition and it really is the way I see it*). It does not doubt, it parenthesises:

Nevertheless the positing undergoes a modification: while it in itself remains what it is, *we, so to speak, 'put it out of action,' we 'exclude it,' we 'parenthesize it.'* It is still there, like the parenthesized in the parentheses, like the excluded outside the context of inclusion. (*Ideas*, p. 59)

This act of suspension, Husserl calls the phenomenological *epochē*.

Simply put, the phenomenologist, in his or her effort to be rigorously scientific and to hold his or her attention only upon those things that are fundamentally indubitable, must put out of play all questions regarding the so-called *real existence* of the so-called *real world*, focusing his or her attention only upon the phenomena as they appear to consciousness. These phenomena, *as* phenomena, are themselves undeniably true, as even Descartes had seen in his *Meditations on First Philosophy*. This brings us to Husserl's famous *Principle of All Principles*:

Enough now of absurd theories. No conceivable theory can make us err with respect to the *principle of all principles: that every originary presentive intuition is a legitimizing source of cognition*, that *everything originarily* (so to speak, in its 'personal' actuality) *offered* to us in *'intuition' is to be accepted simply as what it is presented as being*, but also, *only within the limits in which it is presented there*. (*Ideas*, p. 44)

The epochē is this act of suspension that brings us to this indubitabil-ity, and it takes place by way of two 'reductions', the eidetic and the transcendental or phenomenological. The eidetic reduction derives from the Greek word *eidos*, which is the word for 'idea', and in Plato's usage, 'form' or 'essence'. The eidetic reduction *reduces* the object of con-sciousness (whether perceived or imagined) to its pure essence, leaving aside any and all questions of real existence. It makes no difference whether or not the object has *in fact* ever been encountered, and it really makes no difference what *sort* of object is in question. It may be a spa-tiotemporal object, a socio-political object, a song, etc. In the mode of eidetic seeing, one abstracts the essential nature of the thing in question, analysing it in such a way as to make possible *essential* knowledge that is unattainable in principle on the basis of mere empirical observations. Plato's classic text, the *Republic*, can be understood in this way as one of the greatest philosophical exercises of eidetic variation ever undertaken.

The transcendental or phenomenological reduction goes one step further.[10] For while we have discussed the *world* that is the object of consciousness, we have not yet analysed the effects of this act of suspension upon the consciousness *for whom* there is a world. In other words, my consciousness itself, my empirical ego, is, like all the rest of the objects I have encountered and parenthesised, an *intentional* object. It is something *towards* which my consciousness gazes when it looks back upon itself. Likewise, its nature *as it appears in the mode of reduction* can no longer be taken for granted as having or corresponding to a factical reality. Thus, the *real existence* and the *real nature* of the empirical Ego, *my* empirical ego – 'the full stream—the total stream, taken as endless in both directions, which comprises the mental processes of an Ego' (*Ideas*, p. 110) – must be bracketed in the mode of reduction. Nonetheless, when we have reduced *everything* that can possibly be reduced, there remains a leftover residue of consciousness, but it is no longer *my* consciousness or *this* or *that* consciousness, but pure consciousness:

in spite of all that, consciousness considered in its '*purity*' must be held to be a *self-contained complex of being*, a complex of *absolute being* into which nothing can penetrate and out of which nothing can slip, to which nothing is spatiotemporally external and which cannot be within any spatiotemporally complex, which cannot be affected by any physical thing and cannot exercise causation upon any physical thing . . . (*Ideas*, p. 112)

This leftover residue is what Husserl calls the transcendental Ego.

The Problem of Intersubjectivity

An obvious problem now presents itself to us. It is a problem intimated as early in Husserl's thinking as the *Logical Investigations*:

When I listen to someone, I perceive him as a speaker, I hear him recounting, demonstrating, doubting, wishing, etc. The hearer perceives the intimation in the same sense in which he perceives the intimating person—even though the mental phenomena which make him a person cannot fall, for what they are, in the intuitive grasp of another. [. . .] The hearer perceives the speaker as manifesting certain inner experiences, and to that extent he also perceives these experiences themselves: he does not, however, himself experience them, he has not an 'inner' but an 'outer' percept of them. (*Logical Investigations*, p. 190)

When I am in the presence of another person, I encounter a transcendence that cannot be assimilated, incorporated, encapsulated or explained by my own immediate consciousness. This being says and does things that I can neither anticipate nor control, and based upon my experiences of other such beings, is infinitely capable of a whole host of *other* unpredictable behaviours. Yet, given everything we have said about the phenomenological method of reduction, whereby we suspend all judgements regarding the factical existence or non-existence of objects of consciousness, have we not, in attaining to the level of the transcendental ego, reached a plane of consciousness where the *only* thing I can be sure of is that *I exist*? Or, in starker terms, that the only thing that exists *is* me, the absolute consciousness or the monad (a term with a rich philosophical history that Husserl employs meaning 'unit' or 'one' in the sense of absolute)? In simpler terms, does Husserl not commit himself to the position of solipsism?:

When I, the meditating I, reduce myself to my absolute transcendental ego by phenomenological epochē do I not become *solus ipse*; and do I not remain that, as long as I carry on a consistent self-explication under the name phenomenology? Should not a phenomenology that proposed to solve the problems of Objective being, and to present itself actually as philosophy, be branded therefore as transcendental solipsism? (*Cartesian Meditations*, p. 89)

It is not difficult to see the ethical dangers inherent in such a position, nor is it difficult to understand why Emmanuel Levinas worried so much about Husserlian phenomenology. To put the point simply, if other people I encounter in my field of consciousness are merely *objects*, the existences of which I can never be certain, can I ever truly be *responsible* to such things? Can I ever *owe* them anything? What is to stop me from simply disregarding them, or worse, treating them in the most brutal ways?

For his part, Husserl himself worried about this very possibility, and addressed it head-on in his *Cartesian Meditations*. However, in so worrying he does not seek to abandon the phenomenological method. Indeed, he does not believe that he *needs* to abandon it, and moreover, to do so would be to divest ourselves of the possibility of certitude. After all, *how else* could the otherness of another human being present itself *to* me *except* within the sphere of my own consciousness? In other words, *it is from within the phenomenological mode of analysis that we encounter an 'other' who in many senses seems to transcend my own consciousness.* Thus, we can, while faithfully remaining within the phenomenological standpoint, begin to analyse that *otherness* on phenomenological grounds, therefore not abandoning the certitude it affords.

We experience the otherness of the other, Husserl says, by way of *analogical apperception* or *appresentation.* This is best explained by way of a very mundane example. Suppose you are standing in a yard, any given yard, real or imagined, and you are looking at the façade of a house. To the right and to the left of the house you are looking at are other houses, and since you are at an angle with respect to *those* houses, you can see not only the façade of each, but also one of the sides of each of the houses, but for that very reason, you cannot currently see the sides, nor the back, of the house you are looking at face-on. Nonetheless, when you *look* at the façade, seeing only the face of the house, you *intend* a house itself, in its completeness. Your effort to fulfil that intention may be thwarted. You may walk to the side and discover that the front of the house was in fact a very convincingly structured wooden model, and nothing more, propped up in the back by angled beams. You may walk to the back and discover that the majority of the house has been destroyed by a tornado, which miraculously left intact the face of the house. In any number of possible ways, the object you are looking at may *not* in fact be the façade of a house. Moreover, and in a less fantastical way, the back of the house, upon discovery, will most likely not be exactly what you thought. It may be much larger or much smaller, etc. Nevertheless, when you look at the front, you intend the object as at the same time having a back.

A similar thing occurs in our experience of other people, Husserl claims:

the other is himself there before us 'in person.' On the other hand, this being there in person does not keep us from admitting forthwith that, properly speaking, neither the other Ego himself, nor his subjective processes or his appearances themselves, nor anything else belonging to his own essence, becomes given in our experience originally. (*Cartesian Meditations*, p. 109)

In other words, my experience of the other person presents me with merely a 'front', or in this case, strictly speaking, an 'outside', a body that moves, speaks, expresses emotion, cares, hurts, laughs, walks, smiles, eats, etc., *like mine. Unlike* in the case of the house, however, I cannot intend the 'back' or the 'inside' of this object by way of direct presentation. In the case of the house, I can walk around to the back, or even inside, to verify the original intention, 'house'. In the case of the other person as object of consciousness, however, I cannot, now or ever, *get behind* the face, or *locate the Ego* to verify the intention. It takes place, Husserl claims, on the basis of 'pairing':

In a *pairing association* the characteristic feature is that, in the most primitive case, two data are given intuitionally, and with prominence, in the unity of a consciousness and that, on this basis [. . .] as data appearing with mutual distinctness, they *found phenomenologically a unity of similarity* and thus are always constituted precisely as a pair. (*Cartesian Meditations*, p. 112)

My own body is intimately and primordially connected with the operation of my own Ego. When I encounter the other person, I encounter a body like mine:

The appresentation which gives that component of the Other which is not accessible originaliter is combined with an original presentation (of 'his' body as part of the Nature given as included in my ownness). In this combination, moreover, the Other's animate body and his governing Ego are given in the manner that characterizes *a unitary transcending experience.* (*Cartesian Meditations*, p. 114)

By constantly experiencing the pairedness of my own body with a governing Ego, the recognition of another body triggers this same association, especially in light of the fact that the experiences of that body can never be constituted originarily in my own immanent sphere, except as a transcendence: 'It is therefore conceivable only as an analogue of something included in my peculiar ownness. [. . .] In other words, *another monad* becomes constituted appresentatively in mine' (*Cartesian Meditations*, p. 115). I see the body, and immediately intend, without inference, another subject or Ego.

The Influence of Heidegger

Though Husserl trained and influenced many noteworthy successors, the most famous is without question Martin Heidegger, who in 1927 published the monumental work most recognisably attached to his name – *Being and Time* – in Husserl's *Jahrbuch für Philosophie und phänomenologische Forschung* (*Yearbook for Philosophy and Phenomenological*

Research), vol. VIII, dedicating it to Husserl himself. However, the text demonstrates stark methodological and ontological[11] divergences from Husserl's own understanding of the meaning of phenomenology, such that Husserl himself understood *Being and Time* as an act of betrayal on Heidegger's part. While Heidegger, like Husserl, sees the phenomenological project as a return *to the things themselves*, *unlike* Husserl, Heidegger does not subscribe to the notion of 'bracketing' to a presupposed *pure* sphere of consciousness; our experience, Heidegger will claim, is *always* filtered, through our commonplace concepts and assumptions, which are informed by our media, our culture, our politics, our history and our language – these constitutive factors are riddled with the prattle of the everyday. Heidegger will highlight that it is only a particular kind of being, namely, *human* being, for whom questions regarding *the things themselves* occur at all. To this being, he gives the name *Dasein* (which is technically just the German word for 'existence'; Heidegger uses the term only for *human* existence, but not *human* in the anthropological or biological sense, but rather, *human* in the very specific sense as the being in whom the question of Being lights up). Dasein, however, lives an everyday life of *inauthenticity*, from which it follows that the meaning of Being will, for us, *also* be inaccessible. So the first step towards *allowing the things to show themselves as they are in themselves* involves stripping away the everyday, inauthentic, 'public' life of Dasein, as Dasein is the being where Being opens or reveals itself. And the first step towards doing *this*, Heidegger argues, involves authentically taking up one's finitude, the fact of one's own mortality (a point which most of us try to avoid most of the time), in each moment of existence. Admittedly, at first glance, it is not obvious what the relationship is between the affirmation of my own death, and my authentic experience of the meaning of Being. Let us therefore look a bit more closely at what Heidegger means.

Our everyday lives involve a complex, extensive network of relations, with things, tools, modes of transportation, technological devices, other people, etc. Heidegger argues that within these relations, Dasein is constantly taking measure of the ways in which it differs from these others with whom it relates, and evaluating the means of handling that distance. This constant measuring, which he calls, 'distantiality', deprives Dasein of itself, dissolving the singularity of Dasein into the anonymity of *the others*, what Heidegger calls *the they* (or in German, *Das Man*, 'the one'). The *they* is everyone, and it is no one; it is everywhere, but nowhere in particular. It is the person you sit across from on the morning commute, the person you pass in the street or in the town square, even if the two of you never speak. One seeks to like the music that *they* like, to parse political issues the way that *they* do, to appreciate the art that *they* appreciate, etc. Anything exceptional is understood as requiring *normalising*. In the mode of the they-self, Dasein is, by definition, levelled down. This state of affairs constitutes what Heidegger calls Dasein's *publicness*. It is always 'right', in that its most compelling arguments always take the form of 'everybody knows . . .'. It disburdens Dasein, divesting it of any genuine responsibility, as Dasein no longer has to make any genuine decisions; the alternatives are already clearly laid out, and Dasein needs merely to 'pick a side' in the matter. Therefore, Dasein, according to Heidegger, is, nearly all the time, *fallen* away from its own true nature. So, in order to arrive at an authentic understanding of Dasein, we must bring the structural whole of Dasein within our purview. This brings us into the discussion of time and death.

Heidegger will claim that the structure of Dasein is what he calls 'care'. That is to say, Dasein *cares* for the meaning of its existence in ways that other beings do not; it cares for structuring its existence, for *giving a certain meaning* to its existence. Dasein's own experience of its day-to-day life is such that it is constantly projecting itself forward into the future, and making decisions in the present based upon those future possibilities. Likewise, when it does so, it also carries its past along with it, projecting it forth as well. My past decisions, my upbringing, my culture, my religious background, my historical situation, etc., are all factors that I (knowingly or not) project into the future, forming and informing my possibilities whenever I am making a decision. Dasein always finds itself 'thrown' into a world already. Those future possibilities are largely constituted on the basis of those past elements, and both converge in the fact of the present moment of the decision. So in a certain sense, Dasein's past is always out ahead of it in the future. For Heidegger, then, Dasein's temporality[12] is, as he says, *ecstatic*; it is constituted and defined by its being outside of itself. Therefore, as long as Dasein *is*, it is projecting forth into the future, so there is always a structural incompleteness to Dasein. But when there is no longer a future to come (after which time Dasein would be 'complete'), there is no longer a Dasein there to analyse. This presents a conundrum – I *want* to think the meaning of Being, but my experience of Being is always constituted on the basis of my own existential structure, which is always filtered through the inauthenticity of publicness; I must therefore get a complete grasp on my own, authentic, existential structure; my own existential structure is temporally ecstatic, meaning that it is always projecting forward, which means that I can never have a *complete* grasp of my own existential structure, so long as I am alive; when I am dead, my existential structure will indeed be complete, but then I cannot have a complete grasp of my existential structure precisely because I have ceased *to be*. While alive, I am not *complete*; when *complete*, I am not alive.

So ultimately, in order to grasp the totality of my own existential structure, I must seize authentically upon the fact of my *being-towards-death*. What does this *authentic resoluteness* mean? After all, it seems at least a little bit counterintuitive to argue that we are not aware of the fact that we are going to someday die. What Heidegger means is that most of the time, we live as though death is always out there ahead of us; it is something that will happen *to us* someday, not today or tomorrow, but someday. Resolutely taking up one's death means recognising, as a structural essentiality of Dasein, that death (or finitude) is part of the package. Contrary to how this may appear, Heidegger does not mean by this that we should embrace a pessimistic or self-destructive perspective on life, but rather, that we should fundamentally embrace the fact of our own finitude. Death is the one event that singularises each and every one of us, and no one may die *my* death except for me – it is something each person does alone, even if it is in the company of others. It is the unavoidable terminus of all the possibilities of my life. This, Heidegger thinks, is why it is so disconcerting to us, and why we spend so much time and energy trying to avoid thinking about it, preoccupying ourselves with idle chatter and the fascination with the stimulation of the ever-changing stream of public sensory stimuli. By seizing upon one's finitude as one's own, Dasein avails itself of the recognition of its own limitations (because death is the constant *possibility of impossibility* there as an ultimate possible limitation at each moment of existence); but by extension, in recognising the *limitations* of one's own possibilities, one also comes authentically face-to-face with one's *possibilities* as well.

Being and Time is, in other words, a strongly voluntaristic[13] work, with a robust emphasis on the *resoluteness* of Dasein in the face of its own finitude, and though his name only appears a few times in the text, *Being and Time* is deeply indebted to aspects of Friedrich Nietzsche's philosophy (see note 8 to the Introduction of this book). Heidegger never finished *Being and Time* (completing only Divisions I and II of Part I, though the initial outline promised two parts, each consisting of three divisions), as it is shortly after 1927 that Heidegger's thought begins to radically evolve. Already at this time he is beginning to worry about the question of humankind's relationship to technology, fearing that while human beings understand technology as a *tool* at their disposal, they may in fact be mistaken; it *may* be that humankind is losing itself within the grasp of technology. Adolf Hitler came to power on 30 January 1933, and Heidegger infamously embraced the Nazi movement, perceiving it as the movement capable of restoring the proper relation between human beings and technology. Hitler and the Nazi party incorporated, even if in a perverse sense, the mythos of the ancient Nordic gods, and emphasised the elements of 'blood' and 'soil' (*Blut und Boden*) as the tie between a people and its land, while privileging a natural or agrarian way of life at the diminishment of the moral perversity of urbanity. Heidegger is at this time well-positioned professionally and is appointed Rektor at Freiberg University, and he officially joins the party ten days later, on 1 May 1933. He will be asked to step down as Rektor just ten months later.

At some point during this period, Heidegger begins to re-evaluate his own thinking. Though he remained a party member until its dissolution at the conclusion of World War II, he stopped participating in Nazi party meetings when he stepped down as Rektor in April 1934. In the years between 1936 and 1940, Heidegger began a series of seminars on the philosophy of Nietzsche, with the goal of extricating Nietzsche from a certain form of biologism being foisted upon him by his Nazi interpreters. Heidegger ends up dedicating far more research to Nietzsche than he does any other single figure in the history of philosophy, returning to him repeatedly over the course of his life. Heidegger, however, comes to reject Nietzsche for reasons of his own, namely, that with Nietzsche's concept of the 'will to power', or the will's insatiable, inscrutable 'will to will', Nietzsche merely completes the metaphysical paradigm of the modern age, summed up in the language of *power, grasping, seizing, domination* and *will*. Thus, as Heidegger's thinking moves towards the period known as 'the turn', through his criticisms of Nietzsche's concept of 'will to power', Heidegger in fact comes to critique his *own* voluntarism from the period of *Being and Time*. After 1933, Heidegger rarely uses the term *Dasein* any more (typically reserving it for times when he is critiquing or reflecting on his earlier works), and he drops the voluntaristic language of resoluteness from the period of *Being and Time* altogether.

In his later works, Heidegger more explicitly takes up the issue of

technology as the essence of Modern metaphysics, structuring and
revealing the world in such a way that it is to be challenged, harvested
and called forth for the purpose of storing the power of its resources.
The danger therein is that humankind has lost a central aspect of its
own being, namely, its other creative capacities, and risks becoming
nothing more than a *resource* itself. Thus, the dangerous implications
of the technological age are, for Heidegger, already implicit within the
Modern metaphysics of power, and the epistemology of 'grasping' (in
the sense of *grasping* knowledge) that it brings with it. For this reason,
Heidegger's later works will focus on what he calls the 'Releasement' (a
translation of the German word *Gelassenheit*), a letting go or a powerlessness rather than an emphasis on power, letting beings be. He will also
begin to focus more extensively on the question of the essence of language (or meaningfulness), as a differential structure uniting and holding
in relation *word* and *thing*.

Phenomenology as Existentialism

In the late 1920s, phenomenology entered France. The French philosophical scene was at this time ripe for a revolution, in that it had grown
weary of overly intellectualised philosophical abstraction, and was
hungry for a philosophical engagement with the concrete factors of
everyday life. In 1928, Emmanuel Levinas (Lithuanian-born, French-
naturalised, Jewish phenomenologist and later influence on and friend
of Derrida) went to Freiburg to study with Husserl, also studying with
and making an acquaintance of Heidegger during this period as well.
In February of 1929, Edmund Husserl delivered at the Collège de
Sorbonne the famous Paris Lectures, which were assembled in 1930
and published as *Cartesian Meditations*, one of the most important texts
from Husserl's later period. Michel Foucault highlights the magnitude
of this event in French intellectual history, claiming that it 'marked
the moment: Phenomenology entered France through that text'.[14] In
1931, French translations of two of Heidegger's essays appear: 'What is
Metaphysics?' and 'On the Essence of Reasons'.

Around this time, Levinas published his first essay on Husserl,[15]
followed over the next few years by several others. In 1930, Levinas
published *Theory of Intuition in Husserl's Phenomenology*, which had a profound impact on French philosopher Jean-Paul Sartre,[16] who also began
publishing on Husserl shortly thereafter. In 1932, Levinas published

his first essay on Heidegger,[17] and, especially early on, was significantly more taken with Heidegger's philosophy than with Husserl's. In 1933, Sartre wrote his brief but very important essay, 'Intentionality: A Fundamental Idea of Husserl's Phenomenology',[18] followed, in 1936, by his famous critique of Husserl, *The Transcendence of the Ego: An Existentialist Theory of Consciousness*. By this time, the phenomenological approach to philosophy, both Husserlian and Heideggerian, had situated itself firmly in the French scene; and there was no turning back.

As phenomenology begins to take root in France, it transforms - fusing with strains of burgeoning French thought – and begins to bifurcate into two distinct directions: the subjective and the conceptual.[19] On the subjective side are thinkers like Levinas, Sartre and Maurice Merleau-Ponty. Though neither Levinas nor Sartre corresponds to any standard, traditional definition of the term 'ethics', and though there are drastic differences in their approaches, these two thinkers represent the ethical strains of French phenomenology. In the case of Levinas, this amounts to an attempt to expose a radical experience of transcendence towards the Other, formulated out of critiques of both Husserl and Heidegger. The more immediately culturally influential inheritor, however, is Jean-Paul Sartre, the most famous adherent to the general group of conceptual themes that would come to be categorised as *existentialist*.

Sartre is enamoured, early on, with Husserl's notion of 'intentionality', the idea that consciousness is always conscious *of* something. From this it follows, Sartre argues, that consciousness is always, of its very nature, bursting forth, directed *outwardly*. Even if consciousness turns its gaze back upon itself, it can only do so by making a contentful object out of consciousness, in a sense *falsifying* the true nature of consciousness. In the same way that I can only look at my own face by way of a falsification of my gaze (a reflection in a mirror, a photograph, etc.), consciousness can only view itself by way of an act of objectification. Consciousness, he claims, is therefore essentially an *emptiness*. Thus, what defines the human being is not a pre-given or pre-determined essence, but rather, the way in which it employs its intentionality, in its choices. This brings Sartre into intellectual commerce with a strain of thought already beginning to blossom at that time in religious circles in France, that we today refer to as 'existentialism'. 'Existentialism', as many contemporary historians note, is a term broadly applied to a very diverse group, including both the profoundly religious and the militantly atheistic, and though Sartre and perhaps de Beauvoir were the only two thinkers to embrace the term (Dostoevsky, Kierkegaard and Nietzsche all lived and died before the term was ever coined; and Heidegger, Jaspers and Marcel all explicitly rejected it), there are nevertheless certain themes and motifs present in these thinkers that unite them.

Any worthwhile philosophy, the existentialist holds, must be able to adequately reach down into the facticity of the entire sphere of human modes of existence, rather than isolating and emphasising an idealised abstraction such as rationality. Guilt, shame, thrownness, faith, doubt, anxiety, pleasure, self-loathing, fear, death, responsibility, choice, desire, insecurity, etc., are all undeniable aspects of human life, and it is humanity in its totality that philosophy must address, according to the existentialist. It is for this reason that Heidegger's analysis of Dasein's *being-in-the-world*, analysing guilt, anxiety and death, is so influential for Sartre and for existentialism generally.

Second and in a related manner, existentialist thinkers share the conviction that the conceptual abstractions of the tradition of Western metaphysics, in both its theological and philosophical forms, are fundamentally insufficient when it comes to addressing the singularity of the human life, and that philosophy is worthless if it cannot speak to the human condition in this manner. On the religious side of the divide, thinkers like Gabriel Marcel in the late 1920s were beginning to point back to the writings of Søren Kierkegaard, whose emphasis on an ethics based upon the priority of the single individual in relation to God was a repudiation of ethics in both its Kantian and Hegelian forms, but moreover, a rupture with the rationalist tradition generally. On the non-theistic side, existentialist thinkers point back to Friedrich Nietzsche, whose *Übermensch* is a person who has emerged beyond the human need for transcendent, limiting codes of morality; Nietzsche famously contrasts 'master morality' with 'slave morality' in the ancient world in his *On the Genealogy of Morality*. The ideas of both Nietzsche and Kierkegaard were prominent among existentialist thinkers. Karl Jaspers and Heidegger in Germany,[20] along with Jean Wahl, Gabriel Marcel, Simone de Beauvoir and Jean-Paul Sartre in France, took a great deal of inspiration from the emphasis on the singularity of the individual from both Kierkegaard and Nietzsche.

Going along with this is the notion that most of human life is lived inauthentically, and that what is fundamental and essential to human *nature* is its freedom and its responsibility. What is central is not the human being *as* a member of a species, class, race, gender, etc., whose responsibility it is to conform to an essential nature. Rather, what defines the human being is his or her making choices and positing values, in the face of the absolute awareness of his or her responsibility for doing so. Heidegger will analyse the experience of anxiety, the restlessness of Dasein in the face of 'the nothing', wherein all relations, to things in the world, and to others, are stripped away, and one can only respond in the awareness of suspension over a foundation of absolute groundlessness. In Sartre, the notion of 'resoluteness' is imported as authenticity, the recognition that the human individual is ontologically free, or 'condemned to be free',[21] that so long as he or she lives, he or she is bound by no essential elements of his or her nature, defined only by the choices he or she makes. As he famously claims in the same lecture, 'existence precedes essence'.[22]

The 1943 publication of Sartre's *Being and Nothingness* marked the cultural explosion and near-decade-long domination of existentialism in France, and Sartre (like Derrida would in the 1970s) became something of a cultural icon. To his credit, Sartre used his celebrity status to help lesser-known subversive figures, like Frantz Fanon and Albert Memmi, find an audience, writing prefaces to their books, helping circulate subversive literature, and so on. Moreover, because Sartre so explicitly asserted his philosophical parentage in the figures of Husserl and Heidegger, for better and for worse, existentialism in the 1940s *was*, at least in the cultural mindset, French phenomenology.

Above, we mentioned the bifurcation of phenomenology upon its entrance into France. While Sartrean existentialism is enjoying its prominence on the cultural and literary scenes, at the academic level in France, there is another reception of Husserl that is quietly but insistently disseminating. Here, Michel Foucault's distinction bears repeating:

phenomenology entered France through that text. But it allowed of two readings: one, in the direction of a philosophy of the subject – and this was Sartre's article on 'Transcendance de L'Ego' (1935) and another which went back to the founding principles of Husserl's thought: those of formalism and intuitionism, those of the theory of science [. . .] Whatever they may have been after shifts, ramifications, interactions, even rapprochements, these two forms of thought in France have constituted two philosophical directions which have remained profoundly heterogeneous.[23]

In the first category, Foucault counts Sartre and Maurice Merleau-Ponty, while in the second, he places Gaston Bachelard, Jean Cavaillès

and Georges Canguilhem. What characterises and unites these latter
three are a profound *de*-emphasis on the lived-experience of a constituting subject who founds his or her experience of the world, and
an emphasis on the epistemological breaks and structural formations
accompanying the emergences of bodies of knowledge, coupled with
an interest in the natural and human sciences. As Foucault rightly
notes, for these philosophers, the preferred Husserl is not the Husserl of
the subject, but the Husserl whose ongoing project is the quest for the
scientificity of science itself, that which makes science possible. (In *Voice and
Phenomenon*, these two Husserls are brought into a complex and problematic whole.)

A thinker upon whom we have not yet remarked is Maurice Merleau-
Ponty, an interesting case, in that his work represents a shift between the
two divergent French receptions of Husserl. Early on in his career, he
is concerned with the psychological questions regarding behaviour and
perception. By the time that he writes *The Phenomenology of Perception* in
1945, his work is in many ways an attempt to synthesise the insights of
Husserl and Heidegger regarding the intentional relation between body
and world, at the same time enriching these phenomenological insights
with the latest discoveries in neuroscience. For this reason, and moreover, because he at times explicitly aligns himself with Sartre (especially
early on, the two were friends and founding editors of the left-wing publication *Les Temps Modernes*), Merleau-Ponty is often lumped in together
with the existential strain of phenomenology by later philosophers such
as Michel Foucault and Gilles Deleuze. However, such a characterisation
is only partly accurate. As early as 1945, when Merleau-Ponty published
The Phenomenology of Perception, he is already critical of what he perceives
to be Sartre's Cartesian commitments in *Being and Nothingness* (that is,
a dualistic ontology of the human being, and an overly robust sense
of freedom). And shortly after the publication of *The Phenomenology of
Perception*, Merleau-Ponty comes under the influence of the linguistics
of Ferdinand de Saussure (to be discussed shortly), which injects two
significant changes into his thinking: (1) it begins to push his philosophy
in the direction of later Heideggerian reflections on language, a central
tenet of which is that we always find ourselves already *in* language; (2) it
also introduces him to structuralist thinking, which he sees as integral to
disrupting the radical subject–object break which he has sought over the
course of his career to shift beyond. His later thought is far less subject-
centred, and far more ontological. Experience itself, both subject and

sion, a new set of relations is appended to the existing set, thus altering the relationality and positionality of all involved. And as an individual within the system moves, whether laterally or vertically, he or she leaves behind his or her old roles and becomes someone new. On the surface, structuralism may not seem like a particularly controversial idea, especially when we are talking about linguistic signs, corporations or coffee sizes. But it is important to appreciate the impact such a methodological programme has when applied to the more concrete human arena, broadly construed. It is far more controversial to suggest that what an individual human being does, thinks and says in his or her everyday life is largely, if not completely, a result of his or her relations within the various systems he or she occupies – cultural, familial, political, ecclesiastical, etc. It severely attenuates any emphasis on individual choice and responsibility. Moreover, it drastically undercuts *any* purported foundational impartation of meaning by the subject *at all*. Indeed, structuralism is in many respects an explicit and stark rejection of French existentialism. In 1962, Claude Lévi-Strauss writes, 'I believe the ultimate goal of the human sciences to be not to constitute, but to dissolve man.'[26] Structuralism is applied to cultural relations in the anthropology of Claude Lévi-Strauss (who actually coined the term 'structuralism'), to the various constitutive relations of the unconscious in the psychoanalysis of Jacques Lacan, to the philosophies of Marx and Hegel by Jean Hyppolite and Louis Althusser, and to literature by Roland Barthes, and is at its height as Derrida is developing his philosophical voice. Its pervasive and lasting impact can be felt when we look at the names of the two dominant threads of twentieth-century French philosophy *after* 1967, decon-*struct*-ion and post-*structural-ism* (Michel Foucault and Gilles Deleuze), both of which emerge in direct opposition to certain aspects of structuralism.

Conclusion

As we have shown, Husserl's thought was introduced into France in 1930, followed in short order by the philosophy of Heidegger, and it quickly began to settle in and take root, sparking an intellectual wildfire that would last for decades to come. By the 1940s there is little left in French philosophy that is not *in some way* influenced by German phenomenology. On the one hand, there is the culturally explosive existentialist thread which, employing elements of Husserlian intentionality and Heideggerian resoluteness, highlights the centrality of the founding subject, constitutive of itself through the choices it makes, absurdly free, and unable *not* to be so. On the other hand, and antagonistic to the very tenets of existentialist thought, there is the conceptual thread – interested in Husserl's questions of the possibility of science – embodied in thinkers such as Jean Cavaillès and Georges Canguilhem, who in contrast to the founding subject, emphasise the structural and historical ruptures that give rise to systems of knowledge; this second thread will inform the structuralist tradition that, throughout the 1950s and 1960s will unseat the existentialist modes of thought, giving rise to a new revolution in French academic methodology capable of shaping a broad spectrum of disciplines.

Voice and Phenomenon is born out of the dramatic collision of these two strains of French phenomenology.[27] The structuralist movement had engendered the putative 'death of the subject', but the overwhelming success of Levinas's 1961 *Totality and Infinity* had brought the legitimacy of the question of the subject back into vogue. Written in 1967, as structuralism is on the wane, Derrida nevertheless brings the structuralist emphasis on the genesis of knowledge, along with its criticisms of founding subjectivity, into direct communication with and as a challenge to the re-emerging discussion of the founding subject. With this in mind, we are now prepared to embark upon our close reading of *Voice and Phenomenon*.

Notes

1. For the broad, historical background in this chapter, the following sources have been consulted: Vincent Descombes, *Modern French Philosophy*, trans. L Scott-Fox and J. M. Harding (Cambridge: Cambridge University Press, 1980); Gary Gutting, *French Philosophy in the Twentieth Century* (Cambridge: Cambridge University Press, 2001); Gary Gutting, *Thinking the Impossible: French Philosophy Since 1960* (Oxford: Oxford University Press, 2011); Leonard Lawlor, *Early Twentieth-Century Continental Philosophy* (Bloomington: Indiana University Press, 2012); Leonard Lawlor, *Thinking Through French Philosophy: The Being of the Question* (Bloomington and Indianapolis: Indiana University Press, 2003); Alan D. Schrift, *Twentieth-Century French Philosophy: Key Themes and Thinkers* (Malden, MA: Blackwell Publishing, 2006). For further reading on Husserl himself, see also: Dermot Moran, *Introduction to Phenomenology* (London: Routledge, 2000);

Robert Sokolowski, *Introduction to Phenomenology* (Cambridge: Cambridge University Press, 2000); Dan Zahavi, *Husserl's Phenomenology* (Stanford: Stanford University Press, 2003).

2. In writing this section, the following sources have been consulted: Carl B. Boyer, rev. Uta C. Merzbach, *A History of Mathematics*, 2nd edn (New York: John Wiley and Sons, 1991); Howard Eves, *Foundations and Fundamental Concepts of Mathematics*, 3rd edn (Mineola, NY: Dover Publications, 1990); Raymond Wilder, *Introduction to the Foundations of Mathematics* (New York: John Wiley and Sons, 1952).

3. In writing this section, the following sources have been consulted: Claire Ortiz Hill and Guillermo E. Rosado Haddock, *Husserl or Frege?: Meaning, Objectivity, and Mathematics* (Chicago: Open Court, 2000); Dallas Willard, 'Translator's Introduction', in Edmund Husserl, *Philosophy of Arithmetic: Psychological and Logical Investigations with Supplementary Texts from 1887–1901* (Dordrecht: Kluwer, 2003).

4. *A priori* literally translates as 'prior to', and indicates a brand of knowledge knowable apart from experience.

5. Gottlob Frege, *The Foundations of Arithmetic: A Logico-Mathematical Enquiry into the Concept of Number*, trans. J. L. Austin, M.A. (Evanston: Northwestern University Press, 1950), p. x.

6. René Descartes articulated the central problem that would govern philosophy for centuries to come when, in the *Meditations on First Philosophy* (1641), he argued that, *prima facie*, I have no way of ever being sure that my experiences accurately reflect reality, as the senses are often misguided, and even in cases where my experience seems absolutely vivid, it *may* be the case that I am dreaming, or it may even be the case that an omnipotent but maleficent being is constantly assaulting my mind with deceptions. Though Descartes tries to resolve this uncomfortable conundrum, his successors are not satisfied that he has successfully done so, and thus, every thinker of the Modern period (from Descartes to Kant, and even, in their own ways, Hegel, Schopenhauer and Nietzsche) is concerned with how to deal with this question.

7. The word 'epistemology' derives from the Greek word *epistēmē*, meaning 'knowledge'. So whenever the word 'epistemology' or 'epistemological' is used, it means having to do with the role, scope, qualifications and limitations of knowledge.

8. 'Immanence' is the counterpart to the word 'transcendence', and is defined, literally, as 'remaining within', while transcendence might be defined as 'going beyond'. The immanence–transcendence binary has

many applications, even within philosophy proper. For our purposes, what we mean is something like this: for the Modern philosophers (with the exception of Spinoza, perhaps), the world is *transcendent to* consciousness, meaning it is outside of consciousness, and consciousness must *filter* the sensory data that presents the world to it. Thus, the task of philosophy is to figure out how to *incorporate* the transcendent (the world) *within* the immanent (our experience). On the contrary, what Husserl pushes for is to remain purely within *immanence*, meaning, our experience itself, which is *not* outside of consciousness, and hence is apodictically, undeniably certain.

9. 'Intentionality' means something like 'a directedness-towards'. One of the key insights of Husserlian phenomenology is one that Husserl adopts from his own mentor, Franz Brentano, namely, that consciousness is always consciousness *of* something.

10. In *Ideas I*, Husserl does not radically distinguish these two operations, the eidetic from the transcendental. Later, in *The Crisis of European Sciences and Transcendental Phenomenology* (1936), he more rigorously distinguishes them, reserving the term 'epochē' exclusively for the eidetic reduction, and calling the eidetic reduction the 'condition of possibility' of the transcendental or phenomenological reduction. In the *Crisis* text, Husserl offers up self-criticisms of his own earlier explication of the reductions.

11. The word 'ontology' derives from the Greek word *ontos*, meaning 'being'. So whenever the word 'ontological' or 'ontology' appears, it means having to do with the question of being, or the fundamental nature of reality. In other instances, it may have to do with the nature of a specific thing in question, where what we mean to say is that thing *x* is of a fundamentally different *kind* than thing *y*. For instance, one might say, 'There is an ontological distinction between the body and the soul,' by which one would mean that the soul is a different *kind of thing* than the body is.

12. Its experiential structure of time.

13. 'Voluntarism' is a term used to characterise philosophical orientations rooted in a robust notion of subjective 'will'. Much of what Derrida is critiquing in *Voice and Phenomenon* will be the Western tradition of voluntarism.

14. Michel Foucault, 'Introduction', in Georges Canguilhem, *The Normal and the Pathological* (New York: Zone Books, 1991), p. 8. This introduction is an earlier version of Foucault's final essay, 'Life: Experience and Science'.

15. Emmanuel Levinas, 'Sur les "Ideen" de M. E. Husserl', *Revue philosophique de la France et de l'étranger*, CVII (1929), 54th year, no. 3–4, March–April, pp. 230–65.

16. Simone de Beauvoir tells the story of Sartre's introduction to Husserl, writing that a friend, Raymond Aron, had talked of phenomenology with them over drinks, claiming that, 'if you are a phenomenologist, you can talk about this cocktail and make philosophy of it'. Sartre was apparently so taken with the notion that philosophy was capable of actually touching the concrete everydayness of human life that he immediately went out and purchased Levinas's book on Husserl, reading it with great fervour as he walked. Sartre published his first essay on Husserl just one year later. Simone de Beauvoir, *The Prime of Life*, trans. Peter Green (New York: World Publishing, 1962), p. 112.

17. Emmanuel Levinas, 'Martin Heidegger et l'ontologie', *Revue philosophique de la France et de l'étranger*, 113 (1932), pp. 395–431.

18. *Journal of the British Society for Phenomenology*, vol. 1, no. 2, May 1970, pp. 4–5.

19. Foucault, 'Introduction', *The Normal and the Pathological*. Thank you to Alan Schrift, whose book, *Twentieth-Century French Philosophy*, points to Foucault's Introduction for this bifurcation.

20. German psychologist, and off-and-on friend of Martin Heidegger, whose early work on the psychology of worldviews begins in the early 1920s to assume a more strictly philosophical form.

21. Jean-Paul Sartre, *Existentialism and Human Emotions*, trans. Bernard Frechtman (New York: Philosophical Library, 1957), p. 23. Here we should note that this citation and the following one as well are taken from Sartre's well-known lecture, 'Existentialism Is a Humanism', delivered on 28 October 1945. When Heidegger read this essay in print, in which Sartre 'claims' Heidegger as one of the atheistic existentialists, Heidegger sharply rejects the association. First, Heidegger is critical of the unreflective use of the word 'humanism', which itself has a long history, and contains metaphysical presuppositions that Heidegger rejects. But moreover, he rejects the existentialist employment of the Dasein analytic. Where Heidegger analyses topics like anxiety and guilt, he does so from a more strictly ontological perspective, while Sartre's analyses often tend in the direction of the more broadly psychological. See Martin Heidegger, 'Letter on "Humanism"', trans. Frank A. Capuzzi with John Glenn Gray, ed., rev. William McNeill and David

Farrell Krell, in ed. William McNeill, *Pathmarks* (Cambridge: Cambridge University Press, 1998).

22. Sartre, *Existentialism and Human Emotions*, p. 13.

23. Foucault, 'Introduction', *The Normal and the Pathological*, pp. 8–9.

24. Ferdinand de Saussure, *Course in General Linguistics*, ed. Charles Bally and Albert Sechehaye, with the collaboration of Albert Riedlinger, trans. Roy Harris (La Salle: Open Court Press, 1972), pp. 116–18.

25. This conference is Derrida's introduction to America. The conference was held in Baltimore, at Johns Hopkins University, over the period of 18–21 October 1966. It was titled, 'The Languages of Criticism and the Sciences of Man', and many of the significant papers from this conference as well as the discussions that follow them, including Derrida's own piece, are collected in the volume, ed. Richard Macksey and Eugenio Domato, *The Structuralist Controversy: The Languages of Criticism and the Sciences of Man* (Baltimore: The Johns Hopkins University Press, 1970). Derrida's essay is 'Structure, Sign and Play in the Discourse of the Human Sciences', and is also included in *Writing and Difference*.

26. Claude Lévi-Strauss, *The Savage Mind* (Chicago: The University of Chicago Press, 1966), p. 247.

27. This collision in Derrida's own thinking is most readily witnessed in the back-to-back publication, in 1963 and 1964 respectively, of 'Cogito and the History of Madness', on Foucault, and 'Violence and Metaphysics', on Levinas.

2. A Guide to the Text

Introduction

There are various strategies by which an author may write an introduction to his or her work. Sometimes an introduction attempts to provide a historical background to the work, laying out the history of the problem and the stakes associated with the articulation of the problem, as a way of laying the basic groundwork for what will follow in the argumentation of the book itself. Introductions written in this mode typically require of the reader only a very basic knowledge of the subject matter at hand, and the author's intention is usually to fill in the lacunae that may exist in the general reader's knowledge. Such an introduction is then something of a historical précis; providing the background of the problem, it is required only in order to contextualise the author's argument and see its significance. This kind of introduction then is very basic, not particularly deep or demanding, and hence it is designed to be broadly comprehensible, sometimes even for the largely untrained reader. However, there is another kind of introduction that authors sometimes write. With this second strategy, the author attempts to very succinctly articulate the major points of the entire argument, *which he or she is about to present in what follows in the text*. In an extremely truncated manner, the author presents, in the smallest units but broadest strokes possible, the most significant elements of the entire work. The *virtue* of this latter strategy is that, prior to even beginning the book proper, the reader already has a sense of what the author proposes to argue, and why and how he or she plans to do so. However, since the reader has not yet read the work, an introduction such as this might very well create as many lacunae as it fills in. In short, the reader may well find such an introduction terribly confusing.

The 'Introduction' to *Voice and Phenomenon*, in a certain, very complicated sense, combines *both* of these strategies. The combination of these two strategies in the 'Introduction' is in part due to the fact that, in engaging with Husserl's thought, Derrida is in point of fact engaging with the entire history of the Western philosophical tradition; hence to 'lay out the stakes', as we said above, *requires* a certain historical contextualisation which, for the sake of conciseness, can only be, almost reductively so, cursory. At the same time, in a project where the author attempts to in very broad strokes assimilate a specific thinker to an entire tradition, to, as Lawlor says, 'homogenize the history of Western philosophy' (*VP*, p. xiv), to lay out the stakes is also, by necessity, to argue for the reasons as to *why* Derrida reads Husserl as the inheritor of the entire metaphysical tradition. But to do this, in light of Derrida's overall project of deconstruction, is to already begin to point the way out, towards the 'how' and the 'what' of the concepts that deconstruction attempts to formulate. Hence part historical précis, part argumentative compendium, the 'Introduction' to *Voice and Phenomenon* is perhaps one of *the* most difficult parts of the book.

Having said all of this, the reader is by all means encouraged to carefully engage with the 'Introduction'. But the reader is also encouraged to not give up in the face of the difficulty and complexity of the 'Introduction'; to take as much away from the 'Introduction' as able, and then to dive into the argument of the book itself, which is much more meticulously and exhaustively laid out. Given its aforementioned *virtue* of summarising the main points of the argument, the reader may even be well advised to return to the 'Introduction' once the reading of the text proper is complete, as doing so may help concretise and solidify the main points of the arguments explored throughout the book. Finally, we should keep in mind that Derrida's writing style is such that he often, through the course of the 'Introduction', and into the body of the text as well, employs rhetorical questions – *Is it not the case that . . . ?*, *Does it not . . . ?*, *Can we not say that . . . ?*, etc. – for purposes of aiding the reader in understanding Derrida's motivations, we can advise that in *almost* all cases that Derrida uses a rhetorical device such as this, it can be read as, *I shall argue that . . .* Let us now turn to the reading of the 'Introduction'.

As Derrida notes in the opening paragraph, one of the core premises of the argument of *Voice and Phenomenon* is that the project of phenomenology, despite its many modifications, is born with the 1900–1 publication of the *Logical Investigations*. Despite the fact that Husserl lives (and publishes) for almost a full four decades after its publication, there are, Derrida argues, no substantial *breaks* in Husserl's thinking after the

Logical Investigations; reformulations, perhaps, but no breaks. This is true, more than of anything else, of Husserl's reflections on *language*, and on *the sign*, which by and large are operative from the publication of the *Logical Investigations* until the end of Husserl's life. As the subtitle of *Voice and Phenomenon* indicates, the text is a reflection on the 'problem of the sign' in Husserl's thought.

This *problem of the sign* stems from an ambiguity, the fact that, as Derrida notes, 'the word "sign" (*Zeichen*) would have a "double sense" (*ein Doppelsinn*). The sign "sign" can mean "expression" (*Ausdruck*) or "indication" (*Anzeichen*)' (*VP*, p. 3/4/2). As we shall see in our analysis of Chapter 1, an *indication* is a sign that points the receiver to some state of affairs, as a fever in the body points *to* some kind of infection or illness; while an *expression* is a sign that makes intelligible a linguistic meaning. In summary fashion, we can say that expressions are signs that *mean* while indications are signs that *point*. Prior to articulating this 'essential distinction', Husserl proposes to put out of consideration all constituted knowledge and all presuppositions, wherever they may come from – whether 'from metaphysics, from psychology, or from the natural sciences' (*VP*, p. 4/4/2). He then argues that the fact that our analysis must begin in the 'starting point' of language (*VP*, p. 4/4/2) is not an impediment to this commitment to avoid presuppositions and constituted knowledge. So long as we heed the contingency of the linguistic sign, we are safe to analyse the structures of sense and knowledge, apart from this empirical starting point:

The analyses thus carried out keep their 'sense' and their 'epistemological value'—their value in the order of the theory of knowledge (*erkenntnistheoretischen Wert*)—whether languages exist or not, whether beings such as humans actually make use of languages or not, whether humans or a nature exist really or merely 'in the imagination and on the basis of the mode of possibility'. (*VP*, p. 4/4/2)

And with that stroke alone, the general structure of the problematic of *Voice and Phenomenon* is already laid out in full for us. Let us look at *why* this is.

To, in one and the same stroke, insist upon the absolute absence of presuppositions in one's theory, while at the same time arguing that one's immersion in language as the necessary starting point does not count as a presupposition, is to assert, without argumentation, that language does not qualify as a constituted knowledge, which is to say that it is merely a vehicle for such knowledge. Put differently, to insist, as Husserl does, upon putting out of play all constituted knowledge, and *then*, to insist that the *ideal senses* and *epistemological value* of the analyses to be carried out are *unaffected* by the *contingency* of language, is to presuppose, from the very beginning, that meaning, sense and knowledge are all 'untouched' or 'uncontaminated' by the use of the sign, that is to say, by language. It is to imply, in other words, that there is such a thing as meaning as such, prior to the intervention by the *sign* that would secondarily attempt to *communicate* that meaning to the self or to someone else, and that *knowledge* is possible, over and above the use of language. The sign, then, would be merely a *supplemental tool*, something that humans *employ* in order to *make known* a knowledge that subsists, essentially, *prior to the sign*.

This, Derrida argues, is a metaphysical presupposition through and through, as is, Derrida suggests, anything that would go by the name of a 'theory of knowledge'. It is metaphysical because it assumes that an ideal object (which by definition transcends experience), in the form of the unwavering *presence* of a fulfilled intuition, constitutes knowledge, while representation or language is essentially excluded from this structure, and is secondary and supplemental to it. Hence:

[the] most general form of our question is thus prescribed. Do not the phenomenological necessity, the rigor and subtlety of Husserl's analysis, the demands to which it responds and the demands we must first of all satisfy, nevertheless dissimulate a metaphysical presupposition? (*VP*, pp. 4/4/2–3)

As Derrida goes on to demonstrate in this paragraph, however, the argument of *Voice and Phenomenon* is not – and we must be absolutely clear on this – the argument is not that these metaphysical presuppositions somehow 'intrude' accidentally into the phenomenological project, as though from outside of it, as something foreign to the phenomenological project. Rather, the entirety of the phenomenological project is, Derrida will argue, oriented, constituted and sustained by a somewhat unacknowledged 'metaphysical heritage' (*VP*, p. 4/5/3).

Husserl's adoption of a very traditional philosophical view of the sign and of language is one of the key indicators of this heritage, according to Derrida, and it is an aspect that will cause Husserl himself theoretical and terminological difficulty. For instance, as we shall see later in our analysis of *Voice and Phenomenon*, for reasons of structural necessity, Husserl will subordinate the operation of the sign to a notion of a 'pure logical grammar'. We must keep in mind that the phenomenological project is constituted on the basis of the reduction or bracketing of the so-called existence of the so-called real world, in order to isolate pure structures of meaning as the conditions of apodictic knowledge. Hence the theory of language undergirding this impetus must be able to provide us with a framework for evaluating the meaningfulness of a given discourse such that it: (1) does not rely upon any reference to the bracketed empirical world – its meaningfulness, in other words, can have nothing to do with the degree to which it does or does not correspond with the 'real world', as this relation is precisely what will have been 'bracketed'; (2) might at least potentially provide us with knowledge. Thus, Husserl will remain firmly committed to the position that meaningful discourse must accord with pure, *a priori*, logical laws of syntactical and grammatical connection and configuration, laws which form the backbone of all empirical languages, insofar as they are meaningful.

However, as Husserl recognises, to subordinate the functioning of the sign to a *logic* is also to radically exclude from the domain of 'sense' as 'meaningless' a whole host of non-logical uses of the sign, such as rhetoric, poetry, etc.; not to mention a multitude of non-literary arts, such as dance, music, cinema, photography, architecture, sculpture, etc. It is therefore only on the basis of presupposition that one is able to, without criticism or caveat, fundamentally subordinate the operation of the sign to a 'logic'. For Derrida, this presupposition is the *teleological faith* on Husserl's part that meaningful discourse must point thinking in the direction of that which might at least potentially be given as a fulfilled, 'present' object of intuition. Hence Husserl repeats what Derrida refers to as the founding gesture of the metaphysics of presence.

Even when Husserl speaks critically of the metaphysical tradition, it is always only a certain form of metaphysics that he decries, namely, a metaphysics rooted in an insufficient mode of ideality. What we might call 'bad' metaphysics then, for Husserl, is what he refers to in *Cartesian Meditations* as metaphysics in the 'usual sense: a historically degenerate metaphysics which by no means conforms to the spirit in which metaphysics as "first philosophy" was originally instituted', arguing that 'Phenomenology's purely intuitive, concrete, and also apodictic mode of demonstration excludes all "metaphysical adventure," all speculative excess' (*VP*, pp. 5/5–6/4).[1] The characteristics of degenerate metaphysics, Derrida argues, will always amount for Husserl to the historically prevalent failure to recognise that the *non-reality* of the ideal is what makes it infinitely repeatable across all empirical variations; hence its non-reality is the most essential feature of the ideal. Its non-reality, however, is of a very special sort – it is not a fiction, which is to say an illusion, but it does not come from some other realm either – it is not from 'another mundanity' (*VP*, p. 5/6/4); it would not, as it were, fall ready-made from the sky, as it might be thought to do so within the framework of an oversimplified form of Platonism. Its sole claim to ideality subsists precisely in its pure possibility of repetition, that it 'can be *repeated* indefinitely in the *identity* of its *presence* because of the very fact that it *does not exist*' (*VP*, p. 5/6/4). In order that the ideal may be infinitely repeatable in the face of the ever-changing empirical realm, 'it is necessary that one ideal form secures this unity of the *indefinitely* and the *idealiter*' (*VP*, p. 5/6/4), and this ideal form, in which the ideal is infinitely repeatable, Derrida says, is the *ideal of the living present*, the structure we analysed above as consisting of the core or nucleus of the primal impression, surrounded by the halo of retention and protention – primary memory and primary expectation.

As the contents of experience infinitely arise, diminish and pass away, what secures the ideality of the meanings they impress is the structural element of repetition inherent to the Husserlian 'form' of the living present. In order that a sense can even be initially impressed within a primal impression, it is necessary and essential to it that it will be retainable (which is to say, repeatable) in the mode of retention. This structure of the living present thereby provides the form of lived-experience, and the contents, its matter; therewith repeating uncritically 'the inaugural opposition of metaphysics—between form and matter' (*VP*, p. 6/6/5). The form/matter distinction has manifested in myriad ways throughout the history of philosophy. The most famous and earliest example is Plato's, but a version of this very same distinction – between a 'form' that is pure and unchanging, and a 'matter' that is fleeting and impermanent – is central also for Aristotle, most of Christian theology, Augustine, Aquinas, Descartes, Leibniz, etc. With the ideal form of the *living present*, therefore, Husserl repeats a very traditional move, reaffirming the 'founding value of presence' (*VP*, p. 6/7/5), which will uncritically assert a fundamental distinction between reality (or presence) and representation, and hold that presence comes first and representation second.

This 'presence of the living-present' will be the ultimate metaphysical engine that drives the phenomenological project in its entirety: 'Presence has always been and will always be, to infinity, the form in which—we can say this apodictically—the infinite diversity of contents will be produced' (*VP*, p. 6/6/5). The structure of the living present secures 'presence' in both its senses: (1) spatially, it secures the presence of the object as an object of intuition by way of the essential possibility of repetition that conditions ideality itself; (2) temporally, it secures the self-presence of transcendental life in the temporal present. In both these senses, Husserl's living present reaffirms the founding value of presence. A bad metaphysics for Husserl then is one in which the presence of the present is not fully secured. This is why Husserl's thought, for Derrida, represents 'metaphysics in its most modern, critical, and vigilant form' (*Positions*, p. 5). Whenever Husserl critiques metaphysics, it is ultimately only in order to purify it, or to give back its true self; and whenever the value of presence is at risk in Husserl's thought, he reanimates it by way of what Derrida calls the 'Idea in the Kantian sense' (*VP*, p. 8/9/8) – a concept that of its very nature goes beyond the possibility of experience.

However, the heart of *Voice and Phenomenon* lies in the arguments, conducted through Chapters 4, 5 and 6, 'that phenomenology appears to us to be tormented if not contested, from the inside, by means of its own descriptions of the movement of temporalization and of the constitution of intersubjectivity' (*VP*, p. 6/6/5). In the movement of temporalisation, Husserl designates a radical difference between 'reproduction' as representative memory, and 'retention' as primary memory; this in order to allow 'retention' as the structural possibility of repetition, to subsist in essential commerce with the present-now of the 'primal impression', in order that it may remain within the living present as the ideal form of lived-experience; and yet, to the extent that the primal impression designates the absolute core or nucleus of perception, the 'source-point' as we said, of perception, it follows that retention is – Husserl says so explicitly – a 'non-perception'. This means that the presence of the primal impression remains, essentially and continuously, in relation with a non-perception or non-presence – and the relation that produces these is constituted continuously in the movement of temporalisation. This institutes an originary lack in the heart of presence, or we might say, a 'blindness' at the heart of the inner vision of self-knowledge. Therefore, in the self-relation of the inner life, the self-presence of the subject can only relate to itself as it would to an *other*, across the movement of temporalisation. This otherness therefore becomes an essential condition of the self-relation. But this is not to reject, outright, the founding value of presence. As Derrida notes:

It does not cut into the founding value of presence. [. . .] What is at issue, however, is to make the original and non-empirical space of non-foundation appear, as the irreducible emptiness from which the security of presence in the metaphysical form of ideality is decided and from which this security removes itself. (*VP*, pp. 6/7/5–6)

The purpose is to demonstrate a certain relation to absence as constitutive of presence, a certain relation to death as the condition of life.

By opening this question of life and its relation to death, we have landed upon what is likely *the* central challenge of *Voice and Phenomenon*, which is a reformulation of the question of life itself. It is crucial to note the importance of the concept of life to the phenomenological project, and therefore for Derrida's project as well. The concept of life is central to the phenomenological constitution of sense – 'the source of sense in general is always determined as the act of a thing that *lives*, as the act of a living being' (*VP*, p. 9/10/9), and hence it is central to many of the core phenomenological concepts from the *Logical Investigations* forward – 'life', 'transcendental life', 'the living present', 'experience' ('*Erlebnis*' – *leben* meaning 'life'), 'lifeworld', etc. As Derrida says, 'we must consider that phenomenology, the metaphysics of presence in the form of ideality, is also a philosophy of *life*' (*VP*, p. 9/10/9). To conclude our discussion of the 'Introduction' to *Voice and Phenomenon*, let us look at the role that the concept of life plays for Husserl, and at the ways in which Derrida's analyses call for a new, as yet unnameable, concept of life. We must begin by looking to the various parallelisms that govern Husserl's thinking, as these parallels are united in the concept of life.

Above, we described in a very brief manner the eidetic and transcendental reductions. The eidetic reduction, we said, suspends the question of the real existence of the empirical world, and reduces all objects of consciousness to their pure *essences* (*eidē*) in order that they and their intentional meaning-structures might be analysed purely, without presuppositions or concerns regarding the *veracity* or *adequation* of the objects with respect to the external world. What Derrida calls 'Phenomenological psychology' (*VP*, p. 9/11/10) and at other points 'psychological consciousness' (*VP*, p. 11/13/12) operates at this level of the eidetic reduction, *describing* the operations of the *psychē*, but in a phenomenological mode that has bracketed the questions concerning the correspondence of the psychē to the objects of which its contents would purport themselves to be representations. But though this reduction brackets the empiricity of the 'world', the psychē itself, however, is at the same time an empirical *thing*. This is why Derrida says that the essences which the eidetic reduction 'settles *intrinsically* presuppose the existence of the world in that kind of mundane region called the *psychē*' (*VP*, pp. 11/12–13/12). Therefore, in the mode of eidetic reduction, there remains nevertheless a residue of the empirical world.

The transcendental reduction, on the other hand, reduces even this, my empirical Ego or psychē, thereby opening access to a pure mode of consciousness without which no world, as such, would be possible. As Derrida notes, in this mode, 'the *totality* of the world is neutralized in its existence and reduced to its phenomenon' (*VP*, p. 11/12/12); that is to say, in the mode of the transcendental reduction, everything, including my empirical Ego, is completely reduced to its status as 'sense' or 'meaning', and this mode of consciousness (which we above referred to as the 'transcendental Ego') is what Derrida calls in many places, 'transcendental consciousness' (*VP*, p. 11/13/12). What, then, is the relation between these two modes, psychological consciousness and transcendental consciousness? Transcendental consciousness or pure consciousness is what makes possible the empirical or psychological consciousness. It is the ground, without which no world, and hence no psychological consciousness, would be possible at all. Nevertheless, Husserl also claims that the eidetic reduction, which exposes psychological consciousness, is the *condition of possibility* for the transcendental reduction, which, as Derrida notes, neutralises the totality of the world in its existence, thereby exposing the transcendental consciousness that grounds the psychological consciousness. The eidetic reduction that exposes the psychological consciousness is a *condition* for the transcendental reduction that exposes the transcendental consciousness that, reciprocally, grounds the psychological consciousness.

Between these two spheres Husserl claims, there is a parallel relation:

In the last analysis, between the pure psychical—a region of the world that is opposed to transcendental consciousness and is discovered by means of the reduction of the totality of the natural, transcendent world—and the pure transcendental life, there is, Husserl says, a relation of *parallelism*. (*VP*, p. 9/11/10)

This parallelism is extremely complicated. Psychological consciousness, as Derrida notes, conditions every other domain of experience. Insofar as it reduces *all* objects of consciousness to their status as phenomena in order to purely analyse their essences and intentional structures, the generality of this domain (of psychological consciousness) 'dominates all other regions' (*VP*, p. 10/11/10) and all lived-experiences. Moreover, in the shift from the psychological consciousness to the mode of transcendental consciousness, announced in the transcendental reduction, nothing more regarding the essences or meaning-structures themselves is revealed or exposed. Nevertheless, this domain of transcendental consciousness must be exposed in order to completely neutralise all vestiges of the empirical world, in order to isolate the pure structures of meaning. For these reasons, 'the dependence of the purely psychical in regard to transcendental consciousness, which is the archi-region, is absolutely singular' (*VP*, p. 10/11/10). Given the fact that *nothing more* of the essences or meaning-structures is exposed in the shift from the eidetic to the transcendental reduction, 'The domain of pure psychological experience in fact coincides with the totality of the domain of what Husserl calls transcendental experience' (*VP*, p. 10/11/10).

But in spite of this parallelism, and in spite of this perfect coincidence of the domains of psychological consciousness and of transcendental consciousness, it is nevertheless necessarily the case that between the two spheres 'a radical difference remains, which has nothing in common with any other difference. This is a difference which in fact distinguishes nothing, a difference which separates no being, no lived-experience, no determinate signification' (*VP*, p. 10/11/10) – in the mode of transcendental reduction, we find a perfect coinciding of the spheres, and yet a radical difference between them. This *radical difference*, strictly speaking, has no reality, that is to say that it has no substance. For if there were a substantiality to the difference between the two spheres, the difference would then amount to a real relation, which would thereby permit communication and contamination between the two spheres. But there can be no contamination between the two spheres, for such contamination would result in the very error that the *Logical Investigations* set out to abolish – the reducibility of the transcendental to the empirical, the error that Derrida calls 'transcendental psychologism' (*VP*, p. 11/13/12).

This is a difference, Derrida says, that, 'without altering anything, changes all the signs' (*VP*, p. 10/11/10). Husserl's *radical difference* alters nothing – it does not provide any sort of real or ontological doubling of the Ego, only a doubling of *sense*. This doubling of sense 'changes all the signs', which is to say, it transforms the signs of language from *indicative signs* that can only point, to *expressive signs* that purely mean. That this difference 'alters nothing' and yet 'changes all the signs', indicates that this difference is not 'real' or does not 'inhabit the world, but only language, in its transcendental restlessness' (*VP*, p. 12/14/13). It is a difference found only in language, and thus we could say that it is made possible *by* language. Yet this difference, exposed in the operation of the transcendental reduction, opens the sphere of transcendental consciousness, thereby opening up the pure possibility and structures of meaning that make language itself possible. This is what Derrida means when he says, 'Language keeps watch over the difference that keeps watch over language' (*VP*, p. 12/14/13).

This 'radical difference that distinguishes nothing' is therefore made possible *by* language, and at the same time, it makes language possible. In the face of this paradox, therefore, language can only point to this difference by way of analogy. It is only through the use of analogical language that the operation of the transcendental reduction can be announced; that is to say, one must speak *as if* the Ego were doubled in the operation of the transcendental reduction, recognising all the while that this doubling does not amount to an ontological reality, and hence that this announcement of the reduction is conducted by way of metaphor. For this reason, however, these metaphors must efface themselves in the moment they are employed; necessary though they may be, they nevertheless remain metaphors which, if pushed to the point of substantialising that difference to which they analogically point, if taken *too* seriously, they risk cancelling or attenuating the radical difference that Husserl needs in order to ground the transcendental project. It is for this reason that 'If language never escapes from analogy, even if it is analogy through and through, it must, having reached this point, and at this very point, freely take up its own destruction and cast metaphors against metaphors' (*VP*, p. 12/13/13). This is tantamount to a war of language against itself, as Husserl, in a repetition of a very traditional philosophical gesture, will attempt to exclude language in its entirety from the purity of meaning – to use language in order to subvert language.

This brings us back to the point that opened the 'Introduction', where we noted that, as far as Husserl is concerned, there is such a thing as 'meaning', as such, prior to the contaminating intervention of a language which would attempt to grasp or communicate it. Now we see that this gesture *must* be made and sustained by Husserl in order to secure this radical difference between psychological consciousness and transcendental consciousness, the radical difference that distinguishes nothing *in fact*. Nevertheless, while attempting to maintain this pre-expressive, that is to say pre-linguistic, stratum of sense, the phenomenological project will, in another repetition of a traditional gesture, maintain an 'essential link between the *logos* and the *phonē*' (*VP*, p. 13/15/14). This too follows from the necessity to sustain this *radical difference*. Since self-consciousness for the phenomenological project only ever operates by way of the intentional structure that relates it to an object, ideal and repeatable, and these idealities are linguistic in nature, 'the element of consciousness and the element of language will be more and more difficult to discern' (*VP*, p. 13/15/15). But, as we have said, for Husserl they must be discernible. Since the ideality that Husserl seeks is understood in the sense of *pure repeatability*, these objects must be constituted and repeated in a medium that protects the presence of the object as an object of consciousness, and the self-presence of the intuitional acts to themselves. This medium must not permit the contamination of the transcendental with the empirical. Therefore, in order to respond to this apparent indiscernibility between the psychological consciousness and the transcendental consciousness, Husserl will employ the *voice*.

In the opening line of his *De Interpretatione*, Aristotle writes, 'Spoken words are the symbols of mental experience and written words are the symbols of spoken words.'[2] The *voice*, in other words, is most intimately connected to the *soul* or the sphere of mental experience. Mental experience is primary, the voice utters a spoken sign that represents that experience, and the written sign is inscribed in order to represent the spoken sign. This same gesture appears in Plato, and is repeated by Rousseau, by Hegel, etc. Husserl therefore repeats a move that is very much in line with the philosophical tradition. But, as Derrida notes, Husserl *radicalises* this privileging of the voice, in the most critical and rigorous way possible: unlike the rest of the tradition before him, Husserl forbids the passage of the voice through the exteriority of the world. It will not be the communicative voice, or the bodily voice that Husserl will valorise, 'rather the originative affinity will be recognized in the phenomenological voice, in the voice in its transcendental flesh, in the breath, in intentional animation which transforms the body of the word into flesh . . .' (*VP*, p. 14/16/15).

So, as the radical difference between the two spheres appears to be announced by language, which appears increasingly analogical and hence metaphorical, and as the element of language and the element of consciousness become more and more difficult to discern, Husserl will attempt to ground these differences in the silent voice of the interior life of the soul, which, Husserl will argue, operates without any passage through exteriority (therefore without any diminishment of self-presence), expressing its meanings in an absolutely *pure* manner. This is the voice of the title, *Voice and Phenomenon*, as Lawlor notes in his 'Translator's Introduction' (*VP*, p. xxi), and this is why Derrida conducts such a careful analysis of the operation of *hearing-oneself-speak* in Chapter 6 of *Voice and Phenomenon*. But we must keep in mind that, when it operates, the phenomenological voice must still use language, for which Husserl never provides an extended theoretical account. It is therefore Husserl's problematic relation to the question of language itself that he leaves unresolved; and it is problematic inasmuch as Husserl's project contains two irreconcilable commitments with respect to the nature of language. First, a formalist pole: according to the formalist aspect of the phenomenological project, a discourse can be meaningful, *with or without* the fulfilment of intuition that would make knowledge possible. But if discourse can be meaningful with or without this intuition, this is another way of saying that the fulfilment of intuition is not an essential component of meaningful discourse, and indeed Husserl gives no shortage of examples of discourses that, though meaningful, can designate no object, whether for *a priori* or empirical reasons. Moreover, given that the ideal for Husserl only ever takes the form of the Idea in the Kantian sense, which by definition can never be given in experience, the very form of ideality itself would in fact *preclude* the fulfilment of intuition. The establishment of presence is always infinitely deferred. Second, an intuitionist pole: according to the intuitionist pole of this tension, the very possibility of meaningfulness is established on the teleological basis of the fact that the discourse is structured in such a way that it might at least possibly point to an object that would come to presence in a fulfilled intuition. The opposition of these two commitments underlies as presupposition Husserl's entire understanding of language. Therefore, 'Despite the vigilance of the description, a perhaps naïve treatment of the concept of "word" has no doubt failed to resolve in phenomenology the tension between its two major motives: the purity of formalism and the radicality of intuitionism' (*VP*, p. 14/16/16). This conflict will open onto the question of the infinite, as the *telos* of the infinite presence of intuition opposes the infinite deferral of Husserl's formalism, and this engagement with the infinite brings us to the completion of the concept of life.

The centrality of 'life' for the phenomenological project lies in the fact that 'life' is what finally unites the parallelism between the 'psychological life' and the 'transcendental life'; 'life' lies at the root of each. '"Living" is therefore the name of what precedes the reduction and escapes finally from all the distributions that the reduction brings to light' (*VP*, pp. 13/14–15/14). Life, for Husserl, escapes from the reductions and from all their 'distributions'. But 'life', as Derrida will think it in *Voice and Phenomenon*, through the representative character of language in Chapter 4, the movement of temporalisation in Chapter 5 and the operation of hearing-oneself-speak in Chapter 6, is self-relation, and in relating *to* itself, this *to* will constitute a productive difference at the heart of life. In this sense life is self-distributing, but the fact that life distributes itself entails that it relates itself constantly and essentially to what is *not* life, that is, to death. 'Life', that is, can never reach a full and secure moment of absolute self-presence; its presence, insofar as it is self-distributing, is infinitely deferred.

This concept of life will point towards an opening to a new infinity beyond the *positive infinite* of the metaphysics of presence, which takes the form of the *absolute wanting-to-hear-itself-speak*. This engagement with the *infinite* is intrinsically connected with the operation of *hearing-oneself-speak*. In his *Metaphysics*, Aristotle argues for an 'unmoved mover' that is *noesis noeseos* – self-thinking thought. The prime mover in Aristotle's *Metaphysics* thinks – and to think is to *mean* or *to want-to-say*,[3] and to at the same time *hear* or *understand* – constantly and eternally about what it means to be divine, and in so doing, it draws the rest of the cosmos to an ordered operation as the whole of being attempts to imitate this divine self-thinking thought. Aristotle's prime mover therefore eternally carries out the operation of *hearing-oneself-speak*.

Hegel then pushes this notion of the *noesis noeseos* to the level of the infinite – where Aristotle's self-thinking thought had operated without mediation, in an eternity of pure and simple immediacy, for Hegel the Absolute must posit itself as absolutely other, in order to ultimately surmount this otherness. This passage through exteriority, Hegel holds, is what has occupied the entire progression of the history of thought, conceived as the unfolding of Absolute Spirit. It must *express* or *speak* the infinite as absolute otherness, and then it must ultimately *hear-itself*, thereby overcoming this otherness and subsuming this difference into a higher moment of identity, at which point this act of *wanting-to-say* would be brought to completion. It is only in this way that the 'Absolute' for Hegel can truly be thought – that is, the positive infinite must think itself.

Thought must reach throughout the whole of Being, but it can only do this by passing through its own absolute otherness. Hegel therefore discovers a necessary passage through difference or mediation. But in finally coming into possession of itself in the fullness of *hearing-itself-speak*, the Absolute abolishes the difference, and the infinite becomes finally its own object of intuition.

This means that the 'positive infinite' of the metaphysical tradition amounts to an absolute auto-affection that is *both* Absolute life *and* Absolute death. It establishes the necessity of the movement through difference, or through mediation (or distribution), only so that it can ultimately cancel that difference. The absoluteness of the metaphysical concept of life, when presence becomes fully present to itself in a fulfilled intuition, thereby abolishes the difference that made it possible. The infinite, for Hegel, is thus a *telos* that, once completed, is also cancelled.

The concept of life that emerges in deconstruction, from out of Derrida's engagement with Husserl, will be what Derrida will call the 'différance' of auto-affection. The infinite, as it functions in Husserl, indeed functions as a *telos*, but a *telos* which, by definition, can never be attained. The ideal, whenever it appears, can only do so within finitude. The notion of 'transcendental life' in the form of the living present is itself an ideality that is therefore never, for Husserl, given as such in a moment of fulfilled intuition. That is to say that the 'presence' of the transcendental life is itself constituted on the basis of an essential structure of infinite deferral. But if the presence of 'life' must be understood on the basis of the essential deferral of that presence, then life itself must be thought as essentially finite. Life, for Derrida, is that which constantly distributes itself, and it does so on the basis of and in relation with that which is not-life, *death*. As Derrida says, 'Life, however, is its own distribution and its own opposition to its other' (*VP*, p. 13/15/14). This, however, points thought in the direction of a concept of life that would make possible both the 'psychological life' and the 'transcendental life' of the phenomenological project. It is for this reason that deconstruction attempts to name a concept of life that would serve, we might say, as the *condition of possibility* for the *transcendental*, that Derrida will call this concept of life the 'ultra-transcendental concept of life' (*VP*, p. 13/15/14). But insofar as it is the transcendental consciousness in the phenomenological project that is responsible for the constitution of meaning, there can quite literally be, for Derrida, *no names* by which this concept of life could be named: hence 'and if it has never been inscribed in any language, this concept of life perhaps calls for *another name'* (*VP*, p. 13/15/14). *Voice and Phenomenon* will mark the opening of a passage of thinking that attempts to *name* that which cannot be *named* – this passage itself will go by the *name* of deconstruction.

Let us now turn to our reading of *Voice and Phenomenon*.

Sign and Signs

Opening the first chapter is an argument as to why Derrida retains the German of Husserl's terminology, rather than employing straightforward and accepted French (and for us, English) translations. This multiplicity of languages in Derrida's texts is one aspect of his writing that can seem frustrating to the first-time reader, so let us explore this further. To begin, as we have noted in the previous chapter of this book, there is an ambiguity within the notion of the 'sign' (*Zeichen*), in that it contains two different senses: that of *expression* (*Ausdruck*) and that of *indication* (*Anzeichen*). Then we are quickly introduced to two more German terms with a very rich and complicated history in late nineteenth- and early twentieth-century German thought: *Bedeutung* and *Sinn*. These two terms may both be translated, roughly if imprecisely, as 'meaning' or 'sense'. In his influential article, 'On Sinn and Bedeutung',[4] Frege had distinguished between *Bedeutung*, which he understands as the object towards which a reference points, and *Sinn*, understood as the way in which a given term characterises that object. So, for instance, the phrases, 'the victor at Jena' and 'the vanquished at Waterloo', share, in Frege's sense, a *Bedeutung* (in that they both point towards Napoleon Bonaparte), but they do not share a *Sinn*, because they each tell us something different about Napoleon – they characterise him in a different way.

Husserl rejects Frege's distinguishing between *Sinn* and *Bedeutung* in this way, and in the 1900–1 *Logical Investigations*, he makes his refusal of this Fregean distinction explicit (*VP*, pp. 16/18–19/18–19). Moreover, even when Husserl finally *does* come to draw a distinction between *Sinn* and *Bedeutung*, with the 1913 publication of *Ideas I*, it is not the Fregean distinction he employs, but rather, a specifically Husserlian distinction, between *Bedeutung* as 'ideal sense content of *verbal* expression, while sense (*Sinn*) covers the whole noematic sphere, including its non-expressive stratum' (*VP*, p. 16/19/19). In other words (and this is one of Derrida's primary targets in *Voice and Phenomenon*), *Sinn* for Husserl will eventually come to refer to that *layer* or *region* of inner experience that Husserl

argues for that does not employ signs at all, a sense-stratum of pure presence within the interiority of the soul, while *Bedeutung* for Husserl refers
to the ideality of meaning to which our signs point, when that stratum
of inner experience is brought into expression.

But even *this* terminological distinction for Husserl does not appear
until the 1913 publication of *Ideas I* (even if, conceptually, it is already
operating in 1900). In the earlier *Logical Investigations*, there is no such
distinction: *Sinn* and *Bedeutung* are synonymous. The difference, for
Husserl, between expression (*Ausdruck*) and indication (*Anzeichen*) is that,
while indication is indeed a type of *sign*, it is a sign that has no *Bedeutung*
or *Sinn*: it is '*bedeutunglos, sinnlos*' (*VP*, p. 15/17/17). Thus, we can speak of
a sign as either having or not having a *Bedeutung*. However, the standard
French translation of *Bedeutung* is, as Derrida notes, *signification*,[5] which, if
followed, obscures the terminological precision of Husserl's text – while
a sign can either have or not have a *Bedeutung*, it cannot possibly be
without a *signification*. The phrase 'signifying sign' is a redundancy, while
the phrase 'non-signifying sign' is a contradiction. A similar imprecision
occurs in English as well: both *Bedeutung* and *Sinn*, as we said, are roughly
rendered in English as 'meaning', but an indication, in the Husserlian
sense, though it may not point to an *ideality*, nevertheless would not likely
be said to *have no meaning* – a red light in traffic *means* that one is supposed
to stop, for instance.

For this reason, Derrida will frequently insist upon employing
Husserl's German terminology. But then, Derrida moves straightaway
to offering an alternative French word as an equivalent to Husserl's
notion of *Bedeutung*. *Bedeutung*, Derrida claims, is for Husserl intimately
bound up with the concept of 'spoken discourse' (*Rede*, *VP*, p. 16/18/18)
– Husserl, remember, distinguishes between a non-expressive stratum of
sense (later identified as *Sinn*) and a domain of ideal meaning to which
the signs point by which we *express* or communicate that non-expressive
stratum – this is *Bedeutung*. *Bedeutung*, then, is indistinguishably tied up
with linguistic communication: 'Expression is a purely linguistic sign
and, in the first analysis, this is precisely what distinguishes it from
indication' (*VP*, p. 16/18/18). Since *expression* is linguistic in nature,
and since *Bedeutung* refers to the sphere of ideality to which an *expression*
points, Derrida argues, 'one could define, if not translate, "bedeuten" by
"vouloir-dire" at once in the sense of a speaking subject that *wants to say*,
"expressing himself," as Husserl says, "about something"—and in the
sense of an expression that *means*' (*VP*, p. 16/18/18). *Vouloir* in French

means 'to want', 'to will' or 'to intend', while *dire* means 'to say', such that *vouloir-dire* means literally, *to-want-* or *to-intend-to-say*. Here, Derrida's footnote points to a fortuitous equivocation in English, whereby *to mean* can be understood in two ways: (1) as 'indicating a specific *sense*', as when we say, for instance, 'the word "cold" *means* "lacking in heat"'; (2) in the sense of 'to intend' or 'to will', as when we might say, 'I did not *mean* to hurt your feelings.' But already, in the second paragraph of the text proper, Derrida has drawn a tight relation between *Bedeutung*, as Husserl understands it, and the traditional, metaphysical concept of the 'will'. This affinity will become increasingly important as the text progresses.

An *expression*, then, is a sign that *wants to say something*, while an indication does not *want to say something*, but merely points the receiver to some other state of affairs – an expression *means*, while an indication *points*, we might say. But it quickly becomes obvious that any such rigorous distinction between expression and indication is difficult if not impossible to sustain. As we noted above, every single time we employ *expressions*, we use them in an indicative manner, if for no other reason than that we are using the signs to *point towards* our psychological states, in an effort to recreate them as closely as possible in the mind of the listener:

We therefore already know that, *in fact*, the discursive sign and consequently the meaning <*le vouloir-dire*> is *always* entangled, *gripped* within an indicative system. The expressive and logical purity of the *Bedeutung* that Husserl wants to grasp as the possibility of the *Logos*[6] is gripped, that is, contaminated—*in fact and always* (*allzeit verflochten ist*) insofar as the *Bedeutung* is gripped within a communicative discourse. (*VP*, pp. 17–18/20/20–1)

Derrida's employment of the words '*in fact*' here is technical, and not to be quickly bypassed. He uses the phrase twice in the passage we have just cited. Often, when we use the phrase 'in fact', we are simply re-emphasising that what we are saying is true – almost as a synonym for the word 'indeed'; but this is not what Derrida means. 'In fact' (especially when it is emphasised with italics), for Derrida, following Husserl's line of argumentation, means 'empirical' or 'occurring empirically', and could be distinguished from 'essentially' or 'ideally'. In the preceding chapter, we said that the contamination of expression by its indicative function, though it occurs every time we use expression to communicate with others, is for Husserl an *accidental* or *non-essential* part of the expressive structure. In other words, we can rephrase Derrida's sentence to say, '*Whenever it occurs in the empirical realm*, expression is always contaminated by the function of indication. *But*, it need not, *essentially*, always occur in the empirical realm.' And indeed, this is precisely what Husserl thinks: the factical contaminative nature of the expression–indication relation does *not* entail an *essential* contamination.

At this point, Derrida provides one of his most important claims regarding the *stakes* of his own analysis – it returns in full in the Conclusion to *Voice and Phenomenon* – and it is a claim that, given its density and complexity, the first-time reader may be prone to read past. As we said, for Husserl, the fact that expression is contaminated by its indicative function is merely an accidental or non-essential characteristic. It *must be* possible, *by right of essentiality*, Husserl thinks, to isolate a function of expression that is *purely expressive*, that is, non-indicative – the function of a sign that only *means*, and does not *point to* anything else. This is what Derrida means when he talks about 'this hiatus between fact and right, existence and essence, reality and the intentional function' (*VP*, p. 18/21/21). This hiatus, Derrida claims, characterises the whole of the phenomenological project – this means that the entire weight of the phenomenological project rests on the ability to sustain this hiatus. This is indeed a bold claim, so let us follow Derrida closely.

Recall that for Husserl in the *Logical Investigations*, the central problem – *and this problem never goes away in Husserl's thought afterward* – is the 'relationship, in particular, between the subjectivity of knowing and the objectivity of the content known' (*Logical Investigations*, p. 2). Here we see first-hand the centrality of this hiatus that Derrida characterises. Even if, Husserl argues, objectivity is only *ever*, *in fact*, given in the subjectivity of the subject, it nevertheless remains the case that, *by right of essentiality*, the content towards which that knowing subject intends must be *ideal*, essential and non-empirical. Objectivity is *not* agglomerated from out of the subject's experience of the empirical realm, even if *in fact* that is how the subject first comes to *recognise* and deal with objectivity. This cannot be overstated: this relationship to the ideality of objectivity demands the use of *signs* that *do not point elsewhere*, but only *mean*, purely. It demands, in other words, the sustainability of the *essential distinction* between indication and expression. This is why Derrida says that this hiatus between existence and essence:

does not preexist the question of language, and it is not inserted into phenomenology as within one domain or as one problem among others. It is opened up, on the contrary, only in and by the possibility of language. And its juridical value, the right to a distinction between fact and intentional right, depends entirely upon language and, in language, on the validity of a radical distinction between indication and expression. (*VP*, p. 18/21/21)

Therefore, if it turns out to be the case (as Derrida will argue), that expression is always, *and essentially* (that is, not just *in fact*) caught up in indication, then any radical breach between existence and essence, fact and right, will itself be unsustainable. Hence the entirety of the phenomenological project will be in danger. Thus, this moment in the text, early and difficult though it may be, is paramount.

We proceed – every expression, used communicatively, is contaminated by its indicative function, but the converse is not true. Expressions are always indicative, but indications are not always expressive. Expressions are always indicative, in that when we use them in a communicative manner, we are using our signs to *point* the listener to something else, whether our own psychological states, some state of affairs in the world or some combination of these. Indications, however, are not *always* expressive; they *can* be, to be sure. *Any* written mark on a piece of paper, for instance, is an indicative sign – indicating the presence of another person at some point in time, the type of instrument he or she used to make the mark, the demonstration of intended order or meaning, etc. But it is quite often also an expressive sign, as when someone leaves a note for another, makes a grocery list, writes a journal, etc. These marks are still indications in the above sense, but they are also *expressive* in that they communicate linguistic meaning. However, indications are not *always* expressive, and in the previous chapter we listed several such examples (a fever, animal tracks, etc.). Even marks on a paper are not always expressive (in the Husserlian sense) as, for example, when a small child scribbles randomly with crayons.

Given this seemingly unilateral assimilation (that expressions are always indicative, but indications are not always expressive), it might appear that one ought to think of signs as *essentially* indicative, and expressions as a *species* of the *genus* 'indication'. This of course is entirely unacceptable for Husserl; for if it were the case that expressions were merely subspecies of indications, this would mean that *all* signs *point to* something else, and that *no* signs express meaning in a simple, unmediated manner. In order to successfully *reject* this unilateral assimilation, however, Husserl will need to isolate 'if there is any, a phenomenological situation in which expression is no longer tied up in this entanglement, is no longer interwoven with indication' (*VP*, p. 19/22/22). Since the contaminative relationship arises due to the fact of communication, that is, that the signs *go forth* into the world – pointing to the content that is present in the soul of the other, and forever hidden from one's own lived-experience – Husserl will carry out the reduction of the sign's *going forth* into the world. Put otherwise, since the contamination occurs because of the *communicative* use of expressions:

it is in a language without communication, in a monological discourse, in the absolutely lowest register of the voice of the '*solitary life of the soul*' (*in einem Seelenleben*) that it is necessary to track down the unmarred purity of expression. (*VP*, p. 19/22/22)

This means that the essence of expression will be isolated only when the relation of the soul to what is *outside* the soul is suspended. Derrida calls this a 'strange paradox' (*VP*, p. 19/22/22), that the essence of *ex-pressivity* (literally, *pressing outwardly*) is discovered only when the 'outwardly' is eliminated. But this suspension is not absolute, and this *paradox*, as Derrida notes, constitutes the heart of the phenomenological project: 'Only to a certain outside, because this reduction will not erase and indeed shall reveal in pure expressivity the relation to the object, the aim of an objective ideality, over and against the intention of meaning <*vouloir-dire*>, over and against the *Bedeutungsintention*' (*VP*, pp. 19/22/22–3). Above, we discussed the notion of 'intentionality', that consciousness is always conscious *of* something, and that for Sartre, this entails a constant *outward directedness* of consciousness. Thus, *even when the real existence of the world is bracketed*, in the mode of the epochē, the subjectivity of consciousness is nevertheless constituted essentially by an openness to an ideal objectivity which is, *in some sense*, outside the interiority of the subject. This is why the suspension is only to a *certain outside*:

phenomenological transcendental idealism responds to the necessity to describe the *o*bjectivity of the *o*bject (*Gegenstand*) and the *p*resence of the present (*Gegenwart*)—and the objectivity in presence—on the basis of an 'interiority' or rather on the basis of a self-proximity, of an *o*wnness (*Eigenheit*) which is not a simple *inside*, but the intimate possibility of the relation to an over-there and to an outside in general. (*VP*, p. 19/22/23)

The interiority of the soul, Derrida argues, is not *simple* in the sense that it is not self-contained or self-identical, because there is an essential *openness* in the interiority of the subject that reveals an *essential* relation – of the inside, to a *certain* outside – but only on the basis of the *exclusion* or reduction of *another* outside, namely, the totality of the *existing world*.

So, as we have hinted, Husserl must carry out the reduction of the indicative domain (this will occupy Chapter 2 of *Voice and Phenomenon*). Prior to this explication, however, Derrida pauses to reflect on two possible readings of the Husserlian moves we have discussed thus far. On the one hand, Derrida notes, Husserl *seems* to hastily avoid any reflection on the meaning of the 'sign' in general. In all of the material we have discussed so far, we have pursued the fact that Husserl notes an ambiguity in the notion of the 'sign', in that it contains two heterogeneous types of signs, indications and expressions. But at no point does Husserl reflect at any length on what it means for something to be a 'sign' in general. In other words, in noting that the word 'sign' encompasses two heterogeneous terms, Husserl, problematically perhaps, does not reflect on what it is that makes them both *signs* in the first place. We can, for instance, certainly discuss the differences between the species of 'chimpanzee' and 'horse'; we can talk about all the various things that make them *essentially* different from one another; but we can likewise equally discuss the reasons for which both are united under the genus of 'animal', because we can describe what makes an animal, an animal.

In a similar way, given that 'indication' and 'expression' are both, according to Husserl, types of the form 'sign', and given that Husserl matter-of-factly announces at the opening of the *Logical Investigations* the ambiguity within the notion of the 'sign', it follows that 'we must already have a relation of pre-understanding with the essence, the function, or the essential structure of the sign in general' (*VP*, p. 20/23/24). Derrida himself does not, however, propose to answer the question, or even to *pursue* an answer to the question 'what is a sign in general?' Not at this point in the text, at least. He simply notes the peculiarity of the absence of such a reflection. As Husserl notes, 'every sign is a sign for something' (*VP*, p. 20/23/24), but the status of this *being-for* is left unaddressed. It would appear that we would require some kind of an understanding of 'this structure of substitution or of referral so that, in this structure, the heterogeneity between indicative referral and expressive referral becomes consequently intelligible' (*VP*, p. 20/23/24). Again, we meet with difficult translation issues; but here, Derrida notes Husserl's German word *Zeigen*, which is closely related to the word for 'finger' or 'to point', and can mean generally 'to show' or 'to exhibit'; Derrida is using it in the sense of 'to refer'. *Hin* is a prefix meaning 'there', 'away' or 'out', so *Hinzeigen* means *expressive referral* or referral *outwardly*; while *An* is a prefix meaning 'to', such that *Anzeigen* means *indicative referral* or referral *to*. At root in both these words is the word *Zeigen*, the definitional status of which is left untouched by Husserl.

On the other hand, Derrida notes, perhaps our *question itself*, regarding Husserl's elision, and *not* the elision itself, is problematic, and perhaps it betrays an ontological presupposition on *our* part. We must keep in mind that, for Husserl, the starting point of phenomenology is the elimination of presuppositions. The question 'what is a sign?' presupposes an essential unity to the concept of the word 'sign' that perhaps Husserl does not believe is there to be found. Perhaps, Derrida argues, the whole *point* of these *essential distinctions* that Husserl draws is that there *is* no unity to the concept of the sign, that these two heterogeneous concepts of indication and expression, which have perhaps hitherto been *believed* to possess some essential unity, are in fact completely and irreducibly heterogeneous to one another.

Moreover, the question itself might betray a more surreptitious presupposition, namely, that the question 'what is x?' is *the* question, and the *form* of the question, that we ought always to be asking; and indeed, this is the way in which philosophy since Socrates has conducted itself. When Socrates demands of Euthyphro that he provide, not *examples* of pious actions, but the *form* of piety, he is asserting the priority of the question 'what is x?' As Derrida says, 'This would be a classical way of proceeding. We would subordinate the sign to truth, language to being, speech to thought, and writing to speech' (*VP*, p. 21/24/25). The question 'what is a sign?' presupposes that there is an *answer* to the question, that is, a *true* answer to the question. This in turn, however, assumes first that we know what *truth* means and, moreover, that we know that truth is something distinct from the notion of the 'sign'. In other words, what it means to be *true* would have to precede and condition, or make possible, what it means to be a *sign*. If it were not so, 'if the sign somehow preceded what we call truth or essence, it would make no sense to speak of the truth or the essence of the sign' (*VP*, p. 21/24/26). So, if there is a *truth* to the question of the essence of the sign, truth must then precede and condition the sign, and hence the sign can only ever *signify*, or *refer to*, the 'truth'. But, as we have said, what makes possible the very constitution of objectivity or ideality for Husserl is what we just described as the *openness to a certain outside* that characterises the intentional structure of consciousness. Intentionality itself is thus structurally similar to the *Zeigen* or the referral of the sign itself; and understood as *referral*, the sign would not be a *thing*, any more than intentionality is a *thing*, but rather a *relation*. Considered this way, might it not very well be the case, Derrida challenges,

that the sign, for example if we consider the sign as the structure of an intentional movement, does not fall under the category of the thing in general (*Sache*), that the sign is not a 'being' about whose being we would have just posed a question? Is not the sign something other than a being? Is it not the sole 'thing' which, not being a thing, does not fall under the question of a 'what is'? (*VP*, pp. 21–2/24–5/26)

But this possibility reveals something even more interesting: if ideality or objectivity is constituted always in the intentional relation, and if the sign is the structure of an intentional movement, *then the sign would become the very condition of truth itself.* 'Truth' then becomes a production that is conditioned by the functioning of the sign, rather than the sign merely *representing* a truth, considered as fully present and self-contained, to a knowing subject. But to say as much is to challenge all traditional understandings of the concept of truth; and *this*, Derrida argues, is the most important insight of the phenomenological project of Husserl. In its more daring moments, 'Husserl will give a growing attention to what in signification, in language, and in inscription as it writes ideal objectivity down, *produces* truth or ideality rather than *records* it' (*VP*, p. 22/25/26).

Nonetheless, and almost in spite of himself, Husserl also remains committed, Derrida argues, to the *metaphysics of presence* that Derrida claims has guided philosophy since antiquity, the metaphysical tradition that considers presence as primary and absence as secondary or derivative; and, accompanying this, that *presence* or *presentation* is first, and *re-presentation* second. Phenomenology is thus committed to two motivations: on the one hand, 'the return to an active constitution of sense and validity, to the activity of a *life* that produces truth and validity in general through its signs', and on the other hand, 'without being simply juxtaposed to this movement, another necessity confirms also the classical metaphysics of presence and indicates that phenomenology belongs to classical ontology' (*VP*, pp. 22/25–6/26–7). That it is not a *simple juxtaposition* is extremely important for Derrida's argument: Husserl is not simply committed, in a way unrecognised on his part, to two incompatible positions, as when we might casually note that someone's professed ethical beliefs do not correspond to their lifestyle, for example. What Derrida means is that, *because* Husserl is so deeply committed to the classical metaphysics of presence, his thought is constantly undermined and contested, *but from within*, by the commitment to the active production of sense and validity. Rather than simply *opposing* his commitment to the metaphysics of presence, this Husserlian commitment to the active production of sense *constitutes, while at the same time fragmenting*, this pursuit of presence.

That this is so is revealed in the final sentence of the first chapter (and as we move towards the end of the book, the remainder of Derrida's argument). Derrida claims, 'We have chosen to be interested in this relation in which phenomenology belongs to classical ontology' (*VP*, p. 22/26/27). It is important to note that Derrida has, by this time, already written on Husserl's *commitment* to a certain form of classical metaphysics ('La phenomenology et la clôture de la métaphysique'), and Derrida himself notes this in the 'Introduction' to *Voice and Phenomenon* (*VP*, p. 5/5/3). In this article, as at this point in the 'Introduction', Derrida marks a number of ways in which Husserl, while ever critiquing a *degenerate* or *naïve* form of metaphysics, nevertheless remains committed, by his own admission, to a purified form of metaphysics. If following Husserl's commitment to a certain type of metaphysics were *all* that Derrida hoped to accomplish in *Voice and Phenomenon*, he would not be doing anything particularly new. But *Voice and Phenomenon* does much more than this, and it comes down to Derrida's use of the word 'choice'. Accompanying the classical metaphysics of presence is the voluntaristic metaphysics of *choice* and intention, as Derrida will reveal in Chapter 3 (*VP*, p. 29/34/37); and voluntaristic metaphysics is, as we have noted in the previous chapter, a significant part of what Derrida's thought attempts to deconstruct. Yet, here, Derrida emphasises, we have *chosen* to concern ourselves with Husserl's commitment to the metaphysics of presence. But what Derrida will do throughout the remainder of *Voice and Phenomenon* is demonstrate that, by *choosing* to focus on the pursuit of Husserl's commitment to the metaphysics of presence, we will at the same time unavoidably find Husserl's undermining and constitutive commitment to the active production of sense; in other words, however sincere our *choice* may be, it will not, in the end, be sustainable.

Let us now turn to Chapter 2.

The Reduction of Indication

In turning to the second chapter, we turn to the shortest chapter of *Voice and Phenomenon*. The brevity of Derrida's treatment of the notion of 'indication' parallels Husserl's own brevity – yet this moment is nevertheless crucial for Derrida's argument. As Derrida notes, 'Husserl devotes only three sections to "*the essence of indication*" and, in the same chapter, eleven sections are devoted to *expression*' (*VP*, p. 23/27/28). This 'reductive' treatment should by now come as no surprise: given what we know about Husserl's motivations, that phenomenology seeks always to bracket the merely empirical in favour of the ideal and objective, that it is centred around the isolation of the pure, essential possibility of meaning; and given his essential distinction between expression and indication, that expressions *mean* while indications *point*, it stands to reason that Husserl's primary object of concern should be *expression*, rather than indication. But as we have said, rigorously distinguishing the two is a difficult, perhaps seemingly impossible, endeavour.

As such, Chapter 2 of *Voice and Phenomenon* sets out to accomplish two distinct but related tasks. First, it heightens the stakes of the expression/ indication distinction, demonstrating how inextricable the remainder of the phenomenological project to come is from this distinction. We have now discussed numerous times the *in fact* contamination of expression and indication – the fact that in communicative discourse, expression is always entangled with indication. If this is *always* the case, essentially, structurally and necessarily, the entirety of the Husserlian project, Derrida here argues, falters:

> Husserl's whole enterprise—and well beyond the *Logical Investigations*—will be threatened if the *Verflechtung* attaching indication onto expression is absolutely irreducible and in principle inextricable, if indication were not added onto expression as a more or less tenacious bond, but inhabited the essential intimacy of the movement of expression. (*VP*, p. 23/27/28)

This brings us to the second task of Chapter 2: at the same time as it heightens the stakes of the distinction, it deepens the tremendous difficulty of extricating expression from indication, thereby intensifying the magnitude of this extrication or reduction.

That it is necessary to *reduce* indication (as Chapter 2 announces), entails that there must be an isolable *essence* that makes indication what it is, so Derrida begins by reiterating the basic functioning of indication. There are *natural* and *artificial* indications, and we have alluded to both types above: animal tracks, or a fever, would be examples of *natural* indication, while the written pen-mark is an example of *artificial* indication. Uniting both of these forms of indication, however, is the concept of 'motivation' (Husserl's word is *Motivierung*). Indications, whether natural or artificial, *motivate* (or *put into motion*) the thought of the thinking subject from one thing to another, one knowledge (actual) to another knowledge (non-actual). The actual knowledge of the present sign motivates the thought of the thinking subject to a non-actual knowledge concerning some object or state of affairs. Again, this covers both empirical and ideal objects and states of affairs, which is why Husserl applies it to the sphere covered by the broader, more general German terms for 'being', such as *Sein* ('being'), *bestehen* ('to be') and *Bestand* ('continuance' or 'subsistence'), as opposed to more specifically empirically oriented German words of 'being', such as *Dasein* ('existence', or '*there-being*'), *existieren* ('to exist'), or *Realität* ('reality'). This important distinction is visible in the block quotation that Derrida cites on page 24 (*VP*, p. 24/28/30). So the common element of the different species (natural and artificial) of indication is this *motivation* that moves thought: 'Motivation is what gives to something like a "thinking being" the movement in order *to pass* in thought from something to something' (*VP*, p. 24/28/29).

However, this cannot be the end of it, Derrida argues; 'motivation' in the general sense contaminates the concept of indication with something that is not strictly speaking indication. More precisely, Derrida will demonstrate that the concept of motivation alone cannot be said to be the defining and essential characteristic of indication as such, because there is a species of motivation that exceeds the precise sense of indication for Husserl, that Husserl would never allow to be characterised by indication – this motivation 'overflows indication *in the strict sense*' (*VP*, p. 24/29/30), and this type of motivation that goes beyond indication applies in the case of apodictic demonstration, the type of necessary connections of signs obtaining in geometric proofs, for instance.

Motivation generally, Derrida claims, is a 'because' that can take the form of a *Hinweis* or a *Beweis* (*VP*, p. 24/29/30). The German word *Weisen* means, generally, 'to show', and *Hin* (as we saw above, 'there', 'away', 'out') in combination with *Weisen* means *to show there*, or what Derrida calls 'indicative allusion' (*VP*, p. 24/29/30). This will be Husserlian indication in the strict sense. The German prefix *Be* functions similarly to the English prefix 'be', modifying the verb such that it requires a direct object. *Beweisen* therefore means not just 'to show', but 'to show something definite', in the sense of 'to demonstrate' or 'to prove'. This Derrida calls 'apodictic demonstration' (*VP*, p. 24/29/30). In the most general way, therefore, motivation can move the thought of the thinking subject to accept a conclusion either on the basis of an amassing of *empirical evidence* (showing there), and the persuasive force accruing thereto, or on the basis of the *necessary* connection of the evidence or premises with a definite conclusion. An example of a *Hinweis* might be the presence of specific animal tracks on one's land, coupled with the presence of a specific kind of nest or abode. The degree of presumption of the presence of a certain animal will be directly proportional to the types and amount of evidence related to the species of animal. The persuasive force of this kind of motivation, however, is of an essentially different sort than the persuasive force of a geometric proof, as the latter 'links together evident and ideal necessities which are permanent and persistent beyond every empirical *hic et nunc*' (*VP*, p. 24/29/30).[7] The former is merely *compelling*; the latter *necessary*, and this is the case even if the proposition or proof uses only symbols: 'If A = B and B = C, then A = C' is true under all circumstances, and we need no examples to ascertain its truth – it is true necessarily.

But empirical evidence, no matter how compelling or definitive, can never *produce* necessity. As we have seen, apodictic necessity cannot be amassed from empirical experiences, because, as we have said, it is ideal and hence beyond **every** *here and now*. So, to return to our example of the presence of a species of animal, even if we have the highest possible empirical certainty of the presence of the animal, including repeatedly seeing various members of the species leaving and returning to the animal abode at various times of day, through various seasons, nursing their young, etc., this amassed evidence could never amount to apodictic necessity – indication may motivate empirical certainty, but never apodictic necessity. It is for this reason that Husserl will need to maintain the distinction between *indication* and *demonstration*. This, however, means that the essential characteristic of indication as motivation is over-determined. Motivation, to use Derrida's language, *contaminates* indication with its other

But beyond this difficulty lies another, in the relation of the *Hinweis* to the *Beweis*, as when the thought of a thinking subject is directed *towards* an apodictic demonstration. Here Derrida quotes Husserl: '"An ideal rule is here revealed which extends its sway beyond the judgments linked by motivation *hic et nunc* and embraces as such in a meta-empirical generality all the judgments of like content and moreover all the judgments of like 'form' [*Form*]"' (*VP*, pp. 24–5/29/30).[8] This claim is extremely important, in that it reveals that for Husserl, the *contents* and relations of the signs of apodictic demonstrations fall outside the motivation specific to indication, but the cognitive acts that are directed *towards* the demonstration do not – they are still examples of indication, and this is a matter of essential necessity for Husserl. In order to avoid the psychologism that he sees as paralysing to Brentano's thought, Husserl will *have* to maintain an essential distinction between the *thinking* that recognises a truth, and the truth as such. Put otherwise, the *motivation* that moves the thought of the thinking subject to recognise the necessity of any given apodictic demonstration is always empirical, in that it always takes place in the *here and now* of an empirical present directed towards an outside object – hence and despite the necessary truth of its object (the contents of the demonstration), this motivation itself always falls on the side of *indication*; **but** the sort of *motivation* that relates the contents of those objectivities together is *beyond* all empirical reality, a *meta-empirical generality*. Even when the contents are ideal, the acts that intend them are, at least in some senses, empirical:

> In fact, we know now that, in the order of signification in general, every psychical lived-experience, on the side of its *acts*, even when the acts aim at idealities and objective necessities, is involved only with indicative concatenations. Indication falls outside of the content of absolutely ideal objectivity, that is, outside of the truth. (*VP*, pp. 25/29–30/31)

So the psychical acts directed towards apodicticity are themselves motivated by indication, but these are always radically heterogeneous from the order of their objects: 'even if indication seems nevertheless to intervene in a demonstration, it will always be on the side of psychical motivations, acts, convictions, etc., and never on the side of the contents of truths that are linked together' (*VP*, p. 25/29/31), and this too is a matter of essential necessity. The same impetus of thinking that demands that the contents of apodictic demonstration *not* be conceived beneath the banner of indication (insofar as indication can only, at best, offer empirical certainty and never necessity), dictates at the same time that the *thought* that *thinks* that necessity *must* be considered under the banner of *indication*, as to do otherwise would allow the possibility that the ideal is in some way reducible to the acts of thought that intend it.

We have reached the concluding paragraph of Chapter 2, and the web of entanglements in the analysis has only grown more complex. In Chapter 1, we saw that Husserl's essential distinction between expression and indication is difficult to sustain in practice, as every time we employ expressions in a communicative fashion, we use them in a way that is at the same time indicative: we *point to* psychological states and worldly states of affairs. Husserl will therefore need to separate off indication from expression, and isolate the essence of expression – to do so, however, will require knowledge of the essence of indication as well. Here in Chapter 2 we encounter an analogous difficulty: when we tried to isolate what the essence of *indication* is, we see that it is contaminated by its essential characteristic function of *motivation*, which also characterises the *Beweis* – demonstration or proof – which Husserl, again for essential reasons, must keep distinct from the notion of 'indication' strictly speaking. But then as we just saw, *all* psychical acts directed towards a specific outside object, *even when* they are directed towards objective idealities, fall on the side of *indication* for Husserl.

For these reasons, we can begin to understand why Derrida places such a profound emphasis on the expression/indication distinction. If *indication* is the mode of signification that applies when psychical acts are directed towards a specific *outside* object, then indication bears an essential relation to all of the various phenomenological reductions – eidetic and transcendental – that would follow throughout the rest of Husserl's life. As we have seen, the reduction puts into suspension all questions regarding the real, external existence of the empirical world: that which falls under the grip of the reduction therefore is everything that corresponds in any way to the empirical or factical – the very same domain covered by *indication*. For this reason, Derrida will say, 'indicative signification will cover, in language, all of what falls under the blows of the "reductions": factuality, mundane existence, essential non-necessity, non-evidence, etc.' (*VP*, p. 26/30/32).

Moreover, if what *falls* under the reduction is the domain covered by *indication*, then the mode of signification proper to the sphere *carrying out* the reduction or exclusion would be the mode of *expression* – the reduction, then, 'would be merged with the most spontaneous act of spoken discourse, the simple practice of speech, the power of expression' (*VP*, p. 26/31/32). But if this were the case, it would imply that the phenomenological reduction, and hence the entire sphere of transcendental phenomenology, is opened up and conditioned, 'announced here in the form of a relation between two modes of signification' (*VP*, p. 26/30/32) – expression and indication; in other words, without this *essential distinction*, which is a distinction in the notion of the 'sign', there would be no phenomenological reduction and hence no phenomenology; this would wed phenomenology inseparably to language, thus violating Husserl's *intentions* (and here, we must hear echoes of the word 'choice' at the end of Chapter 1), for two reasons. First, as we have said, Husserl wants to retain a pre-expressive, pre-linguistic stratum of sense. Husserl, like Aristotle,[9] and like nearly all the rest of the philosophical tradition, will want to maintain that primary in human experience is the affection or disposition of the soul or mind, and that *language* is merely a secondary tool employed in order to make the contents of the soul known to others – experience is primary; the language describing that experience is secondary or supplemental. But, if there is no phenomenological reduction without language, that is, if the possibility of the reductions rests upon this *hiatus* between the two types of signs, then Husserl's pre-expressive stratum of meaning becomes problematic. Experience, in other words, becomes contaminated through and through by the use of signs. Second, lacking this pre-expressive stratum of sense, the very notion of 'expression', as the externalisation of an interior meaning, becomes unsustainable in any pure sense. In other words, if experience is *essentially* caught up in a web of signs, then even the most *expressive* expression will be contaminated by indication, as there is no longer any *pure* experience, uncontaminated by discourse, for expression to *express*. If *this* is the case, then there is no longer, even conceptually, any way to sustain the pure and isolated *essence* of expression, which means that expression is contaminated by the function of indication: 'we could almost say that the totality of discourse is gripped by an indicative web' (*VP*, p. 26/31/33).

So among the more controversial and challenging claims that Chapter 2 argues are the claim that there would be no reduction without the expression/indication distinction and the claim that all discourse is contaminated by its indicative function. It is important to note that, at this point, Derrida has not yet *argued* for these claims – this is the task of the remainder of the book. Here we note that Derrida asks, early in the final paragraph of the chapter, 'Do we not already have the right to say that . . . ?' (*VP*, p. 26/30/32), to which he presently responds, 'If we could answer the question in the affirmative, we would have to conclude . . .' (*VP*, p. 26/31/32). The use of the word 'if' here is telling: he has not yet argued that we *can* answer in the affirmative (though that is indeed what he will argue), only that *if* we can answer affirmatively, *then* these paradoxical conclusions must follow. Chapter 2, as we have said, is integral in laying out the stakes of the engagement, which is a crucial stage of the argument of *Voice and Phenomenon*.

Let us now look to Chapter 3, which is where Derrida begins to dissect the notion of 'expression'.

Meaning as Soliloquy

'Let us suppose', Derrida says, that all those inextricable entanglements that we have explored in Chapters 1 and 2 do not obtain, and that it is indeed possible to unproblematically carry out the Husserlian reduction of indication: what are we then left with? 'What remains is expression . . . a sign charged with *Bedeutung*' (*VP*, p. 27/32/34). Indications, we said, *point*, while expressions *mean*. Only expressions have a *Bedeutung*; here in Chapter 3 we begin to examine the status of this *Bedeutung*, and going along with this, the nature of expression. Chapter 3 is divided into two major sections: Section A, which extends from page 27 (*VP*, p. 27/32/34) to page 31 (*VP*, p. 31/37/39); and Section B, occupying pages 31 (*VP*, p. 31/37/39) through the end of the chapter (*VP*, p. 40/47/52).

In Section A, Derrida argues that on the one hand, the sign becomes an expression, or becomes *meaningful*, only in the act of speech, and he will lay out three distinct but related reasons as to why this must be the case for Husserl, related in that they are united 'within the profound unity of one and the same intention' (*VP*, p. 27/32/34). Whenever we see this word *intention*, we must pay careful attention to it, as Derrida is almost always making use of the plurality of senses of the word: on the one hand, in the phenomenological tradition, *intention*, as we have said above, means simply *consciousness of something* or the *directedness-towards*; but at the same time, Derrida utilises the voluntaristic sense of the word, as when one says, 'I intend to . . .'. Though this is discussed in the 'Introduction' and has been implicit all along, Chapter 3 is the first point in the text proper that this voluntarism becomes explicit as an object of analysis. Here in Section A, the meaning of this phrase, 'one and the same intention', is double. On the one hand, it is a singular intention of the philosopher, Edmund Husserl. In other words, Derrida claims that the three 'reasons' that he is going to examine as to why the sign becomes a meaningful expression only in the act of spoken discourse are in fact variations of a single motivation on the part of Husserl. There is a single impetus that unites these three points. On the other hand, this single Husserlian motivation, unifying these three 'reasons', is itself the valorisation of *intention*, or voluntary acts of the will. In other words, what these three points will have in common is ultimately the conviction that signs become meaningful only when they are immediate expressions of a *will*.

The first 'reason' Derrida offers as to why the sign only becomes expression in the act of speech is that ex-pression literally means *to press outwardly*. This is the case with Husserl's German word as well: *Ausdruck*, the German word for 'expression', is comprised of the prefix *aus*, meaning 'out of' and the participial form of the verb *drücken*, meaning 'to press' or 'to force.' So an expression is a sign that presses outwardly; it 'imprints in a certain outside a sense which is discovered first in a certain inside' (*VP*, p. 27/32/34). This 'certain outside' is the conceptual counterpart to the other 'certain outside' mentioned in Chapter 1 (*VP*, p. 19/22/22), where Derrida notes that the concentrated purity of expression is disclosed 'only when the relation to a certain *outside* would be suspended' (*VP*, p. 19/22/22). This turn of phrases, having to do with insides and outsides, is extremely complicated and potentially confusing, so let us look at them very carefully.

When Derrida writes in Chapter 1 that the *purity of expression is revealed only when the relation to a certain outside is suspended*, the 'outside' to which he refers is the totality of the existing world, which will eventually (with the publication of *Ideas I* in 1913) be bracketed in the mode of phenomenological reduction. But as Derrida makes clear in Chapter 1, this is 'only to a certain outside, because this reduction will not erase and indeed shall reveal in pure expressivity the relation to the object ...' (*VP*, pp. 19/22/22–3). In other words, when the relation to the *outside* of the existing world is suspended, there is a relation to another *certain outside* revealed, but this outside is one of pure meaning, found within consciousness itself. 'Here is the place to specify this outside' (*VP*, p. 27/32/34), Derrida says, as this outside within consciousness is itself multi-dimensional.

In the intentional act, the *bedeuten*, or the *meaning-intention* (above we saw that Derrida employs the French term, *vouloir-dire*, 'to-want-to-say' or 'to-intend-to-say'), intends an ideal object. This ideality itself subsists in an *outside* that is not part of consciousness itself, but neither is it part of the world. But when the *bedeuten* intends this ideality, thereby turning it into an *object* of conscious regard, this ideal object then enters into *another* outside, an outside which is at the objective pole of the conscious regard (insofar as it is an object of the gaze), but which is still within consciousness, because it is not 'out there' in the world. Therefore, as we have so far seen, there are three senses of the word 'outside': (1) the 'outside' of the external world; (2) the 'outside' of an ideal meaning or object; (3) the 'outside' as the way in which that ideal meaning becomes an explicit object of consciousness. This latter outside is part of consciousness itself, which is why the interiority of consciousness for Husserl 'is not a simple *inside*' (*VP*, p. 19/22/23).

When the *bedeuten* intends an ideal object, therefore, the ideality shifts from the second sense to the third sense of the word 'outside', becoming an object of consciousness: 'this outside then is ex-pressed, passes outside of itself into another outside, which is still "in" consciousness' (*VP*, p. 27/32/34). Thus, within the *solitary life of the soul*, we have what we have referred to as the *pre-expressive stratum of sense* (an inside), which is the dimension of experience *prior* to language that we said (in Chapter 2) is crucial for Husserl; the *bedeuten* then brings that 'sense' (*Sinn*) into the mode of *expression* by *intending* an ideal object (an outside), which thereby passes into the mode of object of conscious regard (another outside). This explains Derrida's difficult formulation, that expression 'is therefore a double exiting of sense (*Sinn*) outside of itself in itself, in consciousness, in the with-itself and the nearby-itself that Husserl begins by determining as the "solitary life of the soul"' (*VP*, pp. 27/32–3/34–5).

Given that the sign only attains the status of expression in the act of speech, it is very important to note, as Derrida does, that for Husserl, the mode of *expression* adds nothing in the way of meaningful content or structure to the sense (*Sinn*) found in the interior life of the soul, in its double passage outside of itself. The *Sinn* does not transform in becoming a *Bedeutung*. In other words, the mode of expression does not in any way enrich, alter or embellish upon the significance of the experience that it expresses; it merely transposes a sense that, within an *inside*, is in itself complete: the stratum of expression is 'unproductive', meaning that it is a '"*productivity that is exhausted in the expressing and in the form of the conceptual* which is introduced with the expression"' (*VP*, pp. 27–8/33/35). The only thing *produced* in the act of expression is the sign itself, in other words, which puts the sense of the experience in contact with its ideal form; it merely externalises a sense that is already *present* in the interiority of the soul. As Derrida notes, however, despite its centrality to Husserl's argument, this 'unproductivity' of the expressive stratum is in no way obvious, and we shall see this particular point raised again later in the text.

The second 'reason' given under Section A, as to why the sign becomes an expression (or meaningful sign) only in the act of speech, is that the voice, which could potentially remain silent, or completely internal, is **intentionally** *animated*, literally, given *life*, and the thing to which it gives life is 'an ideality that does not "exist" in the world' (*VP*, p. 28/33/36). Here again, Derrida's words are absolutely important. 'To animate' derives from the Latin word *animus*, meaning 'soul' or 'mind', which is itself closely related etymologically to the Proto-Indo-European word *ane*, meaning 'to breathe', hence the Latin word *anima*, meaning 'living being' or 'spirit'. In ancient Greek and Hebrew as well, the words meaning 'soul' are very close etymologically to the words for 'life', 'breath', 'spirit' and even 'wind'. A voice that is animated is thus one that is immediately connected to, and an expression of, the breath and life of a subject; hence it is connected in an unmediated way to a *will*, unlike an indication – 'In indication, animation has two limits: the body of the sign which is not a breath, and the indicated, which is an existence in the world' (*VP*, p. 28/33/35). The 'limits' here are those aspects of indication that make it, we might say, *corruptible*: on the one hand, the *sign* itself is not a breath (which is an expression of the soul), and so it is corruptible in that its meaning is not complete and definite – not being connected to an *animating soul*, its meaning may be ambiguous or over-determined. On the other hand, that towards which it points will be an *empirical* existent, as opposed to an *ideality*. In the mode of expression, these two limits do not obtain – the sign itself is *charged with meaning*, and it is so charged immediately by a living, breathing soul that wilfully and intentionally manifests an ideal object that does not derive from the empirical realm.

The third 'reason' has to do with the possibility of interpretation, which truly obtains, Husserl thinks, only in spoken discourse (the German word for 'interpretation' that Derrida notes is *Deutung*, a component of *Bedeutung*, the *intended meaning*). Objections immediately abound: what, for instance, about facial expressions? Do we not *interpret*, for instance, our significant other's body language and facial expressions in certain ways ('She is being passive aggressive', 'He is happy to see me', etc.)? Or what about more specific and intentional bodily gestures, such as the gesture of the raised middle finger, almost universally recognised as a phallic representation intended to convey a specific obscene exclamation? Do we not interpret *this* gesture?

Husserl's response, Derrida claims, is that we of course *do* interpret such things, but there are two key components of that interpretation that trap it within the domain of expressivity or oral discourse. First, we only *interpret* such things by first *endowing* the acts with a linguistic or conceptual meaning that is not proper to the act itself ('passive aggressive', 'happy', 'loving', etc.) – we *turn* a non-spoken sign or event *into* a spoken act. In other words the interpretive web we cast over the bodily act

makes a latent expression be *heard*, a wanting-to-say (*bedeuten* <*vouloir-dire*>) which was still holding itself in reserve. Non-expressive signs want to say (*bedeuten*) only insofar as one can make them say what was murmuring in them, what was wanting to be said in a sort of mumbling. (*VP*, p. 30/36/38)

Second, as was just implied in this citation, the second key component of such interpretation is that the interpretation is applied precisely to an *intention* of meaning, without which there is no meaning as such. One interprets the gesture or expression in order to determine what it 'wants-to-say', and if there is no such wanting-to-say behind the gesture, then the gesture, as Husserl understands it, has no meaning: 'The essence of language is its *telos*[10] and its *telos* is voluntary consciousness as wanting-to-say' (*VP*, p. 30/36/38). For Husserl, these two components of *indicative* interpretation, along with the examples adduced, do not *undermine* his understanding of expression, but confirm it, insofar as they imply that *all* meaningful interpretation requires the spoken, linguistic component, thus confirming that the sign only becomes *meaningful* with the spoken expression.

Before looking more closely at the notion of 'intention' and the role it plays in Husserlian phenomenology, we must note that for Derrida, the interpretability, however that may be understood, of the indicative sign itself (the bodily indication, the facial expression, etc.) complicates Husserl's designation of expression as a *linguistic sign*, if it is implied that the indication is to be understood as the *non-linguistic sign*. To the extent that the indication is *interpretable* (and *all* indications, it would seem, are interpretable), the indicative sphere is always caught up in the domain of *expression*, and hence of language, even as Husserl understands it: 'For it would be difficult—and *in fact* impossible—to exclude from language all the indicative forms' (*VP*, p. 30/36/39). Here again we see the italicised use of the words, 'in fact', and this has a double sense: it is *in fact* (that is to say, 'indeed') impossible to exclude from language all its indicative forms, but this is because it is impossible *in fact* (in the communicative, everyday use of language with others) to so exclude them. The distinction then, Derrida says, might be between the express and the non-express – the expression being *expressly* linguistic and the indication being *non-expressly* linguistic – but certainly not between language and non-language.

As we begin to shift towards Section B, we must look more closely at the motivation *animating* the expression/indication distinction, for Husserl. We note that the primary reason in Section A for which the gesture and the facial expression fall on the side of indication and not expression for Husserl is precisely that they are not immediately connected to *intention*, and thus they are not subject to the *pure* animation, Derrida says, 'by the *Geist*[11] which is the will' (*VP*, p. 29/35/37). Many of the bodily indications we have mentioned elsewhere, such as sweating from nervousness, blushing with embarrassment, turning red with anger, etc., are in no way intentional – on the contrary, they are often explicitly *un*intentional and undesirable in themselves, and when the subject *intentionally* tries to take control of them, they do not diminish, but rather intensify. Facial expressions and bodily indications 'do not want *to say* anything because they do not *want* to say anything' (*VP*, p. 30/35/38).

But, even in the case of the more specific and intentional bodily gestures, such as our 'raised middle finger' example, the intended meaning is only communicable by way of the intermediary of the body, present for all to see, in the *external* world – it is a physical expression, in some sense distanced from the soul from which it originates, or in other words, it is not *pure* animation. As such, what both of these types (facial expressions and intentional gestures) share, and what deprives them of their pure expressivity, is the loss of the immediate self-presence of the soul, directly and immediately connected to the meaningful expression to which it gives life by way of the breath of the voice: 'Visibility as such and spatiality as such could only lose the self-presence of the will and of the spiritual animation which opens up discourse. *They are literally the death of that self-presence*' (*VP*, p. 29/35/37). This is an extremely important moment in the text, so let us pause briefly to take stock of what we have done so far.

Recall that the way we articulated the distinction between the two types of signs is that expressions *mean* while indications *point*. But while this is a tidy way of cataloguing the definitional distinction, we noted that, in practice, every time we use expressions in communicative discourse, we use them to *point* the listener to our psychological states or states of affairs in the world, such that it would at least seem as though expressions *too* point in an indicative manner. Nonetheless, we noted that

Husserl (in an effort to isolate the pure possibility of meaning) is committed to the conviction that this is merely an accidental, non-essential feature of expression that in no way corrupts the *essential* functionality of the expression, considered in its pure sense. As he goes on to argue, this *indicative* functionality of expression arises only as a result of the empirical *fact* of communicative discourse, which, we noted, is not the *essential* characteristic of the functioning of expression, and which Husserl will attempt to bracket in the examination of the inner monologue.

Now, in this third chapter, Derrida is doing something more. What these three 'reasons' that we have discussed in Section A share (and here we are already anticipating what will come in full force in Section B) is that they demonstrate a more *metaphysical* impetus behind Husserl's conviction as to the essential absolute distinguishability of indication from expression, and it is an impetus inseparable from the body/soul opposition, ubiquitous throughout the tradition of Western metaphysics. What would separate the expression from the indication is that the expression is, in Husserl's sense, alive or living, while the indication is not. This is because the sign *as such* is akin to a 'corpse', or a dead, material body. In and of itself, it has no *life*, strictly speaking, just as the 'dead' matter of the Western tradition. That body (the sign) is animated or given life by the intention of the living being – as immediate expression of the soul, the intention of the subject is thus to the sign what the soul in the metaphysical tradition is to the body: it 'transforms the *Körper* into *Leib* (into flesh)' (*VP*, p. 29/35/37). In the act of communicative expression, the 'life' of the sign is immediately manifested by the 'life' of the soul.

This also goes further in helping to explain why for Husserl, the communicative *use* of expression will not, strictly speaking, constitute the *essential* functionality of the expression. In the empirical, communicative employment of language, we sacrifice the pure expressivity of meaning in at least three ways. First, as we have seen, we lose the pure expressivity of the sign because we employ the sign in order to *indicate* something to a listener. Second, in addition, we lose the pure expressivity of the sign due to the fact that 'the actuality of discourse keeps in itself something of *involuntary* association' (*VP*, p. 29/34/37). When I speak to another, there is always the possibility that what I say will be misunderstood, poorly understood or understood in ways that I did not intend – I *lose control*, as it were, of the interpretations and meanings of my expressions. Finally, these two ways are bound together in that they both derive from the *fact* of the sign's *passage through externality*, its passage through the world – this separation of intention (the soul) from sign (the body) is tantamount, Derrida argues, to a kind of *death* (to be explored further in Section B). What makes speech *expressive*, essentially, whether it is used to actually *communicate* with another or not, is the *intention* of meaning *willed* by the speaker; and everything (including empirical communication) that falls *outside* that intention (understood in this double sense), will also fall commensurably outside the sphere of expression proper. Hence the meaning-structure of intentionality is synonymous with and insepara-ble from the *will* that brings it forth – the intentionality that directs its regard towards an internal, pre-linguistic sense, and *chooses* to give life to that sense outwardly in the world, is inseparable from the traditional, metaphysical concept of the *will*. As Derrida says, 'the concept of intentionality is still taken in the tradition of a voluntaristic metaphysics, that is, perhaps taken simply in *the* metaphysics' (*VP*, p. 29/34/37). This concludes the discussion of Section A proper, but as we shall see, it opens the discussion that occupies Section B.

Section B continues this line of enquiry having to do with the notion of 'self-presence' and 'non-self-presence' of meaning. While the latter part of Section A focused on the self-presence of expression, Section B will begin to explore in greater detail the non-self-presence of indica-tion and of the indicative sphere, articulating the Husserlian themes and threads that will guide the remainder of the reading of *Voice and Phenomenon*. As Derrida says (and as we have suggested from Section A), 'They are going to make us think that what, in the final analysis, separates expression from indication is what we could call the immediate non-self-presence of the living present' (*VP*, p. 31/37/40).

The thrust of Section A was that '*Bedeutung* comes upon the sign and transforms it into expression only with speech, with oral discourse' (*VP*, p. 27/32/34). Above, we referred to this as the *on the one hand* of Chapter 3. Here in Section B we find the *on the other hand*, for Derrida writes, contrary to Section A, 'In fact, it is not enough to recognize oral discourse as the milieu of expressivity' (*VP*, p. 31/37/39). In a certain sense, this apparent contradiction is not at all surprising, given the moves that Husserl has so far made. The contradiction is resolved (or at least finessed) by recalling that, for Husserl, *Bedeutung*, strictly speaking, applies only to what is *express-ible*, that is, a linguistic, conceptual, *ideal* object, capable of being entered into a communicative discourse. This was why, in the case of the bodily indication or facial expression, the notion of 'interpretation' for Husserl (*Deutung*) could be applied only to the extent that the bodily indication is capable of being transposed *into* conceptual, linguistic content. So there is indeed a sense in which the sign becomes an expression only with oral discourse. However, when we *in fact* speak to others in the world, we use these expressions in an indicative manner, such that this exceeds the pure *expressivity*, strictly speaking, that Husserl seeks. As we have now noted many times, '*All discourse, insofar as it is engaged in a communication and insofar as it manifests lived-experiences, operates as indication*' (*VP*, pp. 32/37–8/40). Despite the fact that Husserl admits that expression is '"originally framed"' for communication, Derrida will note that 'expression is never purely itself insofar as it fills this originative function' (*VP*, p. 32/38/41). We must pause to note the use of the word 'originative', taking into consideration that the title of Chapter 7 of *Voice and Phenomenon* is 'The Originative Supplement'. Here on page 32 of *Voice and Phenomenon* we encounter this word 'originative' for the first time in the text proper; this lets the reader know that Derrida is beginning to anticipate the arguments of the latter part of the book.

To return to our line of discussion, given that communicative discourse always operates as indication, it is *not enough to recognise oral discourse as the milieu of expressivity*, as Derrida here notes, for even excluding the non-discursive forms of communication (such as gestures, bodily indications and facial expressions), there remains, 'this time within speech, a non-expressivity whose scope is considerable' (*VP*, pp. 31/37/39–40).

Moreover, the non-expressivity of oral communication is not *exclusively* – not even essentially, Derrida will argue – tied to the physicality of the communicative signs themselves; the fact that, in communication, we produce in the world a *visible* or an *audible* sign, having a *physical* status. In other words, the indicative nature of communicative expressions is not *only* (even if it appears to have been suggested in this manner hitherto) connected to the fact that we, as speaker, put forth a *physical* 'thing' into the world that subsequently functions for the listener or reader as a sign that *points* to something else (as does an indication) in the form of psychological states or states of affairs in the world. Rather, Husserl will also seek to exclude that which makes *possible* that very production of that physicality, 'all that arises from the *communication* or the *manifestations* of psychical lived-experience' (*VP*, p. 31/37/40), everything, in other words, that has anything to do with the *manifestation* of *Bedeutung* will, as a matter of essential necessity, not *count* in the expressive domain.

Therefore, Derrida embarks upon a phenomenological examination of what takes place in the conduct of communication. In communication, 'Sensible (audible or visible, etc.) phenomena are animated by the acts of a subject who endows them with sense, and simultaneously another subject must understand the animating subject's intention' (*VP*, p. 32/38/41). A subject, from out of the solitary life of the soul, intends a specific meaning and ex-presses that meaning by giving life to a particular group and configuration of signs by way of the voice or the written word, upon which time another subject *hears* or *sees* the signs and more importantly (for genuine *com-munication*), must interpret the signs as *meaningfully intended*, and then must understand the intended meaning. There are two poles to this operation: the animation/expression pole, and the reception pole.

The expression of the signs is dependent upon the animation whereby a sign is endowed with a sense. But this animation is not, Derrida says, 'pure and total' (*VP*, p. 32/38/41). That is to say, the movement of animation is not abrupt, not punctuated or rigidly divided, the moment of intention from the moment of expression. In its passage from intention to expression, the movement of animation 'must traverse the non-diaphaneity of a body and in a certain way be lost there' (*VP*, p. 32/38/41). In other words, before the expression has even become, in the communicative sense of the term, an 'expression', while it is still in the process of becoming animated (of being given 'life'), on the way to becoming an external expression, it must do so by moving through the physicality of the body; it is *corrupted*, that is, before it is 'born'. This movement through physicality must accompany every aspect of every expression that is intended to manifest one's interior experience to another. Hence 'The manifestation function (*kundgebende Funktion*) is an indicative function' (*VP*, p. 32/38/41).

At the other pole of the communicative operation is the auditor, who must interpret the speaker's signs as meaningful, and understand the intended meaning. This brings us to the problem of intersubjectivity, discussed above. When I, as a listener, am in a communicative relation with another person, I can have originary intuitions only of those aspects of the person which are exposed in the world: his body, his gestures, his facial expressions and the physical (visible and audible) signs that he expresses for my understanding. However, no matter how clearly, deliberately, articulately and honestly he may express his signs, his own *experience* can never be assimilated and experienced by me directly, or in an intuitive manner, nor mine by him:

But the subjective side of his experience, his consciousness, the acts by which in particular he endows sense to the signs, are not immediately and originarily present as they are for him and as mine are for me. Here we have an irreducible and definitive limit. (*VP*, pp. 33/38–9/42)

Above, we said that, *unlike* the case of a house, we can never get *behind* the face of the person and have immediate intentions of their Ego; we can only *ever* have what we called *analogical appresentations*, which arise on the basis of pairing associations – a body *like mine* is likely paired with a soul *like mine*; everything that constitutes the *solitary life of the soul* of the other person, however, forever alludes the listener in communicative discourse. Here is Lawlor's revised translation, with some of the key words and phrases in bold, of Husserl's passage on this matter from the *Logical Investigations*, partially cited above:

The hearer **perceives the manifestation** in the same sense in which he perceives the very person who manifests—**even though the psychic phenomena** which make him a person **cannot fall**, for what they are, **in the intuitive grasp of another**. [. . .] The hearer perceives the fact that the one who is speaking is externalizing certain psychic lived-experiences, and to that extent he also perceives these lived-experiences. He **does not**, however, **live them himself**; he has **no 'internal' perception** of them, **only an 'external' perception**. Here we have the **big difference between the actual grasp of a being in adequate intuition, and the intended [*vermeintlichen*] grasp of a being upon the foundation of an intuitive but inadequate representation**. In the former case, we have to do with a being given in lived-experience, in the latter case with a **presumed [*supponiertes*] being, to which no truth corresponds at all**. Mutual understanding demands a certain correlation among the psychic acts which are unfolded from the two sides of manifestation and in the grasping of the manifestation, but **not at all their full identity**. (*VP*, pp. 33–4/39–40/42–3)[12]

This passage alone provides a great deal of authorisation for the emphasis on *presence* that Derrida locates at this point in Husserl's thought; the distinctions here drawn are quite interesting. We have *adequate intuitions* of our own experiences – referred to here as *internal* perceptions – and here stressed as synonymous with *truth*, and even with *life*; but we have only *external perceptions*, or *inadequate representations* of the sphere of experience of the other person – here synonymous with the absence of truth. For these reasons, Derrida's reading of this passage does not in any way feel strained or forced: there can correspond to the experience of the other no *truth* and no *life* because the experience of the other can never be made adequately *present* in my soul, nor mine in his. The *manifestation* (or *Kundgabe*), strictly speaking, manifests *nothing*, insofar as such expression forbids the adequate attainment of what is purportedly 'manifested'; it is merely a deficient or insufficient manifestation. This same *lack of presence* characterises every single aspect of every act of communication we have with others, and it is this *lack of presence* which makes the expressive sign, when used in communicative discourse, indicative or not *purely* expressive. Thus, Derrida claims:

> The notion of *presence* is the nerve of this demonstration. If communication or manifestation (*Kundgabe*) is essentially indicative, it is so because the presence of the other's lived-experience is denied to our originary intuition. Each time that the immediate and full presence of the signified will be stolen away, the signifier will be of an indicative nature. (*VP*, p. 34/40/43)

We have thus arrived at the core, or the 'root' (*VP*, p. 32/38/41), of indication: indication occurs whenever an intended meaning is manifested in the world by way of an intentional act that, of its very essence, lacks the possibility of ever becoming fully *present* – a meaningful act that does *not* manifest the full presence of meaning is essentially indicative. Conversely:

> Pure expressivity will be the pure active intention (spirit, psyche, life, will) of a *bedeuten* that is animating a discourse whose content (*Bedeutung*) will be present. It is present not in nature, since indication alone takes place in nature and in space, but in consciousness. (*VP*, pp. 34/40/43–4)

The *presence* of pure expressivity consists in the fact that it has 'not exited from itself into the world, into space, into nature' (*VP*, p. 34/40/44).

Therefore we see here confirmed again the reading of the body/soul opposition of the sign that we examined under Section A, and going along with it, the death/life opposition that we drew out of it. We said that the 'body' of the sign ('dead' in itself) is given 'life' by the animating intention of the subject, when it endows it with the *soul* of the *Bedeutung*, *transforming the Körper into Leib*. We have just now seen, *in Husserl's own words*, an explicit connection drawn between the concepts of life, truth and the self-presence of meaning. When the expressed sign *goes forth* into the exteriority of the world, it loses and even sacrifices the self-presence of meaning that essentially constitutes its life and truth. This exiting of self-presence covers the whole of the indicative domain; indication, as

Husserl understands it, is therefore essentially related to the exiting of self-presence, which is tantamount, as we said in Section A, to *death*. Thus:

with all of these 'exitings' exiling this life of self-presence into indication, we can be sure that indication, which covers so far nearly the entire surface of language, is the process of death at work in the signs. And as soon as the other appears, indicative language—which is another name of the relation to death—no longer lets itself be erased. (*VP*, p. 34/40/44)

The indication is the linguistic sign that functions in the *manifestation* of meaning from one subject to another. This is operative every time the other is present to me, and we enter into a communicative relation. Therefore, if the expression constitutes the pure possibility of meaning, and if meaning is the purity of the self-presence of intention that is lost, *as soon as the other appears*, in the indicative domain, it is ultimately the relation to the other that must be *reduced* and excluded from our analysis: 'The relation to the other as non-presence is therefore the impurity of expression' (*VP*, p. 34/40/44). Hence the reduction to the interior monologue; if indication is characterised by the *exiting of self-presence*, then expression will consist of staying that exit, and remaining in the interiority of consciousness. The interior monologue involves the use of expressive signs (that is, meaningful signs), but it does so by at the same time excluding the relation to others. Here again we quote Lawlor's translation of Husserl's passage, with significant moments in bold:

But expressions also play a great part in the life of the soul insofar as it is not engaged in a relation of communication. This **change in function** plainly has **nothing to do with whatever makes an expression an expression**. Expressions continue to have their *Bedeutungen* as they had before, and **the same *Bedeutungen* as in dialogue**. A word only ceases to be a word when our interest is directed exclusively on the sensible, when it becomes a simple phonic form. But **when we live in the understanding of a word, it expresses something and the same thing, whether we address it to anyone or not**. It seems clear, therefore, that an **expression's *Bedeutung*, and what yet belongs to it essentially, cannot coincide with its activity of manifestation**. (*VP*, pp. 35/41/44–5)[13]

A word remains a word, so long as our attention is focused on the *sense* or *meaning* of the word – this entails that the *meaning* of the word comprises the core, or, we might say, the *essence* of the word, and we only *lose* this essence, that is, *the word ceases to be a word*, only when we shift our focus from the *sense* of the word to the *phonic* structure of it, the way in which the specific letters combine so as to produce a specific-sounding auditory sign. An expression retains *what belongs to it essentially*, whether it is manifested or not, so long as one *lives* in the understanding of the word – but this simply entails that any forms of empirical manifestation of a given word have nothing to do with the nature of the word *essentially*; Derrida writes, 'the sameness of the word is *ideal*' (*VP*, p. 35/41/45). It is *ideal* in the sense that it is the immediate unity (because we *live in the understanding* of the word) of word and sense that is infinitely repeatable, bound together by the animating intention of a *will*, and subsisting apart from all empirical manifestations. 'In the "solitary life of the soul," the pure unity of expression as such should therefore finally be restored to me' (*VP*, p. 35/41/45).

Having reduced our analysis to the interior life, we are met with an interesting problem: does the subject *indicate* anything to him- or herself in the interior monologue? For instance, suppose a father shouts at his children, then a few moments later thinks to himself, 'You overreacted, and you should go apologise to them.' The question is, in uttering these words (or in silently *thinking* these words to himself), does the father in fact *indicate* anything to himself? Does he in any way *point* himself to a knowledge that he, in whatever sense, did not formerly possess? The tokens and types of these inner communications are literally limitless: 'You are in love with him', 'You have made a mistake', 'I am hungry for a burrito', etc. Or what about when we seem to actually pose *questions* to ourselves, which we then subsequently *answer*? For instance, one walks into a room, and asks oneself, 'Now, why did I come in here?' and after a few moments' reflection says, 'Ah, yes, I came in here to check the thermostat.' Do we actually *learn* something about ourselves in these sorts of situations? Husserl too poses this question to himself in the course of his analysis, but for reasons that may by now be obvious, he rejects the very possibility of relating to oneself in an indicative manner:

Shall one say that one who speaks in solitude to himself, and that for him also the words serve as signs [*Zeichen*], namely, indications, [*Anzeichen*] of his own psychic lived-experiences? I do not think that such a view must be held. (*VP*, pp. 35/41–2/45)[14]

Husserl *must* insist on this point. For if expressions, used in the interior monologue, *indicate* knowledge *about* the subject *to* the subject who thinks them, then at bottom, *all* of language would ultimately be indicative, and the purportedly 'pure' expressivity of meaning would become entirely unattainable, even impossible as such. This would destroy the expression/indication distinction, but at the same time, to the extent that the phenomenological reductions are inextricably tied up with this expression/indication distinction (as Derrida has attempted to demonstrate), it would ultimately destroy the possibility of the phenomenological reduction in all its forms. Going along with this, it would also entail a severe compromising of Husserl's understanding of the pre-expressive stratum of sense, as this stratum could only be 'experienced' through the use of *indications* which, we have said, essentially entail the *loss* of self-presence in the passage through exteriority. Put another way, the *self* could only relate *to* itself, as it would to an *other*, a proposal entirely unacceptable on Husserl's understanding. In short, if the self must relate to the self by way of indication, as would be the case if interior monologue *taught* the subject anything about him- or herself, the entirety of the phenomenological project would be called into question. As Derrida says, 'The whole theory of signification announced in this first chapter of essential distinctions would collapse' if 'overall the ideal or absolute solitude of "proper" subjectivity still needed indications in order to constitute its own self-relation' (*VP*, p. 36/42/46). Now let us look to *how* Husserl proposes to demonstrate the superfluity of indication. This will bring us through the end of Chapter 3 and lead us into Chapter 4.

The *Hinzeigen/Anzeigen* distinction that we discussed above becomes important again here,[15] and it is accompanied by the distinction between *reality* and *representation*. In order to demonstrate that *pure* expressions do not function indicatively, Husserl announces the distinction between two types of referral: expressive referral, or what Derrida here translates as 'monstration' (*Hinzeigen*), and indicative referral (*Anzeigen*). The fundamental distinction between these two modes of signification is the passage of the *Anzeigen* through the exteriority of the mundane, empirical world. The *Hinzeigen*, on the other hand, as Husserl understands it, does not pass through *mundane reality*, not even in the looser sense of the passage through the body of the intending subject, as when the sign is *on the way* to becoming a communicative expression. But the opposite is true in the case of indication: 'In contrast, in indication, an existing sign, an empirical event refers to a content whose existence is at least presumed' (*VP*, p. 36/42/47). In indication, one *empirical existent* is used in order to refer to another *empirical existent*; while in expressive referral (*Hinzeigen*) a represented sign refers immediately to a pure *Bedeutung*.

'In the "solitary life of the soul," we no longer make use of *real* (*wirklich*) words, but only of *represented* (*vorgestellt*) words' (*VP*, p. 36/43/47).

The empirical nature of indication also entails that an existent sign points to an existent being or state of affairs with greater and lesser degrees of *certainty*, unlike in the expression of the interior monologue,

> when the expression is *full*, non-existent signs *show* the signifieds (*Bedeutungen*), which are ideal and therefore non-existent, and certain, for they are present to intuition. As for the certainty of internal existence, it has no need, Husserl thinks, of being signified. It is immediately present to itself. It is living consciousness. (*VP*, pp. 37/43/47–8)

The expression is 'full' in that it sacrifices or loses nothing in the way of sense, because it does not pass through the exteriority of the world; it is 'certain' for the same reason – the subject *lives* the sense of the experience *in the precise moment* that it happens; it does not and need not first pass through the exteriority of mundanity before arriving in the sphere of the conscious subject. The *Hinzeigen*, insofar as it employs only *represented*, as opposed to *real*, words, is therefore full and certain, and it points in an unmediated manner to a sense that is ideal, not empirical.

This then brings us to the status of this *representation*, and the *imagination* of the word that we employ in the interior monologue. The final few pages of Chapter 3 emphasise the subtle but very important distinction between the *imagination of the object* and the *imagined object* – this distinction pertains to the status of the *Hinzeigen* that the subject represents to him- or herself in the expressions of interiority. Husserl will have to maintain that 'if we need then the *imagination* of the word, at the same time we do without the *imagined word*' (*VP*, p. 37/44/48). Derrida's example of auditory perception helps to illuminate this *imagination/imagined* distinction.

Whenever we *hear* a word, there is for Husserl a distinction between the word-sign itself – the empirical, audible sign in the world, and the *phenomenon* of the perception thereof, the *hearing* of that sign. That is, essentially accompanying the phenomenon of the perception itself is the sense 'existence', which is to say, the sense that the phenomenal appearance of the sound parallels an empirical *thing* in the mundane sphere. Even in the reduced sphere of the inner life, the sense 'existence' is applied to the phenomenal appearance of an audible sign. It is this sense – 'existence' – that *would* apply to the *imagined object*, and this is why it is excluded or reduced in the sphere of *imagination* itself, strictly speaking: 'In imagination, the existence of the word is not implied, not even by means of the intentional sense' (*VP*, p. 38/44/48). But in reducing this *mundane* type of existence, consciousness highlights an *absolute* existence in the lived-experience of the soul; we might say that it *surrenders* mundane life for a *higher* type of life:

> This absolute of existence appears only in the reduction of existence that is relative to the transcendent world. And it is already imagination, 'the vital element of phenomenology' (*Ideas I*),[16] which gives this movement its privileged medium. (*VP*, p. 38/44/49)

This (and all that it entails), separates definitively Husserl's notion of the 'imagination' and the interiority of the phenomenological subject from what Derrida calls a 'classical psychology of imagination' (*VP*, p. 38/45/49). For on such a model, the image is akin to a *picture* contained in the mind, a 'real' indicative sign that *points to* its imagined object, a 'reality duplicating another reality' (*VP*, p. 39/46/50). The imagination is then able to *duplicate* this picture-image, by producing a memory-image or an imagination-image thereof. Therefore, the difference between the image as *perceived* and the image as *imagined* or *remembered* is, for classical psychology, a difference not in *kind*, but in *intensity*. But, as we discussed above in the material on time-consciousness, for Husserl, there has to be an essential difference between *perception* and *re-presentation*, and for two reasons. First, phenomenologically, they are simply different in kind. One's memory of a certain event has a different phenomenology than does the original experience of the event, and conversely, no matter how weak one's perception of a present experience may be, one never confuses a weakened present perception for a memory. Second, the entirety of the phenomenological project is constituted on the basis of this privileging of the pure expressivity of sense, in the *interior life of the soul*. This entails the radical distinction between perception and representation. As Derrida writes, in one of the text's longer footnotes, 'This heterogeneity constitutes the whole possibility of phenomenology which makes sense only if a pure and originary presentation is possible and original' (*VP*, pp. 38–9n*/45n4/49–50nI). This fundamental distinction for Husserl serves as the backbone of the criticism of classical psychology, for the failure to recognise the *absolute heterogeneity* of *presentation* and *representation* derives, Husserl thinks, from the view that holds the *image* as a mental content that duplicates a reality. For Husserl, the image is not something contained *in* the mind.

However, and here we begin to transition to Chapter 4, what Husserl and classical psychology share – 'their common metaphysical presupposition' (*VP*, p. 39/45/50) – is the conviction that *presence is primary*, that perception is *originary* and representation *secondary*. For classical psychology, this is an image *imprinted* upon the mind from the outside world, and the reality of this image points outwardly to its object – memory or imagination thereof is a less intense, secondary version of this image. For Husserl, this presence is a pure intentional sense. Nonetheless, despite the rigour that distinguishes phenomenology from classical psychology, they are united in the conviction that *presence comes first*. This is precisely what deconstruction will set about undermining, as Derrida here announces:

By asserting that *perception does not exist* or that what we call perception is not originary, and that in a certain way everything 'begins' by means of 're-presentation' (this is a proposition which obviously can be sustained only within the erasure of these last two concepts; this proposition means that there is no 'beginning' and the 're-presentation' of which we are speaking is not the modification of a 're' that has *supervened* upon an originary presentation), by re-inserting the difference of the 'sign' in the heart of the 'originary,' what is at issue is not to turn back away from transcendental phenomenology [. . .] In this way we have just designated the primary intention—and the distant horizon—of the present essay. (*VP*, pp. 39/45–6/50)

This announcement is our indication that *Voice and Phenomenon* is entering the second phase of its movement. So far, we have been laying the groundwork. Chapter 1 emphasised the importance of the expression/indication distinction, as found in the 1900–1 *Logical Investigations*, for the remainder of the phenomenological project. We have also attempted to isolate the core or the essence of both indication and of expression, in Chapters 2 and 3, respectively. As we have done so, we have at the same time pointed towards all the complications and entanglements that these concepts bear. Thus, the analysis so far has attempted to highlight the significance of the stakes, and the magnitude of the complications, comprising the phenomenological project.

As we shift to Chapter 4 (and following this, Chapters 5 and 6 as well), a couple of important transitions begin to take place. First, the arguments of Chapters 4, 5 and 6 are all arguments designed to demonstrate in Husserl's terms the superfluity of the indicative sign in the solitary life of the soul. Chapters 1, 2 and 3 were the foundation that *asserted* to us this superfluity, and demonstrated the stakes of this superfluity, but Chapters 4, 5 and 6 begin to pose explicit *arguments* for this superfluity.

These arguments are, respectively: the argument from representation, the argument from temporalisation and the argument from the medium of hearing-oneself-speak. All these arguments operate, as Lawlor notes in the 'Translator's Introduction', 'on the local terrain of Husserl's phenomenology' (*VP*, p. xxiii). In so doing, and just as we saw in our discussions of Chapters 1, 2 and 3, Derrida's analysis draws out and explores the entanglements of Husserl's commitments, those aspects of the arguments that seem to run counter to themselves. But the stakes are now higher because, as Lawlor also notes, 'they [the arguments of Chapters 4, 5 and 6] also operate on the larger terrain of metaphysics in general' (*VP*, p. xxiii). Indeed we have already seen intimations of this, as when Derrida, for instance, writes in Chapter 3: 'the concept of intentionality is still taken in the tradition of a voluntaristic metaphysics, that is, perhaps taken simply in *the* metaphysics' (*VP*, p. 29/34/37). But where Chapters 1, 2 and 3 were more *implicit* in their connections between Husserl and the whole of the metaphysical tradition, Chapters 4, 5 and 6 are much more *explicit*. The names Plato, Aristotle, Descartes, Hume, Kant and Heidegger begin to appear with greater frequency, many of them for the first time in the body of the text. This is not surprising given that, as we have said, for Derrida, Husserl's phenomenology represents 'metaphysics in its most modern, critical, and vigilant form' (*Positions*, p. 5). Phenomenology binds together the metaphysics of presence in both its spatial and temporal senses, and brings them to the point of their logical *telos* inasmuch as the *emphasis* in phenomenology on *presence* and on *the living present* is, unlike most of its forebears, absolute and uncompromising. The *only* truth in phenomenology is that which conforms to the *principle of all principles*, that which conforms to the strictures of the pure interiority of presence. Therefore, given that Husserl is the philosopher who brings this presence to its perfection, it stands to reason that it is precisely at this point in the metaphysical tradition that the *constitutive difference* that Derrida will argue lies beneath the whole of the metaphysical tradition becomes most salient. It is thus not surprising that it is in Chapter 4 that the term 'deconstruction' first appears in *Voice and Phenomenon*. Ultimately then, what Chapters 4, 5 and 6 demonstrate are the ways in which the commitments of the phenomenological tradition are motivated by the metaphysical tradition, but also the ways in which those commitments are undermined by the differential structure that makes them possible in the first place.

Let us now turn to Chapter 4 of *Voice and Phenomenon*.

Meaning and Representation

In Chapter 3, we attempted to isolate the pure expressivity of meaning in the inner voice of the interior monologue, as when one speaks to oneself. This, we said, is an employment of the *expressive* sign that does not *go forth* into the world, not even through the medium of the body. It is a voice that is absolutely present to itself, in the moment that it is expressed, and its *intention* is also *outside* the empirical world in the form of a pure ideality. But at the end, we wondered, still, is it not the case that when I *speak* to myself, I *learn* something about myself, in which case I would obviously *indicate* something to myself? And for reasons of phenomenological emphasis, we said that Husserl could not possibly allow this. If indeed we indicate knowledge *about* ourselves *to* ourselves in the interior monologue, the pure stratum of presence, upon which the entirety of the phenomenological project is founded, falters. Thus, it is a matter of great exigency for Husserl that we are ultimately able to distinguish essentially expression from indication, so that we can finally *exclude* or *reduce* indication and isolate the pure meaning-stratum lighted up by the expressive sign. As Derrida writes, 'In solitary discourse, the subject learns nothing about himself, manifests nothing to himself. In order to sustain this demonstration, whose consequences will be limitless in phenomenology, Husserl appeals to two types of arguments' (*VP*, p. 41/48/53). Now we begin to look to Husserl's *arguments* for the superfluity of indication.

These two *types* of arguments, the first of which is addressed in Chapter 4, are bound together in the following key passage, with significant passages in bold, from Husserl:

One of course *speaks*, in a certain sense, even in the solitary discourse, and it is certainly **possible to think of oneself as speaking, and even as speaking to oneself**, as, for example, when someone says to himself: 'you have gone wrong, you can't go on like that.' But **in the genuine sense of communication, there is no speech in such cases, nor does one tell oneself anything**: one **merely represents oneself** [*man stellt sich vor*] as speaking and communicating. **In a monologue words can perform no function of indicating** the existence [*Dasein*] of psychic acts, since **such indication would there be quite purposeless** [*ganz zwecklos wäre*]. For the **acts in question are themselves lived by us at that very instant** [*im selben Aubenblick*]. (*VP*, pp. 41/48–9/54)[17]

From this, Derrida abstracts two types of Husserlian arguments for the superfluity of indication in the solitary life of the soul. On the first 'type', I do not indicate anything to myself because it is not *possible* to actually indicate anything to myself; at *most*, I can *represent* myself *to* myself *as though* I am communicating with myself, but that is all it is, a representation: 'Here we have only a *representation* and an *imagination*' (*VP*, p. 41/48/53). According to the second 'type', I communicate nothing to myself and can only *imagine* myself as doing so, *because* there is no *need* to do so; and there is no need to do so because the psychic acts in the cases of the solitary life of the soul are lived by the subject at the precise moment that they occur: 'The existence of psychical acts does not have to be indicated (recall that only an existence in general can be indicated) because the existence of psychical acts is immediately present to the subject in the present instant' (*VP*, p. 41/48/53). Chapter 4, as we have stated, addresses the first type of argument. The second type of argument will be the subject of Chapter 5.

According to the first type of argument, I indicate nothing to myself, because it is not *possible* to do so; it is certainly the case that I *imagine* myself *as though* I were speaking to myself, but this is merely a *representation* of self to self, nothing more: 'one represents oneself (*man stellt sich vor*) as being a speaking and communicating subject' (*VP*, p. 42/49/54), Derrida writes. From the outset this is problematic insofar as it raises the question of *representation*, and the precise status of this *representation*, even as Husserl conceives it, is ambiguous. Husserl himself employs various senses of *representation*: (1) representation in the general sense of ideality, as *Vorstellung*; (2) representation as the modification of 'presence' or presentation, as *Vergegenwärtigung*; (3) representation as the placeholder of another *Vorstellung*, as *Repräsentation*. 'Here', as Derrida notes, in the case of one *representing* oneself *to* oneself as though one communicates with oneself, 'we have to consider representation in the general sense of *Vorstellung* . . .' (*VP*, p. 42/49/54). Husserl's phrasing is key for this: *man stellt sich vor* – here we see the components of the word *Vorstellung*, but insofar as *Vorstellung* is the term for ideality in the general sense, it also encompasses *Vergegenwärtigung* and *Repräsentation*, as Derrida notes.[18]

But this ambiguity itself begets further difficulties. We must keep in mind precisely where we are in the analysis – in order to isolate the pure expressivity that constitutes the heart of ideality for Husserl, we have attempted to reduce or exclude the indicative sphere, which covers, we concluded, *all real (i.e. empirical, actual) uses of language in communicative discourse.* In so doing we isolate the essence of expression, and this is kept *essentially* distinct from indication *because* the employment of it in the solitary life of the soul gives us only a *represented* communication, not a *real* communication. Indication, then, would be understood in Husserl's terms as *real* communication and vice versa, while expression would have to be characterised as *represented* communication. For this reason Derrida writes, 'Husserl here seems to apply to language the fundamental distinction between reality and representation' (*VP*, p. 42/49/54). So in order to arrive at the pure, ideal expressivity of meaning, one must, according to Husserl, pass through a sort of *fiction*, in the form of an *imaginary representation* (*Vergegenwärtigung*).

But moreover, Derrida says, this distinction – reality vs representation – does not seem rigorously applicable to language, and especially not in the way that Husserl has set it forth. If it were indeed the case that representation in the general sense of ideality (*Vorstellung*) were the essential component of *expressivity*, then this would entail, Derrida claims, that representation does *not* apply essentially in the case of *indication*, or the *real* use of language:

First, we would have to assume that in communication, in the so-called 'actual' practice of language, representation (in all the senses of this word) would not be essential and constitutive. We would have to assume that representation is only an accident added contingently onto the practice of discourse. (*VP*, p. 42/49/55)

Representation would then be an accidental, non-essential, 'add-on' to the indicative sphere of communication. But this is simply not the case, Derrida claims, because every single employment of signs, whether for communicative purposes or not, entails – and essentially so – a representational component that constitutes the very basis of signification itself: 'from the start I must operate (in) a structure of repetition whose element can only be representative' (*VP*, p. 42/50/55). Let us explore this further.

Contained in the very nature of the linguistic sign is the essentiality that it functions, that is to say, it must be employable and recognisable, a potentially infinite number of times, across a potentially infinite amount of empirical situations, regardless of the presence or absence of the speaker/author, and/or the auditor/reader. A 'sign' that would mean something only one time, to only one person, is not a sign at all. Having said this, however, we note that the *empirical* operation of the sign always, in some sense, *corrupts* its ideality, simply in virtue of the fact that it is an *empirical* employment, that is, in virtue of the sign's *going forth* into the world – the sign may be *pronounced* differently in different geographical regions, it may be *interpreted* somewhat differently depending upon the culture or the time, etc. But all the same, in order for a sign to *be* a sign, it must retain some kernel of ideality:

> A phoneme or grapheme is necessarily always other, to a certain extent, each time that it is presented in a procedure or a perception, but it can function as a sign and as language in general only if a formal identity allows it to be reissued and to be recognized. This identity is necessarily ideal. (*VP*, pp. 43/50/55–6)

Now, given what we have just said, it is clear that the sign is always and essentially operating hand-in-hand with representation, in all three of the forms Derrida discusses above: (1) as *Vorstellung*, in virtue of the fact that it implies the sphere of ideality in general; (2) as *Vergegenwärtigung*, because of its repeatability, its ability to *stand in for* and reproduce the *presence* of experience across a number of situations; (3) as *Repräsentation* because 'each signifying event is a substitute (of the signified as well as of the ideal form of the signifier)' (*VP*, p. 43/50/56) – each time we *use* a sign, we use it as a stand-in in order to point to an ideal concept. Therefore, if Husserl wishes to essentially assign the notion of 'representation' to the expressive domain of the interior monologue, and 'reality' to the indicative domain of actual communication, this will not work, Derrida claims, because the whole of language is bound up essentially with the notion of 'representation' – every use of the sign is an *empirical* (or real) operation, but nonetheless, no use of the sign is possible without a reference to ideality and representation. Language itself is therefore constituted essentially on the basis of this paradoxical entanglement of singularity (irreplaceable, empirical, 'reality' in each of its operations), and ideality – this entanglement, in other words, and hence the essential inseparability of reality and representation, is what makes language what it is. This is what Derrida means when he writes:

> that in language representation and reality are not added together here and there, for the simple reason that it is impossible in principle to distinguish them rigorously. And no doubt we must not say that this impossibility is produced *in* language. Language in general *is* that impossibility—by means of itself alone. (*VP*, pp. 42/49–50/55)

It makes no difference, moreover, if we suggest that perhaps Husserl is simply trying to isolate the 'exclusively representative character of expressivity' (*VP*, p. 43/50/56) in his exclusion of the indicative sphere. In other words, one might suspect that our analysis makes an assumption that Husserl does not make, namely, that *because* representation applies in the sphere of *expressivity*, then it necessarily *cannot* apply to the indicative sphere; but on the contrary, the objection would go, Husserl does not, in point of fact, hold that 'representation' does not apply in the indicative sphere at all – rather, he is simply highlighting that the essential nature of expressivity is its exclusively representative character: while indication might be representation *plus* something else, expression *just is* its representative character. But it makes no difference as to the point that Derrida has attempted to demonstrate. For once one allows the *essentially representative character* of each and every use of the sign, then even if expression would be *purely* representative (which Derrida rejects), any robust distinction between *actual* or *real* discourse, and *representative* discourse becomes instantly problematic.

These two paragraphs, running from page 43 to page 44 (*VP*, pp. 43–4/50–2/56–8), are among the richest and most pregnant paragraphs in the text. Here begins one of the key heralds and one of the most significant turning points of the entire book: the history of metaphysics consists on the basis of this difference between reality and representation, and the very moment that we allow that representation contaminates the whole of language, then within language itself, this radical difference becomes unsustainable: 'Whether what is at issue is expression or indicative communication, the difference between reality and representation, between the true and the imaginary, between simple presence and repetition has always already started to erase itself' (*VP*, p. 43/51/56). The tradition of the metaphysics of presence, stretching from Plato up through Husserl and beyond, is characterised by the 'obstinate desire to save presence' (*VP*, p. 43/51/57). It thusly ascribes to the sign the characteristic of the *representative* of presence, which is considered primary – hence the 'derivative', supplemental or secondary nature of the sign, according to the tradition of metaphysics. The sign, insofar as it can only *re-present* presence, can only ever be considered *deficient*. (This is also why, as Derrida notes a number of times, Husserl is committed to the notion of an inner stratum of sense, ontologically prior to the domain of the expressive sign.)

The distinction between reality and representation can *only* arise through the use of the sign. As Derrida says, 'This is as well to live *in*

the—assured, secured, constituted—effect of repetition, of representation, in the effect of the difference which snatches presence away'
(*VP*, p. 43/51/57). It is only within the security of a closed sign-system
that we are able to definitively ascribe the characterisation of 'reality', in
the sense of pure, unmediated, unmodified 'presence'. But the sign, and
language more generally, is constituted, Derrida has argued, on the basis
of the essential inseparability of reality and representation, such that
the difference between reality and representation is only sustainable by
wilfully forgetting the essential nature of the sign: 'the gesture that sanc-
tions this difference is the very erasure of the sign' (*VP*, p. 44/51/57).
This paradoxical conjunction entails that the metaphysics of presence
can only install the radical difference that it requires (between reality
and representation) by *erasing* the *true* nature of the sign (as representative in nature through and through) in the very moment that it employs
it. Therefore, there are two ways of *erasing* 'the originality of the sign,
and we must be attentive to the instability of all these movements', as
they 'pass in fact very quickly and very subtly from one to the other'
(*VP*, p. 44/51/57).

The first way is the gesture of the metaphysical tradition, which *erases*
the originality of the sign by, as we have said, overlooking its essential
characteristics of reproduction and representation, 'turning them into a
modification that supervenes over a simple presence' (*VP*, p. 44/51/57).
But we must keep in mind that, for Derrida, the founding value of presence is *the defining and inaugural gesture* of the entire history of philosophy,
such that there has heretofore been *no other* concept of the sign. The
metaphysical concept of the sign, in other words, is *constituted*, it is made
possible, on the basis of the erasure of the sign. Hence the second way
is the gesture that restores the originality of the sign *against* the backdrop
of the metaphysical tradition, and the purpose of this gesture is 'to erase
the concept of the sign whose entire history and entire sense belongs
to the adventure of the metaphysics of presence' (*VP*, p. 44/51/57).
This is the gesture of the project that will be called, 'deconstruction', a
term which makes its first appearance on this page (*VP*, p. 44/52/57).

The gesture that would restore the originality of the sign, however,
leaves nothing throughout the remainder of the system untouched –
presence, originariness, identity – these are the values bound up with
the understanding of the sign as derivative. Hence 'this schema holds as
well for the concepts of representation, of repetition, of difference, etc.,
as well as for their entire system . . . a whole system of differences drawn

into the same deconstruction' (*VP*, pp. 44/51–2/57). Though Derrida would not 'define' deconstruction until the interviews collected in the 1972 volume, *Positions*, nonetheless, on this page of *Voice and Phenomenon*, he gives us a few very important details regarding its structural schema. First, we note that the *movement* of this schema, he says, has 'always already begun' (*VP*, p. 44/52/57). The work of deconstruction, that is, is already underway at every moment of the history of metaphysics. This is because the inaugural gesture of the metaphysical tradition, from Plato through Husserl and beyond, is the positing of the concept of the sign constituted on the basis of the *erasure* of the sign (as derivative reproduction and representation). Thus, insofar as the concept of the sign is the *erasure* of the sign, this erasure lurks in the background of every significant gesture that happens in the philosophical tradition. This is why Derrida's later works (on Plato, Aristotle, Augustine, Rousseau, Hegel, Heidegger, etc.), demonstrate that it is the respective *text* itself that undermines itself in the course of its own operation. This brings us to the second key point, namely, that deconstruction is not a *methodology*, nor is it merely a set of *textual interpretations*. According to Derrida, deconstruction is not something *invented* by the subject, 'Jacques Derrida', something that one can simply adopt and *apply* to a text as if doing so forcibly and as an act of the *will*, from outside the text. If deconstruction were simply this, a method of textual interpretation, it would not be *locatable* in Husserl's text (having not been 'invented' by Derrida until 1967), much less Plato's and Aristotle's, as Derrida argues that it is. Third, this is why, according to Derrida, one cannot simply relinquish the *founding value of presence* and move forward in the philosophical tradition. To be a philosopher means to work out of the philosophical tradition; to work out of the philosophical tradition means to work with an inherited set of concepts and problems; these concepts, however, operate on the basis of certain decisions and presuppositions that run throughout the entire history of philosophy. One cannot simply *change* the concepts, because, like it or not, those concepts carry with them elements of the history out of which they have arisen; when Husserl, for example, uses the term 'monad' to characterise subjective consciousness in *Cartesian Meditations*, it carries with it echoes of Leibniz. However, one cannot simply create *new* concepts, because the *rules* of the Western tradition that govern the creation of concepts operate in accordance with the same presuppositions of the 'founding value of presence'. Therefore, finally, deconstruction is nothing less than an attempt to reformulate our very understanding of what it means to *think*. The only way to begin to think anew is to try to *open* the enclosure of the metaphysical tradition of presence, by interrupting it in its operation. The task of deconstruction, therefore, is to try to push thought *outside* the system, which Derrida elsewhere calls the impetus to 'think or deconstruct the concept of concept' (*Limited Inc.*, p. 117). But one can only do this by beginning within the system of metaphysics. This is why Derrida claims that the 'movement of this schema will only be able, for the moment and for a long time, to work over from within, from a certain inside, the language of metaphysics' (*VP*, pp. 44/51–2/57).

Let us proceed – following this announcement, and for the remainder of the book, the moves in Derrida's argument will begin to gain momentum. Deconstruction, we said, erases the originality of the concept of the sign, restoring the essentially reproductive and representative character of the sign; it *erases* the sign by *restoring* the sign. In so doing, it makes representation, reproduction and repetition primary instead of derivative and secondary. This will be based upon an understanding of the notion of 'ideality' in Husserl. The sense of *any* experience, for Husserl, even in the primary mode of presence, will necessarily conform to an ideality which, insofar as it is ideal and non-empirical, is infinitely repeatable, *prior to and as a condition of its being 'experienced', as such, in the mode of presence*. Hence:

re-presentation has a presentation (*Präsentation*) as *Vorstellung* for its represented. In this way—against Husserl's express intention—we come to make *Vorstellung* in general and, as such, depend on the possibility of repetition, and the most simple *Vorstellung*, presentation (*Gegenwärtigung*), depend on the possibility of re-presentation (*Vergegenwärtigung*). We derive the presence-of-the-present from repetition and not the reverse. (*VP*, p. 44/52/58)

According to Husserl, the structure of discourse can only be understood in accordance with the notion of 'ideality', and this in three distinct but related ways. First, the *signifier* (the sensible form of the word) is itself ideal, insofar as it can be repeated as *the same* across a potential infinity of cases. Second, the *signified*, the ideal sense towards which the *signifier* points, is ideal, subsisting in an 'outside' that, above, we said was outside of consciousness, strictly speaking, and outside of the external world as well. Third, the intended object, when that ideal sense, as we said above, *passes outside of itself into another outside*, this time within consciousness as its object. In all three of these senses, the *ideality* of the ideal for Husserl depends upon the essential possibility of repetition. It 'does not *exist* in the world and it does not come from another world' (*VP*, p. 45/52/58). If it *existed* in the world, it would be merely empirical, and could only *ever* be a *this* or a *that*, occurring only once. If it came from *another* world (as in a naïve form of Platonism), this would reinstate an unattainable and unknowable *transcendence* that the entirety of Husserl's thought rejects. The ideality of the ideal depends solely and exclusively upon the pure repeatability of sense itself. Therefore, 'Its "being" is proportionate to the power of repetition' (*VP*, p. 45/52/58).

Being is determined as ideality, and this because of its *permanence* and essential repeatability. But if being and truth are understood in accordance with ideality (and the possibility of repetition), then sensible existence must be understood as, in some senses *false* or *illusory*. This then 'reawakens the originary decision of philosophy in its Platonic form' (*VP*, p. 45/53/59). In the Socratic *Dialogues*, whenever Socrates and an interlocutor are attempting to track a concept, it is quite common for the interlocutor to first offer Socrates *examples* or empirical instantiations of the concept. Socrates always retorts that he does not seek *examples*, but rather the *form* (*eidos*), which insofar as it is the universal, is repeatable, and hence recognisable as such in the empirical world. The things in the empirical world, according to Plato, *participate* in their respective forms, and to precisely that extent, they participate in *being*, but to the extent that they *are not* their respective forms, they also participate in non-being. The ideality of the ideal does not *exist*, for Husserl, because it is not and cannot be *empirical*, but this does not mean that ideality is characterised by *non-being*, for:

When he asserts the non-existence or the non-reality of ideality, he does this in order to acknowledge that ideality *is* according to a mode that is irreducible to sensible existence or to empirical reality, indeed, to their fiction. By determining the *ontos on*[19] as *eidos*, Plato was doing nothing else. (*VP*, p. 45/53/59)

Hence owing to the emphasis on the *being* of ideality, the phenomenological project is imbued through and through with a purified Platonism; in addition, this weds it inseparably to the metaphysics of presence. Derrida claims, 'this determination of being as ideality is merged in a paradoxical way with the determination of being as presence' (*VP*, p. 45/53/59). This fusion is *paradoxical* in the sense that ideality as Husserl understands it is a radical *outside*, exterior to both consciousness and the world, and thus, in a certain sense it is radically and fundamentally *absent*, not present. Nevertheless, Husserlian ideality unites the two modes of *presence* as Derrida characterises them: spatial and temporal. It is *spatial* in the sense that an ideality involves an ideal *object*. 'Object' combines the Latin root *iacere* ('to throw') with the prefix *ob* ('against'), and hence means *that which is thrown against* or *thrown across from*. The same etymological pairing occurs in French (*objet*), and in German as well: *Vor-stellung* combines *vor* ('in front of') with *stellen* ('to set' or 'to place'). Hence the ideality is an *object*, 'standing over and against, being pre-sent in front of, the act of repetition—*Vor-stellung* being the general form of presence as proximity to a look[20]' (*VP*, p. 46/53/59). So the ideality is a *presence* in that it is the object *most present* to the *look* (regard) of the conscious gaze, within consciousness itself, which is *not a simple inside*. But it is also a presence in the sense that it derives from a *look* that is constituted only on the basis of a temporality of the *living present*, which as we saw above, is itself predicated upon the foundation of the *primal impression*, the *now* that is the *source-point* of retention, and of the structure of the living present. These two modes of presence are united in the phenomenological 'principle of all principles'.

The 'principle of all principles', we recall, states:

> that every originary presentive intuition is a legitimizing source of cognition, that everything originarily (so to speak, in its 'personal' actuality) offered to us in 'intuition' is to be accepted simply as what it is presented as being, but also, only within the limits in which it is presented there.[21]

Everything that is *originarily present* to consciousness is a legitimising source of cognition (and we note that the word 'present' or some form thereof, occurs in the 'principle' itself no fewer than three times). It is in the *present* that the ideality of the object is met. That the 'present' as the now-moment of consciousness secures the *a priori* legitimacy of pure ideality entails, Derrida claims, 'first the certainty, which is itself ideal and absolute, that the universal form of all experience (*Erlebnis*) and therefore of all life, has always been and always will be the *present*' (*VP*, p. 46/53/60). The past *is no more*, the future *is not yet*; only the present *is*. I can only be absolutely *certain* of that which I am experiencing *right now*. The future is essentially unknowable, and about the past I can be easily deceived or mistaken. Only the punctuated *now-point* of the present can secure certainty, because only the present *is*; it is all that has ever been, or ever will be.

Furthermore, insofar as, in the presence of the present, I relate essentially to the ideality of sense, as Husserl demands, and insofar as that ideality transcends my *empirical* existence, this punctuated now-point also signifies one's relation to death. Here we must pay careful attention to Derrida's moves, for they are complex, very quick and quite bold. In the mode of *presence*, I relate to an ideality that transcends *my personal being*, an *outside* to which my own experience is and must be referred. So in the very possibility of signification itself, that is to say, hidden within one's *ability* to express one's experience, there is a necessary passage to that which is, strictly speaking, outside the sphere of one's proper self. Whenever I use *signs* at all, in any way, I am relating to a system of signs, infinitely repeatable, that preceded my birth and that will survive my death. Above, we said that in the indicative, which is to say the communicative use of signs, we sacrifice the immediate self-presence of meaning, and separate the *intention* behind the sign (which acts as a 'soul' that *animates* the sign) from the sign itself, because we send the sign forth into the world – this was tantamount, we said, to a kind of *death*. Here in Chapter 4, Derrida is taking this line of argumentation a great deal further. Insofar as we necessarily and essentially relate to an ideality that transcends our own being every single time we use signs at all, the very possibility of the sign itself, as that which is essentially and infinitely repeatable, *implies* the death or the absence of the one who uses it. This is further solidified in the philosophical emphasis on *the presence of the present*. If the present is *what is*, then this would be true even if the present were emptied of all its empirical content, including that of my own life and experience. Derrida writes, 'It is therefore the relation to *my death* (to my disappearance in general) that is hidden in this determination of being as presence, ideality, as the absolute possibility of repetition' (*VP*, p. 46/54/60).

This relation to death, Derrida argues, is what makes signification possible. The self-presence of inner life *must* be allowed to relate to what is other to it (and the 'other' to life is death) in order to be entered into a sign system, such that it can cease being merely empirical, and can be *expressed*. It is important to note that, for Derrida, it is not *the sign itself* that is the relation to death; rather, the *possibility* of the sign: 'The possibility of the sign is this relation to death' (*VP*, p. 46/54/60). The *possibility* of the sign is itself the relation of the self to the *other* of ideality, and this relation, insofar as it is a relation of the inner life of the self, the solitary life of the soul, to what is other to it, is a relation to death. *This relation is cancelled, or concealed, in the metaphysics of presence.* Let us look at why this is so.

The metaphysics of presence, we said, wants to retain an absolute and irreducible distinction between *reality* and *representation*. This was a distinction, Derrida argued, that could only be sustained within language itself by wilfully *forgetting* the essentially representative character of language, in order to secure oneself within the enclosure of the sign system, such that one can definitively ascribe the term 'reality' as an unmodified, unmediated *presence*. To say, '*x* or *y* is what is *real*,' one must actively and *wilfully forget* that the signs '*x*' and '*y*' *are indeed signs* (as is the sign 'real') and that signs are essentially representative in character. That signs are essentially *representative* in character entails that their sense is essentially *relational*, and hence requires *active production*. By casting aside the essentially representative character of language, the metaphysical tradition attempts to cancel this *active production of sense* (see the discussion of Chapter 1 above), which is itself an essentiality of language. It attempts to cancel the productive relation between the subject and the sign – this relation is the relation of the life of interiority to the death of its 'other'. Hence in cancelling the essentiality of the sign, metaphysics attempts to conceal death itself: 'The determination and the erasure of the sign in metaphysics is the dissimulation of this relation to death which nevertheless was producing signification' (*VP*, p. 46/54/60).

There is a still further implication of this relation to death, insofar as it can no longer be considered, Derrida argues, as a *secondary* or *accidental* feature of life. To establish a relation *in* the present, *to* the present, the subject must relate itself to an ideality that transcends it, which, we said, opens the subject to the relation to its own death. This happens *essentially* – not accidentally – every time we employ signs, even when we say, 'I am'; insofar as the present is all that *is*, the word 'am' is related essentially to *presence*, and this to the repetitive structure of ideality. Thus, the affirmation, 'I am; I exist', is one that contains within it the relation of the speaker who utters it, to his or her own death. '*I am* means therefore originarily *I am mortal. I am immortal* is an impossible proposition' (*VP*, pp. 46/54/60–1). This is true, Derrida suggests, *every time* the words are uttered, *no matter by whom*, that is to say, even if the speaker were divine. 'We can therefore go further. Insofar as it is language, "I am the one who is" is the confession of a mortal' (*VP*, pp. 46–7/54/61).[22]

Derrida then brings this line of enquiry back to its point of origin, to the notions of 'imagination', 'fantasy' and 'fiction'; where Derrida will argue that an erasure or a reduction – an active *forgetting* similar to the one that occurs in the case of the repetitive and representative character of the sign – accompanies Husserl's notion of the 'imagination'. In the interior monologue, the imagination, we recall, is for Husserl the faculty through which one *represents* oneself *to* oneself *as though* one were communicating with oneself (even if, in point of fact, one does *not* and *cannot* communicate with oneself). One must therefore, we said, pass through a kind of *fiction* in order to arrive at the pure expressivity of meaning. As Derrida rightly claims, *fiction* (in the form of the imagination and imaginative variation) plays a notably large role throughout the entirety of Husserl's project. In the mode of eidetic reduction, the imagination is employed in order to neutralise the would-be 'existence' of the phenomenal object, so that one might vary the contents of the phenomena and analyse aspects of the *eidos* not currently *present* to consciousness. In so doing, one is allowed thereby to imaginatively separate the essential from the non-essential aspects of the experience. Hence insofar as one is dealing purely in the *eidetic*, which is to say, the ideal and non-empirical realm, the imagination is *neutralising* or *non-positing*, as opposed to memory. The mode of representation in memory is *positing*, Husserl claims, insofar as accompanying the representation itself is also the sense that it refers to an actuality, something that was formerly a *present*, the sense that *this actually happened*. No such sense accompanies the *image* of imagination, Husserl claims, which is what endows the imagination with a phenomenological *privilege* in Husserl's philosophy. Indeed, Derrida argues that, *like* the sphere of ideality, the imagination is essentially constituted on the basis of the *possibility of repetition*; hence it would be *repetition*, rather than *presence*, that would (or should) serve as the basis of imagination: 'The power of pure repetition that opens ideality and the power that liberates the imaginative reproduction of empirical perception cannot be foreign to one another' (*VP*, pp. 47–8/55/62).

Nevertheless, Derrida claims, this 'fiction' always bottoms out for Husserl in a moment of *reality* or presence. Indeed this would presumably *have* to be the case for Husserl, given the problems that would otherwise arise – after all, it would be quite devastating indeed to the phenomenological method, if one were to arrive at ideality, that is, *truth*, by way of a faculty that is constituted by and employs only *fictions*. Derrida therefore provides textual evidence from Husserl that the faculty of imagination, though a faculty of fiction, derives its *fiction* from a primary *truth*, or an originary presence. Like memory itself, imagination is classified for Husserl under the general category of *representation*, in the form of a *Vergegenwärtigung*, which is a modification of presence (*Gegenwärtigung*). It modifies *presence* insofar as it is a deliberate modification of *memory*, which is itself a *positing representation*, for the reason we stated just above:

Consequently, if it is a good auxiliary instrument for phenomenological neutral-ization, the image is not pure neutralization. It keeps within itself the primary reference to an originary presentation, that is, to a perception and to a positing of existence, to a belief in general. (*VP*, p. 47/55/62)

From here, we move to Derrida's four *disconcerting* points regarding the Husserlian employment of the imagination with respect to the interior monologue. First, we note that expressive phenomena are 'considered representations of imagination' (*VP*, p. 48/56/62). In order to separate the expressivity of expression from the communicative use of signs in the mode of indication, Husserl claims that when we employ expressions in the interior life of the soul, we merely *imagine* that we are communicat-ing with ourselves. Second, therefore, the *discourse* that we carry out with ourselves when we communicate with ourselves is merely *fictional*, but this implies that there is a *non-fictional* or actual form of internal discourse that is *purely expressive*. But then, third, if, in the purely interior use of signs, there is a radical and essential distinction between a *fictional* and an *actual* usage or aspect of the signs, then it would seem that this same distinc-tion would apply in the *communicative* use of those signs. After all, in the interior monologue, we employ the very same signs (and hence the very same idealities) that we employ when we use these signs in a communica-tive manner; and hence the very same essential distinctions *within the uses of the signs themselves* should hold, whether they are employed in an interior or exterior manner. Hence if there is an *actual* and a *fictional* aspect of the signs used in the interior monologue, there should be a correlative distinction in the communicative uses of the signs as well. The actuality that characterises the communicative use of the signs would therefore be considered *accidental*, even to the indication. This implies, therefore, that *actuality* is 'like an empirical piece of clothing that is external to expres-sion, just like a body on a soul' (*VP*, p. 48/56/63). Fourth, in the interior-ity of the soul, the role of this *fictional/actual* distinction would manifest as the difference between a discourse that is *actually* expressive, that is to say, actually representative (but, we should note that 'representation' falls on the side of fiction, a deviation from pure presence, such that we might even say, 'actually fictional'), versus a discourse that is *purely* fictional, or, we might say, *fictionally representative*, which would characterise the seem-ingly *indicative* acts of self-communication.

The conclusion of this line of investigation is that there is no longer a rigorous way to distinguish, as Husserl must, between an *actual* use of the sign and a *fictional* (or merely imagined) use of the sign. If even the most *interior* use of language, that is, the *non-communicative* use of expression, is *actually fictional* or *actually representative*, then, like we said in the case of the sign (where the distinction between 'reality' and 'representation' cannot definitively hold), any radical distinction between an *imagined* interior discourse and an *actual* interior discourse will become untenable. This is what Derrida means when he says that 'The erasure (or the derivation) of the sign is thereby merged with the reduction from imagination' (*VP*, p. 47/55/61).

This then begins the movement of Derrida's thought towards the argument that occupies Chapter 5 of *Voice and Phenomenon*. For, despite the essential unsustainability of the radical distinction between the *imagined* and the *actual* interior discourse, Husserl will nevertheless *have* to hold onto this distinction, in order to distinguish essentially between the expressive and indicative modes of signification, and he will have to hang onto *that* distinction, in order to keep intact the possibility of the phenomenological reductions, and the pure possibility of meaning that serves as the backbone of the entire phenomenological project. Hence let us follow Husserl at this time, and hang onto the distinction (actual vs imagined interior discourse). What, then, follows?

It would appear at first glance as though Husserl would be committed to the notion that the consciousness of the solitary life of the soul is, through and through, a self-deceiving consciousness. 'The subject would believe that he is saying something to himself and communicating something to himself; in truth he would do nothing of the kind' (*VP*, p. 49/57/64). In other words, if we use one of our examples from above, if I *ask* myself why I entered a particular room, and then I *answer* myself, it at least *seems*, even to me, the one *producing* these acts of signification, as though I am in *some* senses communicating with myself. Therefore my *experience* of my own acts of signification would be an experience that *I am indicating knowledge of self to self*. The consciousness of this *experience*, Husserl claims, is false or deluded. This might lead us to suspect, therefore, that the *core* of experience, in whatever sense of the term, would then be, in point of fact, *unconscious*:

We might be tempted to conclude on this basis that, since consciousness is then entirely invaded by the belief or the illusion of speaking-to-himself, an entirely false consciousness, the truth of the experience would be of the order of non-consciousness. It is the opposite . . . (*VP*, pp. 49/58/64–5)

While we would be tempted to conclude that, for Husserl, the conscious-ness of the interior life of the soul is a false consciousness, the opposite is the case: the consciousness of the interior life is immediately present to itself in the punctuated now-point of the present, and it is, of its very essence, incapable of being 'affected by illusion since it relates only to itself in an absolute proximity' (*VP*, pp. 49–50/58/65). Hence the representative and illusory use of signs that takes place in the interior monologue would itself be a secondary, supplemental, non-essential, accidental 'add-on' to the interiority of consciousness itself. If the interior monologue is contaminated by fiction and falsity, this does not reflect a correlative fiction within the immediate self-presence of consciousness itself:

The sign would be foreign to this self-presence, which is the foundation of presence in general. Because the sign is foreign to the self-present of the living present, we can say that it is foreign to presence in general, in what we believe to be able to recognize under the name of intuition or perception. (*VP*, p. 50/58/65)

This brings us to the second 'type' of argument that Derrida announced earlier, and carries us therefore into Chapter 5. According to the second type of argument, I cannot communicate anything to myself in the interior monologue, and can only *imagine* myself to be doing so, because the psychic acts in question are lived by the subject at the very moment that they occur. Hence there would be no *gap* or *hiatus* (of time or space) across which a sign would be required; the acts are experienced in an unmediated way at the precise instant of their origin:

if they are not to be informed about themselves through the intermediary of indications, this is because they are 'experientially lived by us at that very instant [*im selben Augenblick*[23]].' The present of self-presence would be as indivisible as a *blink of an eye.* (*VP*, p. 50/59/66)

This would secure an absolute moment of self-presence and it would confirm our assumptions about our capacity for self-knowledge. That is, it would confirm the *appearance* that *I*, the thinking subject, have direct, absolute and immediate access to and knowledge of the interiority of my *own* experience.

This brings us to Chapter 5.

The Sign and the Blink of an Eye

As we begin Chapter 5, we enter one of the most important chapters of the book, and perhaps one of the most important single analyses that Derrida ever carries out; the analysis of temporalisation conducted in this chapter will form the backbone, not only of the argument of Chapter 6, but also of many of the concepts and analyses that will follow throughout the rest of Derrida's life. While in Chapter 4 we were introduced to the term 'deconstruction' for the first time, here in Chapter 5 Derrida introduces two of the most significant and disseminative terms for his thought for many years to come, namely, 'trace' and 'différance'; and they emerge out of the analysis of Husserl's notion of the 'living present'. With this analysis, Derrida turns, for the first time in the book, the discussion from the 1900–1 *Logical Investigations* in order to address the 1905 *On the Phenomenology of the Consciousness of Internal Time* lectures. In point of fact, however, he is *not* shifting the analysis, but rather, he turns to the time-consciousness lectures because of the problem that arises *within* the context of the *Logical Investigations*, but a problem that, 'for systematic as well as historical reasons' (*VP*, p. 51/60/67) is not thoroughly addressed in the *Logical Investigations*, namely, that 'the sharp point of the instant, the identity of lived-experience present to itself in the same instant bears therefore the whole weight of this demonstration' (*VP*, p. 51/60/67).

As we saw in Chapter 4, Husserl argues that when the subject employs signs in the solitary life of the soul, he or she does not *communicate* anything to him- or herself; he or she may, at most, *represent* him- or herself *as though* he or she is communicating with him- or herself, but it is merely an *imagination* or a *fiction*. This made us wonder if it would not follow that the consciousness of the interior monologue would not be an entirely false consciousness, insofar as one always *thinks* that one is communicating with oneself, *even as a precondition of communicating with others*, but of course, Husserl will not allow such a possibility. He will hold, instead, that the entirety of language in the interior life of the soul is a supervenient, non-essential 'add-on' that occurs in a stratum somewhere *above* the consciousness of lived-experience, strictly speaking. This is because the consciousness of interior life is immediately present to itself, *in the very moment* that it is lived. This requires an undivided, punctuated, *now-point* of the present, which thereby necessitates Derrida's shift to the discussion of *time-consciousness*. In addition, we might note that, from the beginning of

Voice and Phenomenon, Derrida has claimed that the *essential distinctions* of Husserl's First *Logical Investigation* bore within it 'the germinal structure of all of Husserl's thought' (*VP*, p. 3/3/1). By extending the tendrils of the problem in such a way as to branch the analysis into the *time-consciousness* lectures, which, it is important to note, Husserl continued to work on until the end of his life, Derrida is also demonstrating the truth of that claim.

Above, we discussed the structure of the living present, noting its 'centre' or 'nucleus' of the primal impression – the source-point or the now-moment in which experience is originally impressed – surrounded by a halo of *primary memory* or retention, and *primary expectation* or pro-tention. About this structure, Derrida in Chapter 5 explores merely a couple of 'points of reference', claiming that he 'cannot examine closely the admirable analyses' of the time-consciousness lectures (*VP*, p. 52/61/68). These *points of reference* have to do with the tension between the punctuatedness of the primal impression, in tandem with the con-tinuity of primal impression and retention. Let us explore these points of reference.

First, 'The concept of *punctuality*, of the *now*, of the *stigmē*, regardless of whether or not it is a metaphysical presupposition, still plays a role there that is major' (*VP*, p. 52/61/68). Husserl, as Derrida rightly notes, more than any thinker in the early twentieth century,[24] was meticulously attentive to the subtleties of the experience of time. As we noted in the discussion of the *living present* above, much of what Husserl is attempting in the exploration of time-consciousness is to provide a phenomenologi-cal account for how time is *experienced*, and the present of time is always experienced, Husserl argues, in a way that is thick with memory and expectation. Lived-experience can *never* have the *experience* of a pure, punctuated, discrete *moment*; otherwise, one could never truly have an *experience* (insofar as experience always requires context) of anything. Nevertheless, and as we have described above, this spread-out structure of the living present is thought on the basis of a punctuated now-point, which serves as the foundation of the whole structure, and this is the primal impression. In Husserl's words:

The primal impression is something absolutely unmodified, the primal source of all further consciousness and being. Primal impression has as its content that which the word 'now' signifies, insofar as it is taken in the strictest sense. Each new now is the content of a new primal impression.[25]

At the centre of this innovative structure of the living present, Husserl leaves intact a self-identical, punctuated *core*: 'Despite all the complexity of its structure, temporality has a non-displaceable center, an eye or a living nucleus, and that is the punctuality of the actual now' (*VP*, p. 53/62/69). It is to this punctuated primal impression that Husserl refers in the *Logical Investigations*, when he argues that psychic acts are experienced in an unmediated way, '*im selben Augenblick*', at that very instant or moment. Incidentally, Husserl's emphasis on the immediate lived-experience of the present informs his rejection of an *unconscious content* that *becomes* conscious after-the-fact, as we find in the texts of Freud (who, we might note, is Husserl's contemporary).

Furthermore, Derrida notes, this emphasis on the present-now is an essential component of the philosophical tradition, in all of its phases. In the discussion of Chapter 4 above, we noted that for Derrida, to be a philosopher means to work out of the philosophical tradition, and that to do *this* requires one to work with an inherited set of problems, concepts and presuppositions. One of these constitutive presuppositions is the 'founding value of the present-now'. This founding value, Derrida claims, is 'systematic with the founding opposition of metaphysics, namely, that of *form* (or *eidos* or idea) and *matter* as the opposition of *actuality* and *potentiality*' (*VP*, p. 53/63/70), and it 'secures the tradition that continues the Greek metaphysics of presence into the "modern" metaphysics of presence as self-consciousness, the metaphysics of the idea as representation (*Vorstellung*)' (*VP*, p. 53/63/70). In Plato, this emphasis on the present-now manifests as the eternally unchanging persistence of the *form* through every new *present*. Throughout much of the medieval tradition, the emphasis on the present-now is summed up in the concept of divine eternality, which, being outside of time, encompasses *all* of time in a single, unchanging *present*. With Descartes, this *present-now* gets shifted from the transcendency of an eternal realm of Plato's forms or of divine omniscience, to the clear and distinct certainty of the cogito (*I think; therefore I am*) in each moment of its *cogitations*. And in Husserl, the emphasis on the living present is an emphasis on a *form* of time that is itself unchanging, while its contents are ever renewed: quoting Husserl, '"The actually present now is necessarily and remains something punctual: it is a form that persists [*Verharrende*] while the matter is always new"' (*VP*, p. 53/63/70). [26] Though its empirical contents have changed, the *form* as the *form* of presence has remained constant throughout most of the history of philosophy. The emphasis on the present-now is thus a constitutive element of the entirety of the philosophical tradition. As a result, one cannot simply *abandon* the notion of 'presence', and we must note, Derrida never pulls back from this claim. To return to Derrida's 'Introduction' to *Voice and Phenomenon*, 'This expression, moreover, "the founding value of presence," is a pleonastic expression' (*VP*, p. 6/7/5); it is, in other words, a redundancy, as presence is *the* founding value of the metaphysical tradition:

> It is *evidentness itself*, conscious thought itself. It governs every possible concept of truth and of sense. We cannot raise suspicions about it without beginning to enucleate consciousness itself from an elsewhere of philosophy which takes away from discourse all possible *security* and every possible *foundation*. (*VP*, p. 53/62/70)

From within philosophy, strictly speaking, there is no possibility of challenging this *founding value*, but this characterisation of philosophy tells us something quite significant about the nature of deconstruction. Derrida's words here are precisely formulated: 'there is no possible objection, *within philosophy*, in regard to this privilege of the present-now' (*VP*, p. 53/62/70; my emphasis). This is why Derrida's thought will seek to shift towards the *outside* of philosophy. As we said in our discussion of Chapter 4, deconstruction, while deriving its impetus from within the philosophical tradition, nevertheless seeks to *disrupt* that tradition from within, thereby interrupting its closure. This disruption operates by 'depositing in the closure, demonstrating in the closure contradictory or untenable propositions, attempting to produce securely insecurity in the closure, opening it up to its outside, which can be done only from a certain inside' (*VP*, 49n/57n/64n), which is what Derrida has done so far in his analysis of Husserl, but strictly by operating on Husserl's own terrain – he has demonstrated *contradictory* propositions functioning in a constitutive manner, at the heart of Husserl's thought. If philosophy is always a 'philosophy of presence', as Derrida argues that it is, then deconstruction, by pushing thought to the outside that makes this system of presence possible in the first place, is 'a thought of non-presence, which is not inevitably its opposite nor necessarily a meditation on negative absence, or even a theory of non-presence *as* unconscious' (*VP*, p. 53/63/70). If there is no possible challenge to presence *within* philosophy, then deconstruction seeks a way out of this enclosure, which does not point *simply* to a non-philosophy or to an *anti*-philosophical stance. Rather, it is the activity of thought that makes *philosophy* itself possible.

The second *point of reference* that Derrida notes regarding the *living present* consists of the constant Husserlian injunction that 'forbids us from speaking of a simple self-identity of the present' (*VP*, pp. 54/63–4/71). There never occurs in experience, *and this essentially so*, a single, punctuated primal impression. The *present* is always surrounded by a halo of retention and protention, respectively primary memory and primary expectation. Recall that much of the impetus engendering this structure is Husserl's rejection of Brentano's view of memory, which we said categorises *all* forms of memory beneath the banner of *representation*. On this view, perception, strictly speaking, applies only to the present, and everything having to do with *memory* falls beneath the banner of reproduction or re-presentation of that present. Husserl rejects this view outright, on the ground that there is (and must be) a difference in *kind*, or an *essential* and irreducible difference, between the type of memory required in order to *recall* a childhood moment, as opposed to the sort of memory utilised when listening to a song or reading a paragraph, for instance. This point is absolutely crucial for Husserl: from a phenomenological perspective, there is experienced in each moment a continuous passage between the present of the primal impression and a *certain type* of memory, which will be called 'retention'. This sort of memory is required in order to experience the present *as such*. Therefore, if there were *merely* a difference of intensity or degree (that is to say, *not* a difference in kind), between memory as *retention* and memory as *representation*, then insofar as retention is in experiential continuity with primal impression, this would also entail a continuity, at a greater distance perhaps but a continuity no less, between the primal impression and representational memory, or between *perception* (in the form of the primal impression) and *non-perception* (as memory in both its retentional and representational modes). This would therefore allow non-presence to *infect* or *contaminate* the presence of the present, which is an unacceptable proposition for Husserl. As Derrida notes, 'This is the *nervus demonstrandi* of his criticism of Brentano' (*VP*, p. 55/64/72). In order to posit and sustain this irreducible difference between retention and reproductive or representational memory, therefore, Husserl will establish an *essential continuity* between the primal impression and retention, in an effort to save the *essential difference* between retention and reproductive memory:

We see very quickly then that the presence of the perceived present is able to appear as such only insofar as it is in *continuous composition* with a non-presence and a non-perception, namely, primary memory and primary anticipation (retention and protention). These non-perceptions are not added on, do not accompany *contingently* the actually perceived now; indispensably and essentially they participate in its possibility. (*VP*, p. 55/64/72)

As a matter of fact, Husserl will go so far as to allow that the term *perception* may be applied to the mode of *retention*, for it is only in the mode of retention that the *past* is constituted and 'perceived' *as* what it is, as *past*. In the living present, therefore, we meet with a *perception* of the past as past. Derrida, quoting Husserl, notes:

'If we call perception *the act in which every origin resides, the act that constitutes originarily*, then *primary memory* is *perception*. For *it is only in primary memory that we see the past*, it is only in it that the past is constituted, and this happens not in a re-presentational way but on the contrary in a presentational way.' (*VP*, p. 55/64/72)[27]

Interestingly, as Derrida notes, this is the one and only point in the entirety of Husserl's thought where Husserl argues for a mode of *perception* wherein that which is perceived is not a *present*, but a past; and again, this is in order to sustain an irreducible difference between retention and reproductive memory, and to fundamentally disallow the passage between perception and non-perception.

Yet, at the same time and in a slightly different context, Husserl will refer explicitly to retention as to a non-perception, claiming:

If we now relate the term perception with *the differences in the way of being given* which temporal objects have, *the opposite of perception* is then *primary memory* and *primary anticipation* (retention and protention) which here comes on the scene, so that *perception* and *non-perception* pass *continuously* into one another. (*VP*, pp. 55–6/65/72–3)[28]

In this textual passage, not only does Husserl remarkably refer, explicitly and against the citation we just addressed, to retention as to a 'non-perception', indeed the very *opposite* of perception; he furthermore allows that this non-perception is in a relation of continuity with the perception of the present, which he elsewhere calls an 'abstraction', and an 'ideal limit', that is never actually given in experience. The following passage from Husserl is very significant: 'Nevertheless, even this ideal now is not something different *toto caelo* from the non-now, but on the contrary is in continuous commerce with it. And the continuous passage of perception into primary memory corresponds to that' (*VP*, p. 56/65/73).[29]

Therefore, on the one hand, the entirety of Husserl's argument for the superfluity of indicative signs in the solitary life of the soul rests upon the punctuatedness of the primal impression, which is indeed a commitment to which Husserl explicitly holds, in the *Logical Investigations*, in *On the Phenomenology of the Consciousness of Internal Time* and elsewhere. But against this commitment, Husserl will also hold that the present is always thickened by its essential commerce with non-perception. This threatens to destroy the security of the discrete now-point that allows for the immediate self-presence of interior life, and the superfluity of the indicative sign. As Derrida writes:

As soon as we admit this continuity of the now and the non-now, of perception and non-perception in the zone of originarity that is common to originary impression and to retention, we welcome the other into the self-identity of the *Augenblick*, non-presence and non-evidentness into the *blink of the eye of the instant*. There is a duration to the blink of an eye[30] and the duration closes the eye. (*VP*, p. 56/65/73)

If retention is a mode of 'non-perception', then it follows that the distinction between the two types of memory, retention and reproductive, cannot be 'the radical difference that Husserl would want' (*VP*, p. 56/65/73) between perception and non-perception, but a difference rather between two types of non-perception. This entails further that non-presence constantly *contaminates* presence. If the sphere of *my own* is constituted by the unmediated self-presence of consciousness to itself in the very moment of its perception, then a compromise of this self-presence by the continuous accommodation of a non-perception would entail an allowance of *alterity* (or otherness) to contaminate the sphere of the self. The self, that is, would relate to itself as it would to an *other*; in the very nature of what it means to be a *self*, there would be contained an essential *folding back* or a *hiatus* that comprises a *constitutive difference* within the self, one that would then make the *identity* of the self possible as such. This identity then would no longer be a *simple* (which is to say 'pure' or 'undifferentiated') identity. As Derrida writes:

This relation to non-presence, once more, does not take by surprise, surround, or even dissimulate the presence of the originary impression; it allows its upsurge and its ever reborn virginity. But it radically destroys every possibility of self-identity in its simplicity. (*VP*, pp. 56/65–6/73)

But given that the superfluity of the indicative sign will rest for Husserl upon the immediate self-presence of interior life, the 'intimacy of non-presence and alterity with presence cuts into, at its root, the argument for the uselessness of the sign in the self-relation' (*VP*, p. 57/66/74).

This brings us to the third *point of reference* regarding the living present, and begins the transition to the completion of Chapter 5 and the beginning of Chapter 6. While so far our analysis has focused on reducing the indicative sign in the interiority of self-presence, beneath this third point of reference we will see that Husserl will also be required to reduce the expressive sign, in an effort to isolate the absolute *silence* of language within the soul. Given its length (occupying nearly three pages of text), the reader may casually forget or overlook the fact that this third point of reference consists of only two paragraphs; these paragraphs are very dense, and introduce the two terms that we announced at the outset of our discussion of this chapter: 'trace' and 'différance'. Let us now look at this third point of reference, before turning to Chapter 6, which Lawlor, in his 'Translator's Introduction', rightly calls 'the heart of *Voice and Phenomenon*' (*VP*, p. xxi).

The third point of reference concerns the fact that, despite the accommodation of presence to non-presence in the temporal structure of the living present, Husserl will nevertheless be resistant to an assumed *necessity* for the sign in the interiority of experience. Ultimately, this will be because the *sign* falls, for Husserl, into the camp of *representation*, and despite all the complications we have seen, Husserl will nevertheless continue to insist upon a fundamental distinction between retention and reproductive memory, opposing 'the absolute validity of primary memory to the relative validity of secondary memory' (*VP*, p. 57/66/74), depositing retention into the sphere of *originariness* and reproductive memory into the sphere of *representation*. Therefore, only reproductive memory will include *representation* and hence will require the use of *signs*, for Husserl. Despite the accommodation of presence to non-presence, in the relation of the primal impression to retentive modalities, the interior life of the soul will nevertheless not require signs, Husserl claims.

This derives, Derrida claims, from two seemingly irreconcilable commitments on Husserl's part: (1) the living present is only ever constituted as the absolute source of epistemic originariness in commerce with 'retention as non-perception' (*VP*, p. 57/67/75); (2) the source of certainty in general *is* the originariness of the living now. Given these two commitments, retention *must be guarded* in the mode of originariness, and the originary/non-originary border must shift, Derrida claims, *from* the primal impression/retention divide *to* the retention/reproductive memory distinction, 'between two forms of re-turn or of the re-stitution of the present, re-tention and re-presentation' (*VP*, p. 58/67/75).

With this, Derrida announces one of the key discoveries of *Voice and Phenomenon*, namely, the *re-* that makes possible *both* retention *and* representation. This essential *re-* lies at the constitutive foundation of the possibility of presence itself. Let us follow this path slowly and carefully. First, it is important to note that Derrida is *not* attempting to simply 'cancel the difference', as it were, between retention and representation, as though they were merely 'the same thing'; quite the contrary, in fact.

Nevertheless, what will make both forms of memory possible is what Derrida here announces as 'the trace', which he defines as 'the possibility of re-petition in its most general form' (*VP*, p. 58/67/75). Since this term 'trace' is announced in tandem with another very significant Derridean term, 'différance', let us look at this passage in full in order to better understand what these terms *do* for Derrida:

Without reducing the abyss that can in fact separate retention from re-presentation [...] we must be able to say *a priori* that their common root, the possibility of re-petition in its most general form, the trace in the most universal sense, is a possibility that not only must inhabit the pure actuality of the now, but also must constitute it by means of the very movement of the différance that the possibility inserts into the pure actuality of the now. Such a trace is, if we are able to hold onto this language without contradicting it and erasing it immediately, more 'originary' than the phenomenological originarity itself. (*VP*, p. 58/67/75)

Immediately, we note the mention, at the close of this passage, of *phenomenological originarity*. The foundation of phenomenological originarity is, as we have seen, the structure of the living present, which provides for Husserl the very framework and possibility of certainty. So by directing thought to that which is more *originary* (with the necessary caveats, of course), than the phenomenological originarity, Derrida is in point of fact arguing that the operation of the trace and différance together constitute the *structural* elements that *found* the living present as such. Before attempting to dissect the meaning of these terms on the basis of this paragraph (and with some help from other texts), let us look to one other place a little further down on the page, where the term 'différance' is used again:

In all of these directions, the presence of the present is thought beginning from the fold of the return, beginning from the movement of repetition and not the reverse. Does not the fact that this fold in presence or in self-presence is irreducible, that this trace or this différance is always older than presence and obtains for it its openness, forbid us from speaking of a simple self-identity 'im selben Augenblick'? (*VP*, p. 58/68/76)

This passage is revelatory for a number of reasons. First, trace and différance *obtain* for presence its openness, Derrida says. They are what constitute the *living* of the living present, the thickness of time that opens the present to the future while at the same time contracting and expanding retention within it. Our reading of the passage above, that the trace and différance constitute the structural elements that *found* the living present, is thus confirmed in this passage. Second, here in this passage we see the following expressions used interchangeably: 'fold in presence', 'fold in self-presence', 'trace' and 'différance'. While we must without a doubt resist any temptation to treat these terms in a simply reductive manner, as though they are mere 'synonyms', nevertheless, the fact that they are used interchangeably indicates for us that, for Derrida, the terms share an essential relation; therefore, let us carefully unpack this final paragraph of Chapter 5, in order to understand exactly how Derrida thinks these terms.

The trace, he says, is *the possibility of re-petition in its most general form*, and this possibility or trace inserts what he calls *différance*, which he understands as a *movement, into the pure actuality of the now*. Complicated though this wording may at first seem, Derrida is here, in this final paragraph, doing little more than formulating, now in his own neologistic terms specific to the project of deconstruction, the discoveries that he has laboriously revealed in the analyses heretofore. We have just seen that for Husserl, the presence of the living present is only ever given in relation with *non-perception*, in the form of retention, such that for Husserl, perception and non-perception pass, and it must be noted, *essentially*, **continuously** into one another. That is to say, there is *continuity* between perception and non-perception; once continuity is established, it forbids any effort to *radically* distinguish one from the other. This constituted, we said, a *duration* to the *blink of the eye* (of the instant), we might even say a blindness at the very heart of the inner *vision* of self-consciousness. But since the sphere of *my own*, as the tradition conceives it, would only be constituted on the basis of an unmediated core of self-presence, this *non-perception* at the heart of the self-relation would amount, we said, to the allowance of *alterity* into the core of the self-relation, such that the self could only relate to the self as it would to an *other*. But it would only be *in* this relation that a self, as such, could emerge at all. This phrase, *self-relation*, in other words, has to be understood in a very literal sense, in the sense that *self* relates *to* itself, and in so relating there *must be* a *re-flective* moment of the self folding back upon the self. Thus, there is, at the very heart of what it means to be a self, a *folding back* or a *hiatus*, a *constitutive gap-ping*, in the self-relation – a *constitutive play of difference*. This *play of difference* is what Derrida now calls the 'différance'. So in that sense we have already seen this term discussed at some length, only not by way of the explicit use of the term. So let us now look at the différance in greater depth.

Derrida does not provide a 'definition' for the term 'différance' at this point, so in combination with what Derrida does in *Voice and Phenomenon*, we shall also employ some of the elements from other texts, where he *does*, more or less, define it (or at least aspects and characteristics of it). 'Différance' is a specifically Derridean neologism (or, as he says, a 'neographism'). While others of Derrida's key terms (such as 'trace', 'pharmakon', 'writing', 'supplement', 'hymen', 'khôra', 'aporia', etc.) assume a technical operation in Derrida's works, such that Derrida without question makes them *his own*, they are nevertheless terms that Derrida locates and explores from within the text of the Western tradition. In this regard, 'différance' is unique, in that it is a term that Derrida himself coins. The French word for 'difference' is *différence*, which, in the French pronunciation of the term, is indistinguishable from Derrida's 'différance'; hence the change of the second 'e' in *différence* to an 'a' is *inaudible*. This alteration is not performed for the sake of cleverness; the shift to the 'a' indicates or establishes the *middle voice* within the différance, as opposed to the strictly active or strictly passive voice – this is crucial because différance, Derrida will argue, precedes and conditions the possibility of both 'activity' and 'passivity'. In order to understand what that means and *why*, we must take note of some of the other things Derrida says about this strange term, 'différance'.

'Différance', as Derrida notes, is a participial form modelled upon the French verb 'différer', itself a verb that is, we might say, constituted by an essential difference. On the one hand, the verb 'différer' means 'to differ', which is to say, 'to not be identical with' or 'to be other to' something else. On the other hand, 'différer' means 'to defer', as in 'to delay', 'to put off', 'to postpone', etc. One sense of 'différer' is hence spatial, while the other is temporal. What Derrida calls the *movement* of différance, therefore, operates along two distinct but related trajectories, both of which upset the metaphysical emphasis on presence. On the one hand, the movement of différance is 'spatial', upsetting the spatial sense of metaphysical presence insofar as it *differentiates*, creates spaces and gaps, separates, distinguishes, institutes differences, etc. While the metaphysics of presence seeks absolute proximity, différance creates ruptures within that proximity. On the other hand, the movement of différance is 'temporal', in that it disrupts the temporal sense of metaphysical presence insofar as the strict *identity* of the present-now is constantly *deferred*. The *presence* of the present, that is, is always put off, we might say, for a later time, but a time that will never 'arrive'. Presence never comes to rest, and is never *completely* solidified. There is always *duration* and hence the present never really *is*. Différance is the *movement* that both differs and defers, in such a way as to *constitute* presence in its movement, but that by virtue of the fact that it *moves*, constantly *forbids* the absolute presencing of the present. This is how Derrida, in his more programmatic essays and interviews, characterises the movement of différance. Let us now look back to *Voice and Phenomenon*, in order to see how this term is discovered and employed therein.

We must recall, the trace is the *pure possibility of repetition*, Derrida claims, and this trace *inserts* différance into the pure actuality of the now. As we saw:

we must be able to say *a priori* that their [retention's and representation's] common root, the possibility of re-petition in its most general form, the trace in the most universal sense, is a possibility that not only must inhabit the pure actuality of the now, but also must constitute it by means of the very movement of the différance that the possibility inserts into the pure actuality of the now. (*VP*, p. 58/67/75)

Above, we demonstrated that the *ideality of the ideal* for Husserl consists in the fact that meaning, as Husserl understands it, is essentially and infinitely repeatable. In order for a sense to be first *experienced* in the presence of the present, that is, in order for it to be *impressed* in the present-now of the primal impression, that sense *must be* essentially repeatable. Hence even *prior to* the moment of primal impression, the *trace* of the re- must already be *inscribed* into any sense that will or might come to be experienced, and this as a condition of its being impressed in the primal impression at all. Rather than retention or representation coming along, after-the-fact, and contingently holding onto or reproducing a sense of experience that has been originally and contingently *impressed* upon the material of consciousness, the essential *repeatability* of that sense, which will eventually comprise and condition both its retentional and representational forms, is already inscribed (marked, or 'traced') within the sense itself. The trace of retention is therefore already inscribed within the primal impression, not merely empirically or contingently, and we might say not even merely essentially, but rather, *necessarily*. This is what it means to say that the trace does not just *inhabit* the pure actuality of the now, but *constitutes* it. The structural component of retention is not an add-on, but a necessary essentiality, of the present. Without the possibility of repetition, the *present as such*, in Husserl's sense, could never be.

Nevertheless, even if the modality of retention falls, for Husserl, beneath the rubric of *originariness*, it does not, strictly speaking, qualify as *perception*, insofar as *perception* in the strict sense applies, and Husserl says so explicitly, only to the moment of impression; and it is for this reason that Husserl even uses the term 'non-perception' to characterise retention. All the same, retention would be a very important 'non-perception' the trace of which, as we have just seen, *makes possible* the primal impression as such. It is a 'trace' (which implies a past, as when we speak about the 'trace' of a particular aroma when we walk into a room, for instance) that precedes the content of the *present* that it conditions. Hence the presence of the primal impression, and with it Husserl's entire structure of the living present, has to be conceived in a much more complex way than it originally appeared.

The trace of this non-perception subsists in an essential relation with the 'presence' of the primal impression. That is to say, as a matter of essential necessity, the primal impression *as such* never appears *as such* without the essential relation with this non-perception that comprises retention. In the very moment, *im selben Augenblick*, that the primal impression is *stamped* by a given experience, it is *at that very same time* in a structural relation with its retention, which, we said, conditions the primal impression in the first place, and is tantamount to its own *non-perception*. Hence the structure of the living present is constituted on the basis of a *movement*, that never rests, of differentiation into the modalities of the now, retention and protention. The movement of this *differentiation* then would itself constitute the basis of the structure – the *living present*; the *gap* across which the relation constitutes the structure of self-relation is not a simple or pure gap, but rather *the fold of presence or of self-presence* to which we have referred.

Lying at the heart of the self itself, this *productive relation* is temporal, insofar as it is the structure of the consciousness and the production of time itself, but it is not *strictly* temporal, insofar as the *self* that is constituted on the basis of this productive relation is, in some senses, a *thing* – a consciousness, in relation both to itself and to other things – it is the condition *on which* a world of things can become present. Hence it is a productive relation of the *self* that subsists as the condition of both time and space – the two contaminate each other indistinguishably and imperceptibly in the midst of this productive relation. This is what Derrida means when he says of the différance that it is the 'becoming-time of space and the becoming-space of time' ('Différance', p. 8). This productive relationality, this différance, produces *self-presence*, insofar as it constitutes the differentiating structure of the living present, but by that very same movement – the 'relationality' of the relation, what constitutes the *relat-ing*, which, as a verb, is in motion – this movement prevents the self's ever *arriving* at full presence. It therefore constitutes, but at the same time undermines, the self and along with it presence and 'the present'.

We are now better situated to understand some of the other aspects of the différance. Above we said that the inaudible 'a' that replaces the 'e' indicates the *middle voice*, and that this is significant for Derrida insofar as the différance is neither strictly active nor passive, and that it precedes and conditions both activity and passivity as Derrida understands it. Insofar as it conditions the constitution of self-presence, which is the *source*, we might say, of *agency*, of freedom and choice, différance is the condition of activity. However, *as* condition, it is not itself, strictly speaking, *active*, insofar as *activity* as the tradition understands it is a term denoting originariness that is rooted in the *constituted self* of an *agent*, complete with a will. Différance is not strictly 'active' for Derrida in the sense that it must be kept completely separate from all notions (which are metaphysical in themselves, we might add) of the 'will' and of 'agency'. Nevertheless, différance is, as Derrida has shown, productive. It conditions both time and space, it constitutes the experience and production of time, and it moreover lies at the constitutive heart of the self-relation whence *agency*, and thus activity, derive; hence différance is not strictly 'passive' either. It is for this reason that différance is the deconstructive basis of the philosophical tradition of voluntarism, as we have said from the beginning, and notably in Chapter 3.

What is the significance of this inaudible 'a'? Différance can only be *recognised* as such *in writing*. The ear can hear no distinction between the French pronunciation of either *différence* or 'différance'; they sound exactly the same. Hence différance is, we might say, demonstrative for Derrida, in that it upsets the traditional philosophical privileging of the *voice* as the primary locus of expression and signification, the privileging that Derrida in this text refers to as 'phonologism' (*VP*, p. 69/80/90). This will be examined more fully in the discussion of Chapter 6, so we will merely introduce its importance at this point. The voice cannot differentiate *différence* from 'différance'. Only the inscription can; only the written mark can. The différance will serve as the basis of signification generally, and hence of the possibility of both the voice and of writing.

But this brings us to our next point. Différance is not strictly 'present', but nor is it strictly 'absent'; it is not strictly temporal, but nor is it strictly spatial; it is not strictly 'active' but it is not strictly 'passive'; it is not simply 'difference', but it is not simply 'identity'; it is neither strictly 'self', but nor is it strictly 'other'; it is not strictly 'vocal', but it is not strictly 'inscribed'; etc. We can see here a common thread in all of these pairings: each term comprises one pole of a binary opposition from the tradition of Western metaphysics, while its 'partner' term comprises the other pole. These binaries are the bedrock upon which the entire tradition of metaphysics has historically 'carved up' the whole of reality. Already in the course of this brief analysis, we have demonstrated, or rather, witnessed Derrida's demonstration of, the way in which the différance constitutes but also undermines these specific binaries. But insofar as différance lies at the heart of the constitution of ideality itself, Derrida will hold that différance operates in a similar manner, for *all* of the binary categories of Western thought (light and darkness, good and evil, etc.). Its movement constitutes, but at the same time undermines, their operation. Insofar as it operates in this manner, we can say that différance is a movement of *originary contamination*.

Now that we have thoroughly unpacked the meanings and relations of these two very important terms, and have seen how they arise out of Derrida's engagement with Husserl and hence their operational role *in* that engagement, we are now in a position to conclude our reading of Chapter 5 of *Voice and Phenomenon*. Given that the presence of the present is *constituted* on the basis of this movement of différance, given that the self is never *fully* present to the self, that its presence is constantly self-differentiating and essentially *deferred*, given that the self can only relate to the self as it would to an *other*, the very basis of Husserl's indication/

expression distinction would appear to be in jeopardy. Given the way in which Derrida has explicated this distinction, and the correlative concepts that have accompanied the understanding of indication (those concepts having to do with its essentially mediating and communicative aspects), it would seem that indication would be an essential component and accompaniment of 'the movement of transcendental temporaliza- tion' (*VP*, p. 59/68/77) which divides self from self, in the constituting movement of the self as such. With the concept of différance, time is no longer conceived as a series of self-contained present-nows, but rather, as a movement of temporalisation that constitutes but only insofar as it ruptures the self-presence of consciousness. As Derrida writes:

> Likewise, is it not the case that all of what is announced in this reduction to the 'solitary life of the soul' (the transcendental reduction in all of its stages and notably the reduction to the monadological sphere of the *'proper'—Eigenheit—* etc.) is not, as it were, fissured in its possibility by what is called time? It is fissured by what has been called time and to which it would be necessary to give another title, since 'time' has always designated a movement thought beginning from the present and since 'time' can say nothing but the present. (*VP*, pp. 59/68/76–7)

In other words, the *self-relation* that constitutes the self is ruptured by the flow of 'time', but this can be said only by way of a drastic reformulation of the very notion of 'time', only by rooting the concepts of both self and time in the productive relationality of différance. The very same *deconstructive* move that disrupts the unassailable presence of *self*, at the same time ruptures the self-contained 'atomistic' understanding of time conceived on the basis of the *now*: 'the concept of pure solitude—and of the monad in the phenomenological sense—is *split open* by its own origin, by the very condition of its self-presence' (*VP*, p. 59/68/77). But more importantly, for purposes of this analysis, if the self can relate to itself only as though to an *other*, across this differentiating relationality of time, it would appear that an analogously communicative use of the indicative form of the sign would be required even in the solitary life of the soul. That is, even the purity of the interior use of the *expression* would seem to be contaminated by an essentially *indicative* aspect. It therefore comes as no surprise that Husserl will ultimately seek to suspend even the opera- tive role of the *expressive* sign in the solitary life of the soul.

Here at last Derrida makes good on his announcement in Chapter 3 that 'the need for indications means quite simply the need for signs' (*VP*, p. 36/42/46). The expressive sign, even on Husserl's explication, cannot be *strictly* expressive. For as we have said from the beginning, Husserl will not only seek to exclude indicative signs from the interiority of the soul, but ultimately, he will also seek to disallow even *expression*, even in its most purified sense, from operating at the most basic and most fundamental sphere of experience, in an effort to isolate a *pre-expressive stratum of sense*. We see now why this is so. As Derrida says:

> He will consider language in general, the element of the *logos*, in its expressive form itself, as a secondary event, and added on to an originary and preexpressive stratum of sense. Expressive language itself would have to supervene on the absolute silence of the self-relation. (*VP*, p. 59/69/77)

If the self is constituted across a movement of temporalisation, then *any* use of signs will be *communicative* and hence *indicative*. Thus, the use of signs must be completely reduced in the interiority of the soul. The phenomenological *voice* must guard an essential silence.

Let us now turn to Chapter 6.

The Voice that Keeps Silent

Leonard Lawlor's 'Translator's Introduction' announces of Chapter 6: 'We have been considering the argumentation found in chapters 4 and 5, but the heart of *Voice and Phenomenon* lies in chapter 6. Chapter 6 concerns the voice of the title *Voice and Phenomenon*, the voice in interior monologue' (*VP*, p. xxi). In addition to the titular *voice* (*la voix*), the chapter title itself is interesting in its use of the French verb *garder*: 'La Voix qui Garde le Silence', which Lawlor appropriately translates as 'The Voice that Keeps Silent'. The French verb *garder* is a polysemous word, meaning 'to keep' in the sense of 'to hold', but also as in 'to guard', as when a child prays, 'I pray the Lord, my soul to keep.' So *garder* can be translated as 'to keep', 'to preserve', 'to maintain', 'to hold', 'to guard', 'to shepherd', 'to watch over' and possibly even 'to protect', etc., and all these senses are no doubt operative in the title of Chapter 6 of *Voice and Phenomenon*, especially when we think back to some of the claims of the 'Introduction', that 'Language keeps watch over the difference that keeps watch over language' (*VP*, p. 12/14/13) and that 'the voice simulates the 'keeping watch' over presence . . .' (*VP*, p. 13/15/15), both of which also use forms of the word *garder*.

Derrida begins the chapter by emphasising once again that Husserl must carry out two exclusionary reductions in order to arrive at the phenomenological inner *silence*. First, the exclusion of the relation to the *other* in the self. We discovered in Chapter 5 that, given the movement of temporalisation, which involved the essential and constitutive play of différance, the self can only relate to the self as it would to an *other*. This self-relation must be suspended for Husserl, for if such a gap indeed obtains in the interior life, it may be the case that the self would *require* the use of signs, employed in an *indicative* manner similar to when we communicate with *others* in the world, in order for anything like 'experience' to take place. This would severely compromise the notion of a 'pre-expressive [that is to say, silent] stratum of sense'. Second, for similar reasons, the exclusion of 'expression' as a later add-on to the inner stratum of sense. Since the opening of the book, we have seen that Husserl has sought (with tremendous difficulty perhaps) to exclude the *indicative* sign from the analysis, because the indicative sign *points*, while the expressive sign, we said, *means*. Husserl's pursuit of the pure possibility of meaning demands that indication be sidelined in the investigation, so that expression in its purity might be isolated. Nonetheless, if an expressive sign is *required* in the interiority of the soul, if it is *indispensable* in order that the subject be made cognisant of his or her *experience*, then the self-sufficiency of this experience as such would be undermined. So in the end, Husserl must also ultimately reduce even the domain of *expression*, treating it as a 'later stratum, superior to and external to the stratum of sense' (*VP*, p. 60/70/78). It is only on the basis of these two reductions that Husserl is able to posit a phenomenologically *silent* stratum of sense at the heart of experience.

Derrida then says, 'Let us at the outset consider the first reduction' (*VP*, p. 60/70/78), by which he means the reduction of the relation to the other within me. Here we see announced a 'two-chapter' strategy, similar to the one we saw in Chapter 4, where Derrida announced the two threads that would occupy Chapters 4 and 5. Here at the outset of Chapter 6, Derrida announces the two 'exclusions' or 'reductions' that Husserl must perform. The first of these exclusions, the relation to the other, will be the subject of Chapter 6, while the second, the supplemental nature of expression (and the nature of supplementarity generally), will be addressed in the final chapter of the book. It is also in these two chapters that Derrida's own, 'positive', philosophy will begin to emerge. Chapter 6 gives us a phenomenological account of the interior monologue, of what happens in the interiority of the soul when one hears oneself speak, *at the very same time that one speaks*. This unique form of auto-affection[31] has been the object of Husserl's (and Derrida's) pursuit all along, and at last we have arrived at the 'heart' of the book. Let us therefore embark upon our discussion of the phenomenology of the inner monologue.

As we have seen, while acknowledging that the expressive sign, when used communicatively, is used in an *indicative* manner, and that expressions are *often* (perhaps mostly) used communicatively, Husserl will nevertheless maintain that there is an *essential distinction* between the two types of signs on the basis of the fact that, when the expression is employed in the interior monologue, it does not *communicate* anything to the subject who uses it. Of this argument, Derrida says:

Indeed, it is necessary to recognize that the criterion of the distinction between expression and indication is in the end entrusted to an all too summary discussion of 'interior life': in this interior life, there would be no indication because there is no communication; and there is no communication because there is no *alter ego*. And when the second person arises in interior language, it is a fiction, and fiction is only fiction. (*VP*, p. 60/70/78)

The example that Husserl uses of what *seems*, falsely, to be an example of interior communication is the self-reproach, 'You have gone wrong, you can't go on like that' (*VP*, p. 60/70/78).[32]

This treatment of the interior life, and the use of these examples, is *all too summary* according to Derrida, in that it is a very particular *type* of interior proposition being employed, and one that, Derrida argues, is chosen quite strategically by Husserl, in order to accomplish exactly what Husserl sets out to achieve. The 'goal' of this selection by Husserl is to ensure that the propositions we encounter cannot possibly count as *indications*. As Derrida notes, the examples are of a *practical* nature: 'In the propositions chosen, the subject addresses himself to himself as to a second person that he blames, exhorts, invites to a decision or to a regret' (*VP*, p. 60/71/79). If we think about the way that a practical proposition functions, we note a couple of interesting points. First, nothing is *made manifest* by way of them. As Derrida says, 'neither *Kundgabe* nor *Kundnahme* are functioning' (*VP*, p. 61/71/79). Saying to oneself, 'do this,' or, 'don't do that,' does not *tell* the self anything instructive or informative *about* the self. Second, nothing empirical or psychological is *pointed to* by way of such formulations, as would be when we use signs in a communicative exchange with others. There is not an existent object in the world to which the propositions point, etc. Given these two characteristics of

142   Derrida's *Voice and Phenomenon*

practical propositions, it is therefore clear that these exemplary propositions that Husserl poses could never count as indications, in the way that
Husserl has articulated the functioning of indication. As Derrida says,
'Husserl needs to choose his examples within the practical sphere in
order to show at once that in them nothing is "indicated" and that these
consist of false discourses' (*VP*, p. 61/71/79).

However, it equally follows, and for the same reasons as we shall
see (this is part of the argument of number 2 on page 62 of *Voice and
Phenomenon*), that these types of propositions are not *expressions* either.
Once we have adopted Husserl's example of the practical proposition,
Derrida claims,

we might be tempted to conclude from these examples, by supposing that we
are unable to find another genus of them, that interior discourse is always essentially practical, axiological, or axiopoetic [. . .] But it is precisely this temptation
that Husserl wants above all and at all costs to avoid. (*VP*, p. 61/71/79)

In other words, once we have followed Husserl's path of thinking on
this matter, and we have assimilated the *practical proposition* with the
functioning of the interior voice, we might fool ourselves into thinking
that *all* interior monologue conforms to this basic pattern. Once we
have the example in tow, we might think that interior monologue *just
is* practical self-direction, that interior monologue *only ever* appears in
the form of practical propositions. But as Derrida says, we would have
missed Husserl's intentions entirely in so doing; and going forward with
our discussion, we must keep in mind that what Husserl has sought constantly to isolate is the use of *expressions* within the solitary life of the soul,
because it is only in the expression that we find a *pure possibility of meaning*.

This *meaning*, however, and the structure of *meaningful language* generally, has to be for Husserl of a very particular sort. There is a fundamental conviction that Husserl retains throughout the entirety of his life:
the structure of all *meaningful* language *must* conform to a 'pure *logical*
grammar that is governed more or less immediately by the possibility of
a relation to the object' (*VP*, p. 61/71/80). This means that there are *a
priori* laws of syntactical connection and configuration that govern *any*
meaningful language. This grammar is, we might say, the *form* of which
all empirical and natural languages are merely instantiations, and the
object here, in *the possibility of a relation to the object*, is a *Bedeutung* or an ideal
meaning. These *a priori* logical laws of grammar are what dictate for
Husserl that a proposition such as 'The quadrilateral is round', though

no doubt contradictory, is nevertheless *meaningful*, while a sentence formulated thusly, 'The hot is slowly', is meaningless. This is because while the former proposition is formulated in such a way that the predicate would at least theoretically be predicable of the subject in the way that it is stated (even if the definitional analysis of the terms forbids such predication), in the case of the latter proposition, this is not so. 'Quadrilateral' is a noun and 'round' is an adjective, whereas 'hot' is an adjective that modifies no noun in the sentence, and 'slowly' is an adverb. Hence we can at the very least *decipher* the meaning of the proposition 'The quadrilateral is round', in order that we might then be capable of saying that it is a contradictory proposition, whereas, in the case of 'The hot is slowly', even such basic, rudimentary deciphering is impossible – this proposition is wholly without meaning.

The point of this explanation and the reason that we have spent such time on it is that Husserl will ultimately reduce the possibility of *all* meaningfulness, both in its indicative and expressive forms, to its strictly theoretical (which is to say, *not* practical) core. So while, on the basis of Husserl's exemplary propositions 'You have gone wrong, you can't go on like that', we might be tempted to conclude that *all* propositions in the interior life of the soul are of a practical nature, this is absolutely not the case for Husserl, as 'Husserl never stopped asserting the reducibility of the axiological to its logico-theoretical nucleus' (*VP*, p. 61/71/79).

From here, we get Derrida's bold argument, 'it is remarkable *that Husserl must, at a certain depth, have recourse to an essential theoretical nucleus of indication in order to be able to exclude it from an expressivity that is purely theoretical*' (*VP*, p. 61/72/80); let us unpack this argument. Our analysis in this book began by noting the seemingly inseparable contamination that obtains between indication and expression. Indications are signs that *point*, we said, while expressions are signs that *mean*. We noted, however, that indications are often *meaningful* (as in the example of inscriptions on a piece of paper), and that expressions almost always *point* (as when we use them communicatively in a discursive way with another person). We then noted that we use expressions in an *interior* way as well, when we talk to ourselves, and established that for Husserl, this counts as a *purely* expressive use of expressions, which thereby *purifies* the notion of 'expression', and rids it of its indicative contamination. We wondered, however, whether or not it is indeed the case that the subject *indicates nothing* to herself, that she *learns* nothing *of* herself, when she uses expressions in an interior way, but also saw that, for reasons of theoretical necessity, Husserl forbids such an interpretation, arguing that we may *represent* ourselves *as though* we are speaking to ourselves, but that this is merely fiction, and that we have no *need* to indicate knowledge *of* ourselves *to* ourselves because the experiences are lived by the subject at the very same instant.

Now, the example *by which* Husserl *makes the case* that expressions in the interior life are not indicative is 'You have gone wrong, you can't go on like that', which is a pairing of practical propositions. Husserl employs these specific propositions in order to demonstrate that these interior propositions are indeed *not* indications, which is an effort to dispel the reader's suspicion (one that Husserl himself entertains) that the subject *indicates* to itself in the interior life. As Derrida says of such propositions, 'in them nothing is "indicated" and that these consist of false discourses' (*VP*, p. 61/71/79); and here is the key point: these propositions consist of false discourses insofar as they are not *purely* theoretical propositions. Therefore, in an effort to *exclude* the indicative sign from the solitary life of the soul, in order to extricate the purely theoretical expressivity of expression from indication, Husserl employs examples of propositions which are not indications, *in part because they are not purely theoretical*. Put a little more simply, Husserl's demonstration *depends* upon the reducibility of the indicative sign to its theoretical core (which partly explains why the propositions in question do not count as indications), *so that* he might ultimately *exclude* the indicative sign *from* the *expressive* domain, in order to isolate that which is, at least according to Husserl, *purely theoretical*; he employs the theoretical core of indication in order to ultimately exclude indication from the *purely* theoretical sphere. Thus, in order to *exclude* indication from expression, he employs a *purity* of indication that paradoxically shares its core with expression.

This is why Derrida says:

Perhaps, at this depth, the determination of expression is contaminated by the very thing that it excludes: pointing the finger at what is in front of one's eyes or at what must always be able to appear to an intuition in its visibility, the *Zeigen*—the relation to the object as indicative monstration—*is invisible only provisionally*. (*VP*, p. 61/72/80)

If, in order to exclude indication from expression, Husserl must use in his argument an essential theoretical *core* of indication, then perhaps these two, expression and indication, are not absolutely and essentially separable after all; it would seem that expression would be *contaminated* by the very *pointing* of the indication it sought to exclude. We ourselves have grappled throughout the book (even if we have not drawn explicit attention to the fact until now) with the fact that Husserl has a serious terminological difficulty in radically distinguishing the terms for 'expression' and 'indication', inasmuch as many of the common German roots of the terms crop up on both sides of the would-be divide. For instance, we saw that the German prefix *Hin*, which means 'there', 'away' or 'out', is operative in *both* the *Hinzeigen* (or 'outward referral') of 'expression' and in the *Hinweisen* (or the 'showing there') of 'indicative allusion'. Likewise, we saw that the German word *Zeichen*, Husserl's general word for 'sign', lies at the heart of the word *Anzeichen*, which is Husserl's technical term for 'indication', but this entails that the 'expression' is also a *Zeichen*. The *Zeigen* itself, we said, lies at root in the *Hinzeigen* of expressive referral *and* in the *Anzeigen* of indicative referral, a point that, at the end of our analysis of Chapter 1, Derrida raised as a possible concern or problem, in that Husserl never reflects on the nature of the sign *as such*. One might suspect that all these terminological intertwinings are accidental or perhaps insignificant, but given all the other conceptual entanglements we have encountered in the course of our analysis, one might also suspect that this inability to radically distinguish these conceptual terms is instead an *essential* entanglement, especially since Husserl never provides an explicit engagement with the question of the sign *as such*. Here Derrida explicitly does so (though, in point of fact, this is what he has been doing all along).

We recall that, in Husserl's words, 'Every sign is a sign for something' (*VP*, p. 20/23/24); every sign stands *in the place of* something – and being in the *place* of this other thing, the nature, or the characteristic activity, of the sign is that it *refers*, and essentially so – as we saw, the *Zeigen* lies at the root of the *Hinzeigen* and the *Anzeigen*. The sign *refers* – in German, *Das Zeichen zeigt*. This *Zeigen* (referral or monstration) is of its very nature a *pointing*, whether it *points* in an indicative or in an expressive manner (but here, we see again the danger of this entanglement, as we have stated that the characteristic specific to the indication is that it *points* while the expression *means*). Derrida says:

The *Zeigen* is always an intention (*Meinen*) which pre-determines the profound essential unity between the *Anzeigen* of indication and the *Hinzeigen* of expression. And the sign (*Zeichen*) would always refer, in the last analysis, to *Zeigen*, to the space, to the visibility, to the field and horizon of what is ob-jected and pro-jected, to the phenomenality as vis-à-vis and surface, evidentness or intuition, and first of all as light. (*VP*, pp. 61–2/72/80)

Thus, we see that Husserl's employment of the theoretical core of indication, in order to extricate expression *from* indication, is problematic for Husserl's project insofar as it *points* to an essential entanglement or contamination, an essential inseparability or *core* underlying both types of sign. The sign *refers* and this referring is an *intention*, that is to say, a relationality or directedness-towards, which unites the gesture and the perception, *the finger and the eye*, whether it does so indicatively or expressively. Thus, 'Paradoxically, the proposition is not indicative because, insofar as it is non-theoretical, non-logical, and non-cognitive, it is as well not expressive' (*VP*, p. 62/72/81). This leads us to the second reason for which Derrida claims that the propositions chosen by Husserl are revelatory.

This reason has to do with the *temporal* dimension of the propositions, inasmuch as these practical propositions (and such propositions generally) do not concern themselves with *the present*. The temporal framing of these specific practical propositions is that of a past wrongdoing, in tandem with an injunction towards future repentance and correction – they concern, in other words, the past and the future, *not* the present; this too is deliberate on Husserl's part, according to Derrida, insofar as it automatically precludes any genuine expressivity of the propositions. Derrida writes:

Now the *temporal modality* of these propositions is not a matter of indifference. If these propositions are not propositions of knowledge, this is because they are not immediately in the form of predication. They do not utilize immediately the verb 'to be,' and their sense, if not their grammatical form, is not in the present. (*VP*, pp. 62/72–3/81)

The practical propositions we have looked at so far, 'You have gone wrong, you can't go on like that', are not *indications*, but neither are they *expressions*, insofar as they are not *purely* theoretical; and they are not *purely* theoretical because they do not conform with, nor are they reducible to, the propositional model of simple predication, set in the present and by way of the third-person singular, present indicative form of the verb 'to be'; this propositional model is 'S is P', which, Derrida claims, is for Husserl 'the fundamental and primitive form, the originary apophantic operation from which every logical proposition must be able to be derived by simple complication' (*VP*, p. 63/73/82). In order to accord with Husserl's understanding of *pure logicity*, a proposition must be ultimately reducible to the form of 'S is P'. For this reason, practical propositions of the form that Husserl proposes, or even of the types that we looked at above ('You are in love with him', 'I am hungry for a burrito', etc.), can never be purely *expressive*, insofar as they employ verb tenses other than the third-person singular, present indicative 'is', indexicals (such as 'I' or 'you'), proper names and mere empiricalities, which can only *ever* be indicative: 'Even more, it is the type of proposition, "S is P," in which the S is not a person for which we can replace a personal pronoun, the latter having in all real discourse a value that is solely indicative' (*VP*, p. 62/73/81).

It is Husserl's emphasis on the third-person singular form of the verb 'to be' that provokes the discussion of the *voice*: 'It is here that one must *speak*' (*VP*, p. 63/74/82), Derrida writes. Through these next few paragraphs, Derrida begins to demonstrate the essential relation between the concepts of 'being' and 'presence', along with their traditional essential relation with the 'voice'. 'Being', in the form of the third-person singular, present indicative word 'is', holds a distinctive relation in the philosophical tradition with the being of the *word* itself (which is to say, with the unity of *phonē*[33] and sense). There is something unique and special about the word 'is', as opposed to any other word or words in the philosophical or even the everyday lexicon. This is a discovery that, as Derrida notes, Heidegger had argued for in *Being and Time*.[34] we *use* the word 'is' all the time, without stopping to concern ourselves with what it means, and this entails that we have *some* sense of what it means, even if it is a pre-thematic or pre-conceptual sense alone. We know quite well, for instance, what it means to say, 'The grass *is* green', or, 'Today *is* Wednesday', or, 'Grandpa *is* no more' (and as the reader will note, each particular use of the word 'is' in these propositions is unique – the first is an 'is' of predication, the second an 'is' of identity and the third an existential 'is'). We must, therefore, have *some* sense of what this word 'is' means, but actually *defining* the word 'is', is a complicated matter. Its sense seems to be found in the word 'is' primarily, if not alone.

Now, one might with good reason wonder, is this not also the case with many other things, for instance, imaginary or non-existent things such as 'mermaid', 'unicorn' or 'Santa Claus'? Is it not the case that, like the word 'is', these things, since they do not in any way *exist*, are found only in the uses of the words that pertain to them? However, there is a

very important difference between these sorts of *beings* and the sense of
the word 'is', and it is this: concepts that apply to *non-existent things* such
as mermaids, unicorns and Santa Claus, are nevertheless *concepts* that are
filled out *by way of* other concepts for which there are indeed *meaningful
senses*, such that the sense of the concept of the non-existent thing itself
is meaningfully developed with conceptual content. For example, when
we say, 'Santa Claus,' a conceptual image comes to our mind, of a portly
man, with longish white hair and a long white beard, wearing a certain
type of clothing (which will vary depending upon one's specific culture),
perhaps smoking a pipe, likely bearing gifts, etc. For this particular
non-existent thing, we might also think of the historical figure upon
whom the mythic figure is based, and the reasons for which he assumed
a mythic status, etc. When you read the words 'Santa Claus', an image
comes into your mind, and it is likely an image not drastically different
from the one that comes into my mind as I type the words. 'Santa Claus'
produces in us a conceptual touchstone that is indeed *filled out* in certain
ways, whereas the word 'is' does not, *even if we have some sense of what it
means when we use it.* As Derrida says, 'Whether we demonstrate this in
the Aristotelian way or in the Heideggerian way, the sense of being
must precede the general concept of being' (*VP*, p. 63n†/74n4/82n2).
In order to even begin explicating the meaning of the word 'is', we have
to *employ* the word 'is', which indicates that we must already have some
vague sense of what the word 'is' means. But it is a word that points,
literally, to *nothing*, nothing conceptual, nothing empirical, etc.:

> Since, however, its sense designates nothing, no thing, no being nor any ontic
> determination, since we encounter it nowhere outside of the word, its irreduc-
> ibility is that of the *verbum* or of the *legein*, that of the unity of thought and voice
> in the *logos*.[35] (*VP*, pp. 63–4/74/82–3)

Hence 'to be' shares an essential and irreducible relation with language
itself. This will entail that the deconstruction of the *language* of Western
metaphysics will necessarily involve the deconstruction of the privilege
of *being* itself.

The privileging of the third-person singular, present indicative 'is'
prompted for us the discussion of the *voice*, where we located the special
relation between the verb 'to be', and the *being* of the *word* and of language itself. But this only raises further problems, concerns and questions. Even if the verb 'to be' shares an irreducible relation with the *being*
of the word itself, why should this entail a privileging of the third-person

singular, present indicative form of the verb – 'is'? Further, why does this unique relation of the 'is' entail the privileged status of the propositional *form*, 'S is P', as the template upon which all genuinely *meaningful* expressions are founded? Finally, how does this all relate to the determination of being as *presence*? 'Why is the epoch of the *phonē* the epoch of being in the form of presence, that is, in the form of ideality?' (*VP*, p. 64/74/83).

In order to begin to answer these questions, we must turn to the concept of auto-affection, as we find in the duration during which the self, in speaking *to* the self, *hears* the self: 'It is here that one must *hear oneself*', as Derrida writes (*VP*, p. 64/74/83). The *objectivity* of the object, or the *ideality* of the ideal, we said above, consists in the object's being *present* to the look of the conscious gaze, and in its being an ideality which, *not of the world*, is infinitely repeatable, in no way dependent upon or contaminated by the empirical, non-essential elements of the *hic et nunc*, or even of the empirical subjectivity intending it. The power of its ideality rests upon its pure power of repetition, as we have noted many times through the course of our analysis. Nevertheless, Husserl does not subscribe to a naïve Platonism, in which the idealities in question would subsist in some *other* realm:

> its ideal-being is *nothing* outside of the world; it must be constituted, repeated, and expressed in a medium that does not impair the presence and the self-presence of the acts that intend it: a medium that preserves at once the *presence of the object* in front of the intuition and the *presence to oneself*, the absolute proximity of the acts to themselves. (*VP*, pp. 65/75–6/84–5)

Therefore, being *nothing outside of the world*, the ideal sense *must* be constituted, which means that it must be *expressed*, but within a milieu or, as he says here, a 'substance', that does not contaminate the purity of the ideal's *presence*, maintaining at once the *presence* of the object to intuition, and the presence of the intuitional acts to themselves.

This brings us back to the question of the nature of expression and the expressive act of the interior monologue. We recall that the stratum of expression, for Husserl, must be conceived as 'unproductive', in that the only thing *produced* in the act of expression is the sign itself, but the sign itself must not be understood to *add* anything to, or embellish in any way upon, the sense that it expresses. As Derrida here says, 'the *telos* of complete expression is the restoration, in the form of presence, of the totality of a sense actually given to intuition' (*VP*, pp. 64/74–5/83). Insofar as the *inner sense* itself is established on the basis of a relation to an ideal object, and this ideal object is *nothing outside the world*, the task of expression then is to 'protect, respect, and restore the *presence* of the sense, *at once as the being-in-front of the object* available to a look, and *as the proximity to oneself in interiority*' (*VP*, p. 64/75/83). It is to bring the presence of sense *back to itself* in the form of the ideal, but all the while never allowing the *sense* to vacate itself or to lose itself in so doing.

This requires a unique *medium*, and, as Derrida says, '*The voice is the name of this element. The voice hears itself*' (*VP*, p. 65/76/85). Whenever I speak to myself, it is an essential component of the act that I *hear* myself *across the time* that I speak – there is no *distance* between speaker and hearer; the sign does not have to *go forth* into the world in order to be *received* and *interpreted* by an auditor, because the speaker and auditor are *the same person*; the signs are spoken, heard and understood at the same time, and the *body* of the signifier does not *leave* the *soul* of the animating intention:

The subject does not have to pass outside of himself in order to be immediately affected by its activity of expression. My words are 'alive' because they seem not to leave me, seem not to fall outside of me, outside of my breath, into a visible distance; they do not stop belonging to me, to be at my disposal, 'without anything accessory'. (*VP*, p. 65/76/85)

This unique relation between the sign, as expressed in the medium of the voice, and the phenomenological interiority of consciousness is unlike any other. Whereas all other signifiers, and more specifically *written* signifiers – even though they may essentially *point* to an ideality that is *not of the world* – include, as an essential component of their senses, a reference to the *exteriority* of the world, this is not the case (at least not obviously so) with the phenomenological voice of the interior monologue. That is to say, for all other, non-phonetic signs, 'the sense of "outside," "in the world" is an essential component of the phenomenon' (*VP*, p. 65/76/85). With the inner voice, however, this does not appear to be so. The signifying substance of the voice, therefore, appears to be one that is wholly singular. Indeed, from a strictly phenomenological perspective, 'the operation of "hearing-oneself-speak" is', Derrida writes, 'an auto-affection of an absolutely unique type' (*VP*, p. 67/78/88). Its uniqueness derives from the convergence of two seemingly paradoxical but essential aspects of its operation. First, 'hearing-oneself-speak' operates in the realm of the universal. The signs that it employs refer to idealities that are *not of the world*, and whose power and objectivity derive from the fact that they are infinitely repeatable, without alteration, even in the presumed absence of the speaker. Second, at the same time, 'hearing-oneself-speak' is a seemingly absolutely *autonomous* auto-affection that essentially subverts the necessity of an act's *going forth* into the world; it is an auto-affection 'without any detour through the agency of exteriority, of the world, of or the non-proper in general' (*VP*, p. 67/78/88). It is at once both absolutely universal and absolutely singular. We might say that hearing-oneself-speak is an auto-affection that embodies the paradox of the *absolute death* (insofar as it deals exclusively in idealities, which transcend the subject as its '*outside*'), and the *absolute life* (insofar as it is a fundamentally *pure* auto-affection) of the subject that enacts it. Every other type of auto-affection, Derrida claims, must sacrifice one of these two components. Let us consider, for instance, the experience of seeing-seen. In order to *see* myself, I necessarily rely upon a *medium* that is not my own. I must have a *substance*, either reflective or photographic, in order to *produce* the image (which must itself be external to me) to become the object of my *look*; I need also *space*, in the form of *distance through the world* (distance from the mirror or photograph, a medium through which or across which to 'see' the image; I cannot *see* my reflection, for instance, if my eye is pressed directly against the surface of the mirror). Similar impediments occur in the experience of touching-touched, as when I might lay my right hand over my left. These two types of auto-affection share in common the necessity of *exposing* the interiority of the self to the exterior world in order to *affect* the self. They include, in other words, an *essential* relation to the exteriority and the 'non-proper' of the world: 'In the two cases, the surface of my body, as a relation to exteriority, must begin by exposing itself in the world' (*VP*, p. 68/79/88). There are, indeed, forms of auto-affection that do *not* rely upon an act's *going forth*. These are forms of auto-affection that occur within our bodies, such as when the heart pumps blood throughout the body, which nourishes the cells, or when the central nervous system sends and receives signals from the various parts of the body. However, this internal auto-affection is purely empirical and cannot operate in the sphere of the universal or ideal, as does the phenomenological voice.

But the result of this paradoxical confluence then implies that even the *spatiality* and the *empiricity* of the body itself, even when considered in its own completely internal operation, is also reduced in the phenomenological voice. The voice, that is, does not rely upon the body, and here it behoves us to remind ourselves of our discussion above of the *non-diaphaneity* of the body that *corrupts* the sense of the expression as it is *on the way to* its manifestation. Such material corruption does not occur in the interior voice:

> it seems to be able to do without this exteriority within interiority [. . .] This is why hearing-oneself-speak is lived as absolutely pure auto-affection, in a proximity to self which would be nothing other than the absolute reduction of space in general. (*VP*, pp. 68/79/88–9)

The auto-affection of the voice is thus *absolutely pure*, inasmuch as it involves the unmediated and direct contact *of* a non-material self *with* the very same non-material self, and without any necessary recourse through the materiality of the exterior world, even the *materiality* of the body itself. This reduction of space does not, it is important to note, entail a reduction of *time* or of the temporal medium, inasmuch as the iterations of the idealities take place across the moments of time. The constitution of the ideal in a non-spatial, purely temporal domain is what solidifies the essential relation between the voice and ideality. Derrida writes, 'When I speak, it belongs to the phenomenological essence of this operation that *I hear myself during the time* that I speak' (*VP*, p. 66/77/87).

In the act of hearing-oneself-speak, the voice is *heard* in the present during which it is *spoken*; it therefore seems that I *affect* myself and am so affected at the same time, in a relationship of absolute self-proximity, such that my *signs* in no way *go forth* into the world or even through the *non-diaphaneity* of the body. This restraint entails the absolute proximity of the *signifier* to the *signified* that is never lost in the expressive act of the interior monologue, a proximity that is not found, for instance, whenever I communicate with others. As we saw above, 'the actuality of discourse keeps in itself something of *involuntary* association' (*VP*, p. 29/34/37). The loss of this *proximity* entails a loss of my *power over* the sign. The *communicative* use of signs entails, *essentially*, the possible loss of sense – there is always the possibility that I will be misunderstood or poorly understood. There is always the possibility that my signs can be *recontextualised* in such a way as to corrupt their intended meanings. At the same time, when I speak to another, even though it is the case that I hear myself speak when I do so, it is also the case that

> if one is heard by the other, it is to make the other *repeat immediately* in himself the hearing-oneself-speak in the very form in which I have produced it. Repeat it immediately, that is, reproduce the pure auto-affection without the aid of any exteriority. (*VP*, pp. 68–9/80/89)

When I speak in the presence of the other, there is a sense in which I stand in a relation of *power* over the other, insofar as I have the power to *force*, whether he or she likes it or not, the *repetition* of the very same *auto-affection* that has occurred within me in the act of hearing-oneself-speak. When I speak, and my words are *heard*, the auditor repeats in the interiority of his or her soul the very same act of hearing-oneself-speak that occurs in the speaker. But, I also *relinquish* power in some ways as well, in that I also sacrifice the pure possibility of sense, inasmuch as the communicative use of the sign entails an essential possibility of *involuntary association*. I force the repetition of the sign, but at the expense of the intended *sense* of that sign. In the act of hearing-oneself-speak, however, I constitute this very same *repetition*, across time, but without the passage through the world that would rob the signs of their senses. This is what we mean by the *absolute proximity of signifier to signified*. I, the speaker, whose *intentions* have given *life* to the sign, *maintain complete and absolute power* over the sign, and hence over the *sense* of that sign – the ideal object: 'This possibility of reproduction, whose structure is absolutely unique, *gives itself* as the phenomenon of an unlimited mastery or an unlimited power over the signifier, since the latter has the form of non-exteriority itself' (*VP*, pp. 69/80/89–90).

The expressive medium (or 'substance') of the voice is therefore also unique in that the immediate presence of signifier and signified entails that the *body* of the signifier is, unlike all other expressive media, seemingly *erased* at the very moment it is given life. Handwritten signs, for instance, leave a mark that might very well survive the *death* of their author. Even when we *speak*, outwardly into the world, the sign *traverses* the materiality of the world, reverberating off empirical surfaces, fleshy substances, etc. With the phenomenological voice, however, 'the phenomenological 'body' of the signifier seems to erase itself in the very moment it is produced' (*VP*, p. 66/77/86). The sign is utilised only in order to deliver the sense up to its ideal form, and at precisely the same moment that the sign is *embodied*, it is effaced: 'It reduces itself phenomenologically and transforms the mundane opacity of its body into pure diaphaneity' (*VP*, p. 66/77/86).

The maintenance of this *power* over the ideal object, in relation to the universality of the ideal, Derrida claims, is why the *voice* is the *basis* or the *possibility* of consciousness and of subjectivity. We must recall that in the introduction, Derrida formulates the definition of *consciousness* as 'nothing other than the possibility of the self-presence of the present in the living present' (*VP*, p. 8/9/8). This formulation, no doubt a para-phrasing of Husserl's *principle of all principles*, emphasises the closeness or, we might say, the *with-ness* of the intuitional acts to themselves. The word 'consciousness' throughout this text is a translation of the French word *conscience*. As is perhaps apparent, therefore, the English word 'consciousness' shares an almost indistinguishable etymological origin with the word *conscience*. Both words derive from the Latin *con* and *scire*, meaning respectively, 'with' and 'to know'. Combining these two roots, *conscire* means 'to be mutually aware'. It is in this sense that we speak of a moral *conscience*, which means an ineffable, indefinable *knowledge* that one supposedly has *within oneself*, an inherent knowledge of right and wrong; one that, moreover, is shared *with* everyone else who can be said to have a *conscience*. We might say, for instance, 'Anyone who would do *that* cannot possibly have a *conscience*.' But, what is important to note is that this sense of *with-knowledge* or *mutual awareness* that is central to our moral understanding of *conscience* also accompanies the sense of the (seemingly morally neutral) word *consciousness*, such that, in French, the two terms are the same. Consciousness is the *with-knowledge* that brings the self into close (that is to say, absolute) proximity to the self. It is the knowledge that one has *with* and *of* oneself, but without which no experience of the sense of the world would be possible. To be *conscious* means that the sense of one's interior experience is relatable and related to idealities that *transcend* the self strictly speaking, but related in such a way as to remain within and reinforce the experience of the interior self itself. This occurs, Derrida has argued, only in the auto-affection of the voice, which is why he says, 'The voice is being close to itself in the form of universality, as con-sciousness <*con-science*>. The voice *is* consciousness' (*VP*, pp. 68/79–80/89).

Ironically, it will be on the basis of the absolute proximity of signifier to signified that Husserl will declare the stratum of expression 'unpro-ductive', and that he

will be able, paradoxically, to reduce the medium with no harm being done and assert that a pre-expressive stratum of sense exists. On this condition too Husserl will give himself the right to reduce the totality of language, regardless of whether it is indicative or expressive, in order to regain the possession of the originarity of sense. (*VP*, p. 69/80/90)

Since the subject maintains absolute power over the ideal object, in that the signifier never *departs* from the signified, the signifier itself, Husserl will claim, *adds nothing* to the sense that it expresses. Since it adds *nothing*, strictly speaking, it is 'unproductive', and hence can theoretically be jettisoned as a non-essential, supplemental feature, an add-on to the stratum of experience.

When Husserl makes this move, he is repeating a traditional Western stance in regard to the relation between meaning, language, voice and writing. Aristotle famously declares, in the opening lines of *De Interpretatione*, 'Spoken words are the symbols of mental experience and written words are the symbols of spoken words.'[36] Looking at this formulation, we can see that the *mental experience* for Aristotle is primary, and language in the forms of both voice and writing are *supplemental* to the stratum of mental experience; that is to say, they are non-essential *add-ons* that somehow secondarily (and tertiarily) *symbolise* the experience. We *have* the experience, and *then* we *symbolise* this experience through the use of symbols. But between these two supplemental symbolising strata, the voice is privileged. The voice first expresses the *symbols* of the mental experience, and the written sign secondarily provides a *symbol* of the spoken sign – it makes the spoken sign *legible*. Writing is thus a supplement twice over, *a sign of a sign*, according to Aristotle; and then, according to the remainder of the philosophical tradition, as this move will be adopted uncritically by most of the rest of the philosophical tradition. This also explains why, for the Western tradition generally, the *closest* that writing can come to the sphere of ideality will be writing in its *phonetic* form, insofar as phonetic writing, unlike pictographic writing, for instance, creates *symbols* that represent the *sounds* of the voice themselves. As Derrida writes, 'If writing completes the constitution of ideal objects, it does this only insofar as it is phonetic writing. Writing comes to stabilize, inscribe, write down, incarnate a speech that is already prepared' (*VP*, pp. 69/80–1/90–1). Here we see Derrida's word for this traditional binary opposition between voice and writing that asserts the pre-eminence of the voice: 'phonologism' (*VP*, p. 69/80/90).

In this sense, writing for Husserl is supplementary and derivative. We might say that, until its senses are *animated* by the intention of the subject who reconstitutes them in the act of reading, the written signs are merely *corpses* on the surface of the expressive medium, whatever it may be. Derrida claims that the letter is a 'symbol that can always remain empty' (*VP*, p. 70/81/91), mere indications that can only be *understood* by being *reanimated* – quickened or resurrected – in the form of expressions once more. Here again we can hear the metaphysical inheritance undergirding

Husserl's project, centred around the body/soul opposition that we have seen above. The privilege of the voice is that it *expresses* ideality within the absolute proximity of self-presence, the presence of the ideal object to the intuition, and the presence of the intuitional acts to themselves. The *sign* is akin to a body that *houses* a sense-intention, as the physical body *houses* the soul. As such, in the absence of the animating intention (which is akin to the soul), the sign is like a corpse, or a dead, material body. Like the 'dead' matter of the Western tradition, it has no life strictly speaking. It requires the animating intention of a subject in order to *give* life to it. Hence insofar as the sign does not *depart* from the *soul* that animates it in the operation of the voice, the words of the voice are most *alive*. Derrida says:

> The word is a body that means something only if an actual intention animates it and makes it pass from the state of inert sonority (*Körper*) to the state of animated body (*Leib*). This body proper of the word expresses only if it is animated (*sinn-belebt*) by the act of a wanting-to-say (*bedeuten*) which transforms it into spiritual flesh (*geistige Leiblichkeit*). But only *Geistigkeit* or *Leiblichkeit* is independent and originary. (*VP*, p. 70/81/91)

The further through time our signs get from their animating intentions, the greater the risk of *death*, in the absolute emptying of sense.

The constitution and transmission of knowledge, therefore – which, we should note, *necessitates* writing – is an endeavour rife with tremendous risk. It requires the 'discoverer', who must first *constitute* the ideal sense of the knowledge that is to be transmitted, who must then *express* this ideality in the medium of speech, and then *translate* that speech into a configuration of written symbols that most 'properly' align with the idealities that they intend to express, all in the hope that the future *receivers* of these symbols will be able to *reconstitute* this very same ideality in the exact same way. The further that the history departs from the *living* source of this intention, the greater the likelihood that this primordial sense will be covered over or lost:

> With the possibility of progress that such an incarnation authorizes, the risk of 'forgetfulness' and of loss of the sense grows constantly. It is more and more difficult to reconstitute the presence of the act that is buried under historical sedimentations. The moment of the crisis is always that of the sign. (*VP*, p. 70/81/91)

This phonologism comprises the traditional dimension of Husserl's project. But already we see, at the same time, that this privileging of the voice is contested from within: the constitution, transmission and accumulation of knowledge *requires*, as Husserl acknowledges, the transposition into the *written* sign, and yet, this written sign threatens the very self-presence of sense that it aims to transmit.

Thus it will be the case that Husserl will also have to acknowledge the *temporal* dimension of the constitution of sense, such that the movement of *temporalisation*, carried out in the reading from the previous chapter, will once again come into play, disrupting the presumed self-presence of sense that gives the voice its privileged status. In the first sense, the accumulation and transmission of knowledge *requires* the entrusting of sense to writing, in order thereby to engender further constitutions and accumulations of knowledge. But even more fundamentally, the movement of temporalisation itself, even within the so-called 'originary' act of constitution – the act that 'first' constitutes an ideality – is itself operative and constitutive. As we have seen, the phenomenological voice of the interior monologue amounts to the *absolute reduction of space*, in that the signifier does not pass through the non-diaphaneity of the body or the materiality of the external world. However, it does *not* amount to an absolute reduction of time or the temporal dimension. The iterations of the signs take place *across the moments of time*, in the constitution of the living present – the nucleus of primal impression surrounded by the halo of retention and protention. As Derrida says, 'The originality of speech, that by which speech is distinguished from every other milieu of signification, comes from the way its fabric seems to be purely temporal' (*VP*, p. 71/83/93). This purely temporal, non-spatial iteration is what ensures and secures their ideality.

But this introduces a further complication into the Husserlian schema. Derrida writes, 'Auto-affection as the operation of the voice assumed that a pure difference came to divide self-presence' (*VP*, p. 70/82/92). This *living present* upon which the constitution of ideality is founded in the operation of the voice is the very same that was explicated and deconstructed in Chapter 5, the *self* of which is constituted on the basis of the play of différance. The temporal nature of the iteration does indeed secure the ideality of sense, but in so doing, it also opens it up to the movement of différance that we discovered in Chapter 5. The movement of différance is a movement of *originary contamination*, which means, an *impurity* that does not happen *to* the given, accidentally *after-the-fact*, but as an essential and constitutive component of the given. *Auto-affection as the condition of self-presence* entails first that there is a difference between the *self who speaks* and the *self who hears*, **and** that the *self-presence of the self who speaks* and the *self-presence of the self who hears* are *essentially insecurable*. Each passes into the other in the constitutive play of différance, which is to say, they are constituted by a *pure difference*,[37] which makes them both possible and hence this différance, as Derrida says, does not 'supervene upon a transcendental subject', but 'produces the transcendental subject' (*VP*, p. 71/82/92). That is to say, it is only *as* self-relation or auto-affection, wherein the self relates to the self as to an *other*, that a self *as such* is made possible.

But this complicates the entirety of the phenomenological project. This 'self' is the condition of the transcendental reduction, but insofar as the pure self-presence of the present-now is disallowed by the play of différance, the transcendental reduction can never be *pure*, because *otherness* is always already worked *into* the constitution of the self. We can *never* hope to 'purely' bracket the world, the body or the other. The possibility of everything that Husserl would have hoped to have exorcised under the designation of *indication* (space, the outside, the world, the body, materiality, empiricity, etc., everything that would be bracketed in the mode of transcendental reduction) is rooted within this différance. Hence 'As soon as we admit that auto-affection is the condition of self-presence, no pure transcendental reduction is possible' (*VP*, pp. 70–1/82/92). Nevertheless, Derrida says, thought must still pass *through* the reduction, because it is only in the mode of transcendental reduction that one can 'recapture the difference in closest proximity to itself: not to its identity, nor its purity, nor its origin. It has none of these. But in closest proximity to the movement of différance' (*VP*, p. 71/82/92). In other words, *passing through* the reduction, Derrida claims, does not get us the *purity* of self that the phenomenological project would want, because of *originary contamination*, nevertheless, it *does* bring us to the realisation of this originary contamination. It is only by passing *through* the reduction that we recognise the *impossibility* of a pure reduction, as well as the reasons *for* this impossibility.

There is, therefore, a sense in which at precisely this point in the analysis, Derrida demonstrates his own deeply philosophical commitments, and there is even a sense in which these commitments reveal a very traditional stance on Derrida's part. Derrida, like the whole of the Western philosophical tradition, is in pursuit of that which is *originary*, that which would provide the *foundation* of the possibility of subjectivity and of thought. There is a very important sense in which every philosopher in history – from Plato through Heidegger – has done nothing else. The passage through the reduction is for Derrida the closest that thought can get to the *originary*, and it is on account of this *proximity* that the passage through the reduction is for Derrida necessary and uncircumventable. Nevertheless, it is also precisely at this moment that Derrida's specific uniqueness emerges as well, as the *originariness* that he discovers is one of *originary* movement and contamination, as opposed to the secure, unmoving foundation,[38] or the *Archimedean point*,[39] the presence of the present, that has always served as the object of pursuit for the Western tradition. We might even say that Derrida's différance is a *non-originary originariness*, inasmuch as it is not a *simple* or *pure* origin, but a *foundational* productive relationality, one that undermines any presumptions to the stability or security of thought, including the security of concepts such as 'origin', 'originary' and 'foundation'. All the same, it is here, in this non-originary originariness of différance, that Derrida locates the possibility of meaning, of truth and of thought.

To close out the analysis of Chapter 6 and begin the movement into the book's final chapter, Derrida notes that our analysis heretofore has *relied* upon the auto-affection in the operation of the *voice*, and poses the question of whether we have not been too myopic in our pursuit – maybe, that is, if we bracket, with Husserl, the operation of the voice and of language – even in its expressive form – maybe we will discover a 'level of pre-expressive lived experience, the level of sense insofar as it preceded *Bedeutung* and expression' (*VP*, p. 71/83/92). Perhaps *prior to* that moment that a sense is brought into expression by way of the voice, there would be *access*, within the interiority of the soul, to an atemporal, self-contained, ideality. This possibility too is disallowed, even within the confines of Husserl's own project, inasmuch as *ideality* is itself, Derrida says, temporal *through and through*.

He notes that the *uniqueness* of the auto-affection and of the voice seemed to be that it unfolded its sense in a purely *temporal* domain, an *absolute reduction of space*, we said. This *temporalisation* is an essential component of the constitution of the ideal in the mode of expression; *but*, more importantly, the *ideal itself*, the sense that is thereby constituted, *does not avoid this temporalisation* for Husserl. In other words, 'this temporality does not unfold a sense that would be itself timeless. Even prior to being expressed, the sense is through and through temporal' (*VP*, p. 71/83/93). Husserl's thought therefore distinguishes the *omnitemporal* from the *eternal*, a distinction that the Western philosophical tradition prior to him, by and large, had not made. *Eternity* for the Western philosophical (and religious) tradition, means 'outside of time'. For the most part, the Western philosophical tradition has assimilated the necessary truths of logic and mathematics under this designation of *eternal* truths; they are *timelessly* true – their truth *transcends* the whole of time. For Husserl, the fact that a truth may be true *throughout all time* does not divest it of the essential requirement that the truth must first be *constituted*, and this constitution is a temporal activity; 'The omnitemporality of ideal objects, according to Husserl, is only a mode of temporality' (*VP*, p. 71/83/93). *True for all time* for Husserl does not mean *true outside of time*. Time is an irreducible component of *truth*.

As soon as we speak of the *movement of temporalisation*, even if we are talking strictly about the ideal, Derrida writes, the discussion of *auto-affection* is unavoidable, and here he takes a lead from Heidegger's analysis of temporalisation in *Kant and the Problem of Metaphysics*. Hence Derrida goes right to the 'source' of the living present, the *source-point*, the 'now' of the primal impression which, Derrida will argue, *can only* be understood as an *auto-affection*. He writes, 'The "source-point," the "originary impression," that on the basis of which the movement of temporalization is produced is already pure auto-affection' (*VP*, p. 71/83/93). In order to argue for this claim, Derrida first points out that the primal impression is a *pure production*. This means that it is a *production* that is not *halted* or, we might say, *contaminated*, by the *terminus* of a product, which would bring to a conclusion the movement of production itself. It has no end (product), and likewise for the same reasons, it has no *origin* (producer) either – it is a *pure* production. The newness of the now, Derrida says, is therefore engendered by *nothing*. Here he quotes Husserl:

'The originary impression is the absolute beginning of this production, the originary source, that starting from which all the rest is continuously produced. But it itself is not produced. It is not born as something produced, but by *genesis spontanea*, it is originary generation.' (*VP*, p. 72/83/93)[40]

The primal impression must, as the nucleic 'now' of the *living present*, be retained as a constitutive element of another *now* that will displace it, and must affect itself so as to assume a new *actuality* in the mode of *non-now*, or past now. Complicated though it may seem, the structure of time itself parallels that of the self-relation that constitutes the subject. The now *becomes* a now only insofar as it relates to itself (an *other now*) in its *otherness*, in a pure auto-affection 'in which the same is the same only by affecting itself with an other, by becoming the other of the same' (*VP*, p. 73/85/95). The living now is a *pure spontaneity*, Derrida says, that creates *nothing*, no *thing*. Neither creator nor created, the living now constitutes *itself* by relating *to* itself in its *own* otherness – by *becoming-other*. Only as such is the *now* ever constituted.

This structure of temporalisation lies at the heart of the production and constitution of sense itself, according to Husserl; it can only be thought as a pure movement, which means that all the names and concepts that would be formulated in the hope of *describing* this movement would have to be *borrowed* from the domain of constituted sense that this movement *makes possible* in the first place. These constituted concepts are of their very nature, we might say, presumed (perhaps even 'required') to be fixed or stable – but insofar as they are solidifications that are designed to describe fluidity, they can only ever be essentially *metaphorical*. For Derrida, this metaphoricity of language is not a deficiency or inadequacy, but an essentiality. As he says, 'We say the "movement" with the terms for what the "movement" makes possible. But we have always already drifted into ontic metaphor' (*VP*, p. 73/85/95). And again, Derrida on this point is simply trying to press Husserl to the logical *outcome* of his (Husserl's) own thinking. In one of the more substantial footnotes in the book, Derrida quotes a long passage from Husserl:

'We are unable to express this in any other way than: *we describe this flow in this way according to what is constituted*, but it consists in nothing that is temporally "objective." This is absolute subjectivity, and it has the absolute properties of something that we have to designate metaphorically as "flow," something that springs up "now," in a point of actuality, an originary source-point, etc. In the lived-experience of actuality, we have the originary source-point and a continuity of moments of retentions. For all of that, names fail us.' (*VP*, p. 72n/84n9/94n1)[41]

We note, and this is very important, that Husserl in this passage is suspicious of *all* terms by which we would attempt to characterise this movement, even of terms such as 'flow' (and presumably, of 'movement'). In our discussion of Chapter 4, we attempted to draw out some of the characteristics of *deconstruction*, one of which we said was that one cannot simply *relinquish* the so-called 'founding value of presence' and move forward in the philosophical tradition as though we were moving forward *without* these concepts. There we said that to be a philosopher means to work out of a *tradition*, and to do *this* means to work with an inherited set of concepts and problems. We cannot simply *change* the concepts we work with, because like it or not, these concepts carry historical baggage *with* them (after all, there must be some *reason* for which we choose to call something by the name of Concept-X, some kernel of the tradition that we perceive it to carry over with it, even if we attempt to attach all necessary caveats before doing so). Likewise, we cannot simply create *new* concepts, because the *rules* in the tradition that govern the *creation* of concepts operate in accordance with the very same presuppositions of the 'metaphysics of presence'.

We should note at this point that this is one of the more controversial aspects of Derrida's thought. The uninitiated reader might very well suspect that Derrida is simply 'rigging the game', as it were, in favour of deconstruction.[42] The deconstructive comportment recognises the movement of différance at the heart of the inherited concepts of the Western tradition. The undecidable quandaries through which the philosophical tradition has been led are a result of the either/or, binary frameworks with which the tradition operates, which, 'deconstruction' discovers, are constituted on the basis of a differential *play*. Why not simply discard them then, and create *new* concepts, or new frameworks, perhaps? Is it not simply the case that Derrida *insists* that concepts *must* be created in the way that they are, only in order to then demonstrate *why* this way of forming concepts is problematic? Is he not just, as we said, 'rigging the game' in his favour? Why not just call this *originary* ineffable that Derrida seeks by the name of a 'flow', or a 'movement'? What is *wrong* with such terms? But here, as we see, this is also to ask the question, why does Husserl put the word 'flow' in scare quotes?

To see *why* such terms are problematic for Husserl and for Derrida, we need only ask what is *contained* within these terms, and when we ask *this* question, we come to see the stealthy ubiquity of the metaphysics of presence. One need only ask oneself, how possible is it to think of concepts like 'flow' or 'movement' in any other terms than those of 'what does not *stand still*'? Concepts of fluidity and movement are themselves constituted against the backdrop of concepts that emphasise solidity and stability. Moreover, insofar as *any* term we would use in order to characterise this *originary non-originariness* would be a *constituted* term, its *definition* ('to define', meaning, 'to *make finite*') would *by definition* be a conceptually *artificial* imposition of stability over a fundamental *instability*. Therefore, as Husserl says, it is fundamentally *unnameable* ('*For all of that, names fail us*'); and yet, *it must be named*, for to fail to do so would be to surrender the highest task of thinking. Here we see the tension that drives the whole of deconstruction: the necessity to name what cannot be named, and to think what cannot be thought, 'plunging in, and groping our way through inherited concepts, toward the unnameable' (*VP*, p. 66/77/86).

Let us conclude the reading of Chapter 6. Given that this *pure movement* lies at the very heart of the production of *sense* itself, sense as such 'is never simply present. It is always already engaged in the "movement" of the trace, that is, in the order of "signification"' (*VP*, pp. 73/85/95–6). The 'trace', as we discussed, is the *possibility of repetition, in its most general form*; it is the *pure possibility of repetition*. This trace essentially and constitutively *inscribes* itself into *each present-now*, and since the production of sense is caught up in this movement, the *trace* is also an essential component of this production. *This entails, however, that sense, even in its 'presence', is always essentially marked by otherness, in the form of the trace.* This is what Derrida means by the term 'archi-writing', the originary *inscribability* that makes sense as such, along with its repetition, possible (*VP*, p. 73/85/95). Hence it is never *simply* present, even in the innermost quietness of the subject. Sense is always marked by its *outside*, which means that sense is always *on the way to ex-pression*, and essentially so. As Derrida says:

Since the trace is the relation of intimacy of the living present to its outside, the openness to exteriority in general, to the non-proper, etc., *the temporalization of sense is from the very beginning 'spacing'*. As soon as we admit spacing at once as 'interval' or difference and as openness to the outside, there is no absolute interiority. (*VP*, p. 73/86/96)

Thus, with Derrida we note a number of important discoveries. First, though we have heretofore said that the uniqueness of the auto-affection of the voice lay in the exclusively *temporal* nature of its operation, we see now that this *temporalisation* is such that it cannot disallow its own *contamination* by the spatial. In its very constitution as time, the *presence of the present* is structured by the movement of the *trace*, which is an opening of the present to its own *exteriority* that marks it originarily. The very *nature* of time, therefore, opens onto what is *other to it*, and this includes *space*; Derrida writes, 'If we now remember that the pure interiority of phonic auto-affection assumed the purely temporal nature of the "expressive" process, we see that the theme of a pure interiority of speech or of "hearing-oneself-speak" is radically contradicted by "time" itself' (*VP*, p. 74/86/96). Second, this *inability* to fundamentally close the *self* off from its *other* infects also the would-be interiority of the subject. While the transcendental reduction of the phenomenological project would seek to reduce the whole of experience down to its bare sense, and this lying at the heart of the solitary life of the soul, this solitary life, constituted as it is on the movement of temporalisation, cannot keep the *outside* out of the *inside*. Thus, going along with the contamination of the temporal with the spatial is, as we have seen, the impossibility of the pure transcendental reduction: 'temporalization is at once the very power and the very limit of the phenomenological reduction' (*VP*, p. 74/86/96). Third, given that the production of sense is essentially always *on the way* to expression, this movement of expression disallows the absolute self-presence of sense within the inner life of the soul. It is therefore impossible to radically reduce the sphere of expression from out of the solitary life of the soul. Hence the sought-after *pre-expressive stratum of sense* becomes impossible. Fourth, given that sense is always in passage to its *outside*, there is no longer a way to radically distinguish *expression* from *indication*. Recall that it was the passage through exteriority that conditioned a sign's being used in an indicative manner. In order to isolate *pure expressivity*, we said that the passage through the outside, the sign's *going forth*, must be reduced. Once the distinction between an absolute inside and an absolute outside is attenuated, the criterion by which one might hope to radically distinguish expression from indication is lost. Fifth, given that the *production* of sense is through and through marked essentially by the notion of the 'trace' (and this on account of its own movement of temporalisation), the notion of 'inscription' (or 'archi-writing') essentially accompanies even the so-called 'first' occurrence of a given ideality, in the form of the *spoken sign*. That is to say, the traditional privilege of the *voice* is lost. To put this in simple terms, whenever we *speak*, we do so through the use of signs that point to idealities, but all the characteristics one would ascribe to these idealities (repeatability, permanence, stability, etc.) are most properly characteristics of the *written*, as opposed to the *spoken*, sign. The spoken sign is the most *alive*, but only because it is directly connected to the *soul* that utters it, which entails also that it is the most *effervescent*, the most *mortal*. The written sign is the most *dead*, because it is inscribed apart from the animating intention, but by this very same token, it is all the more capable of being *preserved*, *repeated* and *passed down*. These are characteristics of *all* signs as such, including the spoken signs of the voice. The production of *sense*, even in the inner voice, is engendered by a kind of 'archi-writing'.

This brings us to the end of Chapter 6, which opens onto the discussion of supplementarity. Derrida writes:

> If indication is not added onto expression which is not added onto sense, we can nevertheless speak, in regard to them, about an originary 'supplement.' Their addition comes to supplement a lack, an originary non-self-presence. And if indication, for example, writing in the everyday sense, must necessarily 'add itself' onto speech in order to complete the constitution of the ideal object, if speech must 'add itself' onto the identity of the object in thought, this is because the 'presence' of sense and of speech has already begun to be lacking in regard to itself. (*VP*, p. 74/87/97)

Chapter 6 (the argument from the medium of hearing-oneself-speak) completes the three arguments that operate on the terrain of Husserlian phenomenology itself. Derrida has now laid the conceptual groundwork that will comprise and constitute the basis of the conceptual originality of his own project, which is made explicit in Chapter 7.

Let us now turn to the final chapter of *Voice and Phenomenon*.

The Originative Supplement

At the beginning of Chapter 6, we noted that there were two *reductions* that the phenomenological project must carry out in order to constitute the phenomenological 'silence'; the second of these was 'that of expression as a later stratum, superior to and external to the stratum of sense' (*VP*, p. 60/70/78). Hence the opening sentence of Chapter 6 announces the analysis of the structure of supplementarity that occupies Chapter 7, and as the conclusion of Chapter 6 and the title of Chapter 7 make clear, this supplementary structure, or the structure of supplementarity generally, will turn out to be 'originary' (*VP*, p. 74/87/97). This originary structure of supplementarity will comprise the basic *form* of the very operation of signification on Derrida's reading of Husserl, and here in Chapter 7, Derrida demonstrates the fundamental tension that this *formalism* in phenomenology bears with respect to Husserl's *intuitionist* emphasis. According to the *formalist* side of the tension, 'a discourse can be a discourse, even if it makes no knowledge possible' (*VP*, p. 76/90/100), so long as it accords with certain logical rules of discursive grammatical construction, a 'pure morphology of significations' (*VP*, p. 76/90/100) – in other words, so long as discourse operates in accordance with certain rules, it can be meaningful discourse, with or without the *fulfilled intuition*; while, on the other hand, according to the *intuitionist* pole of this tension, the very possibility of meaningfulness is borne out by the *telos* of the intuitive *fulfilment* of the intention, the presupposed eventual teleological givenness of the intended object as the content of an intuition – *meaning* of its very nature *tends towards truth*. These two emphases, in tension with each other, occupy the whole of Husserl's philosophy of language. Therefore, in this final chapter, Derrida embarks upon the exploration of the phenomenological tension, which he announced in the final sentences of the 'Introduction' to *Voice and Phenomenon*, the 'tension between its two major motives: the purity of formalism and the radicality of intuitionism' (*VP*, p. 14/16/16). Let us now turn to the discussion of supplementarity.

Here at the outset of Chapter 7, Derrida writes, 'Thus understood, supplementarity is really *différance*, the operation of differing that, at once, splits and delays presence, subjecting it by the same action to originary division and originary delay' (*VP*, p. 75/88/98). So already at the beginning of the chapter, Derrida is gesturing that the différance, which we learned in Chapter 5 was essentially related to the concepts of the 'trace', 'the fold in presence', 'the fold in self-presence', and in Chapter 6, 'archi-writing', is also tied essentially to the notion of 'supplementarity'. The différance, we have seen above, is the differing of both time and space, incorporating both senses of the French verb *différer*. Thus, as Derrida says here, différance 'is to be thought prior to the separation between deferral <*différer*> as delay and differing <*différer*> as the active work of difference <*différence*>' (*VP*, p. 75/88/98). As the productive differing of both time and space, it is also the 'site' or the locus where the two bleed into each other – we saw in Chapter 6 that the very *nature* of time itself is its openness to exteriority or to what it *is not*, and this essential openness cannot disallow the spatial. The relation of auto-affection is a *temporal* relation, but one without which a *world as such* would not be possible. Thus, as we have said, différance is the *becoming-time of space and the becoming-space of time*. It is productive, perhaps even *the* productive itself, but it precedes any radical distinction between the strictly active or the strictly passive – its *actions* are not actions in the sense of 'deriving from an agent', and its *passions* are not passions in the sense of 'being done *to* an agent'. Finally, the différance, we said, is what conditions all of the cherished binary oppositions of the Western tradition. Derrida is thus attempting to *think* the structures that *make thinking possible*. As Derrida here says of 'supplementarity' and 'différance', 'We must now verify, *going through* the First Logical Investigation, in what way these concepts respect the relation between the sign in general (indicative as much as expressive) and presence in general' (*VP*, p. 75/88/98), and we must determine how this differential productive relationality of différance relates to the concept of the 'supplement'.

The supplement (or the supplemental), is considered to be an add-on, something that comes after-the-fact, something that substitutes or makes up for something else that would in whatever way be insufficient. For instance, when a person speaks of a 'supplemental income', he or she means a modest amount of income, just enough to substitute or make up for the deficiency in his or her primary income. This secondary income more often than not comes from a *secondary* mode of employment, one that the person would rather not hold, all things being equal, but which for reasons of economic necessity, he or she *must* hold. The supplemental, then, *makes up for some kind of lack* by way of *substituting* for that which the *lack* is missing. To speak of the 'supplement' as 'originary' then, as Derrida does here, is to assert two things. First, it 'implies the non-fullness of presence' (*VP*, p. 75/88/98). To continue with our economic example, if an income requires a *supplemental* income, it is because there is first a *lack* in the *primary* income; its 'presence' is not full, it is not enough. Likewise, if 'presence' requires supplementation, it can only be because the *presence of the present* itself is not fully present – it must be insufficient. Second, given that the supplement is, by its very nature, a *substitute*, to call the supplement 'originary' is to assert that what is primary is not *originary presentation*, but rather, *originary substitution*. This then relates intrinsically to the discussion of the *sign* in general, and the privilege of representation in Chapter 5, inasmuch as the sign is itself a substitution. Above, and going all the way back to our discussion of Chapter 1 of *Voice and Phenomenon*, we noted the peculiarity of the fact that the *Zeigen* ('referral' or 'monstration'), for Husserl, lies at the root of both the *Hinzeigen* of *expressive* referral and the *Anzeigen* of *indicative* referral, and yet, Husserl never deals with the definitional status of the *Zeigen* itself – he never deals with the basic question of what makes a sign a sign, which is that it is a *substitute for something else*. We noted that 'every sign is a sign for something' (*VP*, p. 20/23/24), but also noted that the status of this *being-for*, or what it means to say that a sign is *in-the-place-of*, that is to say, it is *substitutive*, is never addressed by Husserl. In our discussion of Chapter 6, we noted that Derrida says of the *Zeigen* that it 'is always an intention' (*VP*, pp. 61–2/72/80), which means that the *Zeigen* is a directedness-towards, as in towards an *other*. Therefore, to even speak of the supplement as a *substitutive* structure is to invoke the *substitutive* structure of signification generally, and to say that the supplement is originary is to say that *presence* consists of a primary lack, and that the *presence of the present* is constituted by way of an originary movement or moment of substitution (or signification). As Derrida says:

> What we would like finally to start thinking about is the fact that the for-itself of self-presence (*für-sich*), traditionally determined in its dative dimension as phenomenological, reflective, or pre-reflective auto-donation, arises in the movement of supplementarity as originary substitution, in the form of the 'in the place of' (*für etwas*), that is, as we have seen, in the very operation of signification in general. The *for-itself* would be an *in-the-place-of-itself*: put *for itself*, in the place of itself. (*VP*, pp. 75/88–9/99)

Although it is no doubt the case, as Derrida says, that 'This structure of supplementarity is very complicated' (*VP*, p. 75/89/99), nevertheless, Derrida has thoroughly laid the groundwork to aid us in understanding this complex concept of supplementarity. The analysis in Chapter 5 revealed to us that the *self*, considered in the movement of temporalisation, can only relate *to* itself, as it would to an *other*. This discovery was once again confirmed in the analysis of auto-affection in the operation of the voice in Chapter 6. This point – that the self can only relate to the self as it would to an *other* – entails a primary, constitutive *gap* or what Derrida called in Chapter 6 a 'pure difference' that 'came to divide self-presence' (*VP*, p. 70/82/92). This hiatus or this gap is a necessary component of the establishment of a self *as such*; if one can only relate to the self as to an *other*, then the self can only be thought in terms of its own self-substitution, its recognition of its own *otherness* within the very structure of the self-relation that *makes possible* the self in the first place. It can only *become* a self by *first* substituting itself *for* itself. Let us consider briefly a very simple exemplary analogy – seeing the self in the reflection in the mirror. In order to *see* the self, the self must project an *other* image of itself, and *then*, it must *look at itself* in its otherness. It must *look* into the reflection in the mirror, which, to be clear, provides little more than waves of light, passing from the body, echoing off a reflective surface and reverberating against the retinas of the eyes, such that an image is produced and received, and say, 'There I am'; which is to say, *that image, which is a substitute, stands in for me, and is me*. An analogous distancing and spacing, similar to the one that occurs in the *visual* sphere, though on a much more miniscule scale of course, occurs also in the inner, mental sphere as well, once the radical distinction between inside and outside, space and time, is deconstructed. The self can only *see* the self, and can only *relate* to the self, as to a *substitute*. This 'substitution' is what *makes possible* the self.

To say as much, however, is to completely unsettle everything that we think we know about 'original' and 'copy', and about 'primary' and 'substitution'. But then, once we have a general idea of how the structure works, we can also recognise this same unusual structure of the supplement at work in all of the analyses that Derrida has done so far: representation is the condition of *presentation*; expressivity is the condition of sense; indication is the condition of expression; archi-writing is the condition of the operation of the voice; retention is the condition of primary impression; difference is the condition of the same; the *other* is the condition of the *self* – and in each case of these traditional hierarchical, binary relations, they are in a sense *reversed* such that we see a certain *absence* (in the form of a would-be 'deficient' term) preceding and conditioning a certain *presence*. Derrida writes, 'The strange structure of the supplement appears here: a possibility produces by delay that to which it is said to be added' (*VP*, p. 75/89/99). The structure of the supplement is that the supplement precedes and conditions that which it is believed to supplement. Let us now see how this structure of supplementarity works with respect to signification.

The signifier is a supplement – its task and function is that it points, *ultimately*, to an ideal sense that would not otherwise be presentable. But it is important to note that 'the signifier does not first re-present merely the absent signified' (*VP*, p. 75/89/99). Here Derrida is speaking of the *indicative* mode of signification; inasmuch as the indicative sign does not, itself, *point* directly to a *signified* (the ideal object), it is not primarily a *representation* of that absent signified. At the same time, however, 'the indication is not only the substitute that supplements the absence or the invisibility of the indicated' (*VP*, 76/89/99), the indica*ted* being, as Derrida notes, always an *existent* – an empirical being, psychological states or states of affairs. Rather, the indication also points, by detour, *to* the signified, *through* the expressive mode of signification. This is what Derrida means when he says that the signifier

substitutes itself for another signifier, for another signifying order, which carries on another relation with the missing presence, another relation that is more valuable owing to the play of difference. It is more valuable since the play of difference is the movement of idealization and because the more the signifier is ideal, the more it augments the potency of repetition of presence, the more it protects, reserves, and capitalizes on sense. (*VP*, pp. 75–6/89/99)

The indication is therefore a *stand-in* that stands in for yet *another stand-in* (the expression) that, insofar as it is more *closely* related to the movement of idealisation, is *more valuable*, or, we might say, more *full* of meaning, more *meaning-ful*. This substitution is necessary in colloquy, because, 'as we recall, the sense intended by another and, in a general way, the lived-experience of another are not and can never be present in person. This is why, as Husserl says, expression then functions "as indication"' (*VP*, p. 76/89/99). The speaker thus *ex-presses* a sign that *points* the auditor *to* a lived-experience that is internal to the speaker, and the sign itself, in being expressed, becomes for the auditor an *indication* that points the listener to that lived-experience of the other, which can never be made *fully present* as an object of intuition for the auditor.

There is therefore a sense in which expression is considered to be *more full* than indication, in that it is thought to skip the 'appresentational detour' (*VP*, p. 76/89/100) that is an essentiality of the indicative mode of signification – expression is nearer to the lived-experience of the subject, and it is furthermore nearer to the ideal object towards which that inner lived-experience points. Nevertheless, as Derrida says, what is 'most important' is to determine 'in what way expression itself implies in its structure a non-fullness' (*VP*, p. 76/89/99). This will bring Derrida's analysis of Husserl into direct contact with the concept of 'intuitionism', which Derrida argues, in some sense or at some distance, 'governs Husserl's concept of language' (*VP*, p. 76/89/100). However the uniqueness of Husserl's concept of language, Derrida claims, is that *despite* its intuitionist commitments, it is all the same driven by an uncompromising permissiveness of the 'freedom of language, the outspokenness of a discourse, even if it is false and contradictory' (*VP*, p. 76/89/100), a *freedom* in the sense that it requires of discourse only that it *be meaningful*, and nothing more.

This is to say that in a very important sense, Husserl's conception of language is governed by the willingness to *allow language to do what language does*, without necessarily concerning itself with the speaker or the auditor, or more importantly the *fulfilment* of the intuition. 'Pure logical grammar, the pure morphology of significations, must tell us *a priori* under what conditions a discourse can be a discourse, even if it makes no knowledge possible' (*VP*, p. 76/90/100). This, as we said, is the *formalist* impetus behind Husserl's thought – meaningful discourse *conforms* to certain rules or conditions, and so long as it does so, discourse will be meaningful with or without the fulfilled presence of the intended object. As a matter of essentiality, the expression need not be made *full* by its corresponding to an *object*. Derrida notes numerous textual passages wherein Husserl *reduces* as non-essential components of expression 'the acts of intuitive knowledge that "fulfill" the meaning <*vouloir-dire*>' (*VP*, p. 76/90/100). Citing Husserl:

'If we seek to plant ourselves firmly in the soil of pure description, the concrete phenomenon of expression animated with a sense [*sinnebelebten*] is articulated, on the one hand, into a *physical phenomenon* in which the expression is constituted according to its physical side, and on the other hand, into *acts* which endow it with the *Bedeutung* and **contingently *intuitive fullness***, in which the relation to the expressed objective correlate is constituted. Thanks to these acts, expression is more than a simple *flatus vocis*. It *intends* something, and insofar as expression intends something, it is related to something objective.'[43]

And again:

'Or else, when this is not the case, the expression functions with its charge of sense [*fungiert sinnvol*], and is always more than a simple *flatus vocis*, **although it is deprived of the intuition that founds it**, which provides it with an object.' (*VP*, pp. 77/90/100–1)[44]

From these citations we see that for Husserl the *expression* becomes *more than a simple flatus vocis* (literally, a 'breath of the voice', which is to say, 'a mere word') insofar as there is a *meaning-intention* that animates the expression. The intention might very well be finally *deprived* of the intuition that founds it, that is to say, the *object* that first *motivated* the intention might never come to be fulfilled, but this poses no essential problem, as this intuitive fulfilment is, Husserl claims, merely *contingent* anyway – 'contingent', that is to say, *non-essential*. There is thus an essential distinction between the *intention* that animates an expression and the *intuition* of the object to which it points. Derrida writes, 'The "fulfilling" intuition is not therefore essential to the expression, to the intention of the meaning', going on to say that 'the rest of this chapter is devoted to accumulating proofs of this difference' (*VP*, p. 77/91/101).

We should here pause to take note that this point, that the *intuition* does not accompany essentially the *intention*, is not really surprising given careful reflection, as there are various ways, Derrida notes, in which the *expression*, the *Bedeutung* and the *object* can be combined, which would not at all be the case if the fulfilled intuition of the object were an *essential* component of the intended *Bedeutung*. If a *meaningful* expression required the presence of the intuited object, there could never be any possible *remainder* of signification or, we might say, of *signifying content*, within the parameters of a given expression that would *permit* the exchangeability of one intuited object for another; but clearly *language*, in order to really function *as language*, must allow for this substitutability. For instance, two identical expressions can have the same *Bedeutung* and designate different objects ('X is a man', 'Y is a man'); different expressions can have entirely different *Bedeutungen*, and yet can intend the same object (the well-known 'victor at Jena', 'vanquished at Waterloo' example, both of which expressions, possessing entirely different senses, point to the historical figure, Napoleon Bonaparte); or two different expressions can have the same *Bedeutung* and intend the same object ('blau', 'blue', 'bleu'). These variations in meaningful composition and combination would not be possible without such an intention/intuition distinction.

Moreover, without the intention/intuition distinction, there would be no possibility of the *pure logical grammar* that Husserl seeks. The framework of a pure logical grammar holds that there are *a priori* laws of syntactical connection governing any *meaningful* discourse, insofar as it is meaningful, and this commitment, we should note, is an indispensable component of Husserl's project. We must keep in mind that the entirety of Husserl's methodology brackets the so-called *real existence* of the so-called *real world*. On this basis, Husserl's theory of meaning must establish a set of criteria by which a statement's meaningfulness is assessable *without*, and essentially so, any reference to any corresponding *empirical object*. If a *meaningful expression* required a fulfilled intuition, then any expression whose sense is accompanied by the sense 'existence', insofar as this sense cannot be completely 'fulfilled' in the mode of the transcendental reduction, would have to be considered *meaningless* for Husserl, which would result in absurdity, as any and all statements concerning *empirical* events or objects – 'The tree in the yard is tall', for instance – would by implication be meaningless.

Furthermore, it was on the basis of this pure logical grammar that we said above that statements such as 'the quadrilateral is round' are meaningful, while statements such as 'the hot is slowly' are not. This distinction too would be impossible without the intention/intuition distinction. It is only because we can recognise the *meaning* of the first proposition that we can also recognise *a priori* that it is necessarily false, and we recognise the *meaning* of the first proposition because it accords with framework of pure grammatical laws, according to Husserl. In the case of the second proposition, we are unable to establish any *meaning*, precisely because it does *not* conform to these *a priori* grammatical laws. This is why for Husserl, the statement 'Santa Claus lives at the North Pole' is indeed meaningful – that is, we can understand what it *means* – while for many other philosophers (such as Bertrand Russell, Ludwig Wittgenstein and Rudolf Carnap), a statement can only be meaningful if it can be assigned a truth-value, and a statement such as 'Santa Claus lives at the North Pole', insofar as it is a statement of fantasy and designates no empirical object, is neither true nor false, but therefore simply *meaningless*. As Derrida says:

If we were not able to understand what 'square circle' or 'golden mountain' *means*, how could we come to a conclusion about the absence of a possible object? In *Unsinn*, in the a-grammaticality of non-sense, this minimum of understanding is denied to us. (*VP*, p. 78/92/102)

We must be able to *understand* the *meaning* of the expression 'square circle' in order to recognise that no such object, *necessarily*, exists. If the expression *required* the fulfilled intuition of the object, whether ideal or empirical, then the *pure logical grammar* that is such an important component of Husserl's theory would not be possible.

On the basis of these arguments, Derrida claims, we might want to take the claim even further than Husserl appears willing. If there is an essential distinction between the intention of meaning and the intuition of the object, as Derrida, following Husserl's lead, has argued – if this distinction is indeed rigorous – then not only would we want to say that the fulfilled intuition *need not* accompany the meaning, but that, as a matter of essentiality, it *does not* or even *cannot* accompany the meaning, strictly speaking. In other words, if fulfilled intuition is not an *essential* component of *meaning-intention* then we might say that when the fulfilled intuition *does* accompany the meaning-intention, this is merely an accidental *add-on* to the *meaningfulness of the expression* itself – that the *meaningfulness* is its own thing, while the fulfilled intuition is something *additional*. Let us consider for a moment what happens in cases wherein the fulfilled intuition of the object *does* accompany the meaning-intention. Derrida argues, though once again pursuing the logic of Husserl, that in the *meaningful intention* that takes place in the presence of the *intended object*, the *expression* itself, the *meaningful discourse* itself, evaporates in the moment it is uttered, because its sole task is to point the listener *away* from the meaningfulness in general – the expressivity of the expression – and directly and immediately *towards* its designated object: 'the language that speaks in the presence of its object erases or lets its own originality dissolve' (*VP*, pp. 78–9/92/103). To say, for instance, 'The tree in the yard is tall,' is to, in point of fact, *divert* the attention of the listener *away* from the meaningfulness of the expression itself, and *towards* the object in question. Intention and intuition, when they accompany each other, become something *other* than the pure meaning-intention of the expression itself. Therefore, we might not only want to say that the intention does not *require* the object, but that, structurally, it requires its *absence*: 'The structural originality of the meaning would be the *Gegenstandlosigkeit*, the absence of the object given to intuition' (*VP*, p. 78/92/102).

Derrida then takes the argument one step further still, although again, he is attempting to rigorously follow the implications of Husserl in doing so;[45] in addition to the required structural absence of the *object*, Derrida claims, the absence of the *subject* is also *required* of the expressivity of expression. Derrida examines the unique discursive example of statements about perceptions, posed in the moment of the perception:

I say, 'I see now a particular person by the window,' at the moment I actually see that person. What is implied structurally in what I am doing is that the content of this expression is ideal and that its unity is not impaired by the absence of the *hic et nunc* perception. The one who, next to me or at an infinite distance in time and space, hears this proposition must, in principle, understand what I intend to say. Since this possibility is the possibility of discourse, it must structure the very act of the one who speaks while perceiving. (*VP*, pp. 79/92–3/103–4)

In order for the expression 'I see now a particular person by the window' to function discursively, in order for it to *do what the speaker needs it to do when it is used communicatively*, the expression must convey a *meaning*, but insofar as the expression is *meaningful* – that is to say, that it *points to ideal meanings* – its content is *ideal*, and hence it is meaningful, with or without the *presence* of the object, which in this case would be the *presence* of the perception itself, that within the perceiving subject. Thus, following on the logic of the absence of the *fulfilled intuition* (the object), that we carried out just above, we see that there are also cases in which that *object*, insofar as it occupies the role of a *perception* of a *subject*, entails also the absence of the *subject*. As Derrida says:

> The absence of intuition—and therefore of the subject of the intuition—is not only *tolerated* by the discourse, the absence is *required* by the structure of significa-tion in general, were one to consider it *in itself*. The absence is radically required: the total absence of the subject and of the object of the statement—the death of the writer and/or the disappearance of the objects that he has been able to describe—does not prevent a text from 'meaning' <*vouloir-dire*>. On the con-trary, this possibility gives birth to meaning <*vouloir-dire*> as such, hands it over to being heard and being read. (*VP*, p. 79/93/104)

Another way to make this point would be the following: in order to understand what the expression 'I see now a particular person by the window' *means* in this or that situation, when in the presence of this or that speaker, who is attempting to *indicate* something about his or her own perceptions *to us*, we must first understand what the terms them-selves, and what the expression itself, *means*. For instance, were we to see this expression on paper, 'I see now a particular person by the window', we need not know *who* wrote it, or *when* they wrote it, nor do we need to know *whom* the person was that was seen, or *what* window was being described, in order to understand what the expression itself means. It is only *because* we understand what the expression *means* that we would be able to fill that meaning out with the empirical details, were they pro-vided for us after-the-fact. Here is another example: were we to discover an anonymously hand-written journal, meticulously detailing over a long period of time the emotions and psychological states accompanying one's beloved object of unrequited affection, who is also in the journal anonymously spoken of only as 'her' or 'him', we would very well be able to understand what these expressions mean, even in the absence of the names of either the author or his or her beloved. But, very importantly, this ability to understand what those terms and expressions of perceptions *mean* without the presence of the subject further entails the necessary structural *absence* of the subject in the evaluation of the meaningfulness itself, just as the essential intention/intuition distinction entails the structural absence of the *object*.

On the basis of *this* analysis, Derrida will then move, *through* an exploration of the personal pronoun, 'I' (which is, we might note, the epistemological *foundation* of the Modern period, beginning with Descartes), to the analysis of archi-writing and its relation to death and the movement of idealisation. Husserl, Derrida notes, classifies the 'I' as *essentially occasional*, meaning that '"it is essential for this expression to orient its actual *Bedeutung* each time to the occasion, to the person who is speaking, or his situation"' (*VP*, p. 80/93/104).[46] It is of the very essence of the word 'I', Husserl thinks, that its *Bedeutung*, the *meaning* towards which it points, is reoriented each time, on each *occasion* it is used, on the basis of the zero-point of the person who is *in fact* using the expression. It is, we could say, *essentially plurivocal*. It is hence distinguished from *contingently plurivocal* expressions (expressions whose polysemy can be reduced by way of clarification or further articulation – words with multiple meanings, such as 'rule' or 'light'), and from *essentially univocal* expressions (expressions whose singularity of meaning is incorruptible by empirical circumstances – abstract expressions such as those of pure logic or mathematics). Derrida writes, 'We are able to recognize an essentially occasional expression by means of the fact that we cannot in principle replace it in the discourse by a permanent, objective, conceptual representation without distorting the *Bedeutung* of the statement' (*VP*, p. 80/94/105), and Derrida provides an example of such a distortion: 'Instead of "I am pleased," I would have "whatever person who, while speaking, is designating himself is pleased"' (*VP*, p. 80/94/105). Similar distortions occur with words such as 'here' ('the spatial point at which the person designating him- or herself is located'); 'now' ('the moment in time at which the person designating him- or herself is speaking'); etc. All such expressions are, Husserl argues, *essentially occasional*.

Since they are essentially occasional, Husserl thinks, they can only *ever* be indicative signs, at least, when they are used discursively. In other words, that they are *essentially occasional* means that when we use these signs in communication with others, they cannot function *except* by *referring* the auditor to a particular, empirical, psychological state, object, being or state of affairs – 'I', 'me', 'my', 'here', 'this', 'that', 'there', 'now', 'then', 'yesterday', 'tomorrow', etc. Each of these expressions *begins* from a purely *subjective* locus, and hence is only *comprehensible* by pointing the listener *back* to that locus; as Derrida says, 'The root of all of these expressions, as we see very quickly, is the zero-point of the subjective origin, the "I," the "here," the "now"' (*VP*, p. 81/94/105). They are hence essentially *indicative*, insofar as they are essentially *occasional*. But – and this is very important – for Husserl, this indicative status is reduced, down to its expressive core, *for the person who is using these expressions*, at the moment that he or she is using them. In the footnote on this page of the text, Derrida cites a remarkable passage by Husserl:

'In solitary discourse, the *Bedeutung* of the "I" is realized essentially in the immediate representation of our own personality, which is also the meaning of the word in communicative discourse. Each interlocutor has his I-representation (and with his individual concept of the "I") and this is why the word's *Bedeutung* differs with each individual.' (*VP*, pp. 81n/94–5n5/106n1)[47]

This passage is *remarkable* for three reasons. First, it makes reference to an *immediate representation*. By all appearances, *immediate representation* would be an oxymoron, especially in the context of a traditional theory of meaning. Like the phrase 'original copy', a *re-presentation* would seem, by definition, to not be *im-mediate*, which is to say *without mediation*. That it is a *presenting-again* would seem to preclude its being unmediated. So the very *expression* itself is rife with apparent contradiction. Second, supposing that such an *immediate representation* were in fact possible, why then would the representation require the use of the term 'I'? If it is indeed possible for the subject to *represent* him- or herself *immediately*, that is to say, *without mediation*, **to** him- or herself, why then must he or she accompany that immediate representation with the use of a pronoun? As Derrida says, the 'I' would be 'a supplement whose reason for being <*raison d'être*> is moreover not clear if the immediate representation is possible' (*VP*, p. 81/95/106). Finally, the very notion of an 'individual concept', of a concept that applies to *exactly one thing*, appears problematic. It would seem that a *concept*, of its very nature, would be comprised of a definable *essentiality* or *essentialities* that, on Husserl's system, would be *ideal*, such that the *concept* would then be *applicable*, at least possibly if not *in fact*, to multiple empirical or ideal *things*. To talk about the 'concept of number', for instance, is to attempt to isolate the core, essential feature(s) of what makes a number a number. The concepts of 'horse' or 'person' function similarly; but it would appear impossible to formulate a concept for a specific empirical 'horse' or a specific empirical 'person'. For Husserl to invoke an *individual concept* that is applied, by the subject, *only to him- or herself*, is therefore quite provocative, as is his invocation of a *singular Bedeutung*. As Derrida notes, 'One cannot help being astonished in the face of this *individual concept* and this *Bedeutung* which differ with each individual' (*VP*, pp. 81n/94–5n5/106n1).

But moreover, Derrida argues, the 'I' itself functions, contrary to Husserl's claims, also as an *ideality*. Citing Husserl again, he notes that '"since each person, by speaking of himself, says 'I,' the word has the character of a **universally operative indexical** of this fact"' (*VP*, pp. 81n/94–5n5/106n1; my emphasis in bold). Indeed, it *must*, in order for the receiver to *ever* understand what any given speaker *means* in so using it. In order that the 'I' be used, useable and comprehensible by all persons who speak from the perspective of their own lived-experiences, in order that the 'I' indeed be *universally operative*, as Husserl says that it is, the term 'I' *must point to an ideality*; and here, all of our previous examples return to us. In order to understand statements of perception in the absence of the speaker; in order to empathetically experience the documented expressions by an anonymous lover of unrequited affection for an unnamed beloved; in order to understand *any* first-person narrative, whether fictitious or otherwise, this term 'I' must have some isolable *kernel* of meaning – it must, as Derrida says, be 'able to remain *the same* for an I-here-now in general, keeping its sense even if my empirical presence is erased or modified radically' (*VP*, p. 81/95/106).

This follows, Derrida says, from the intention/intuition distinction. If the meaning-intention does not *require* and structurally *forbids* the accompaniment by the fulfilled intuition, then the utterance or the written expression 'I', inasmuch as it is meaningful at all, cannot require, and indeed must again structurally forbid, the *fulfilment* of that intention, which in this case would be the actual embodiment of the lived-experience which the 'I' is meant to express. The same exact conditions that guaranteed the comprehensibility of the statement of perception 'I see now a particular person by the window', in the absence of the speaker, and in the absence of the *knowledge* of the speaker, also guarantee, Derrida says, the comprehensibility of the 'I' with or without the intuition of the content of the 'I' and for the same reasons:

Just as I do not need to perceive in order to understand a perceptual statement, I do not need the intuition of the object 'I' in order to understand the word 'I'. The possibility of this non-intuition constitutes the *Bedeutung* as such, the *normal Bedeutung* as such. (*VP*, p. 82/96/107)

Moreover, just as the *value* of the statement of perception remains the same, whether it is present or past, actual, possible or fictitious, the same holds also of the statement of the 'I'. The statement 'I see now a particular person by the window', strictly speaking, *means* the same thing whatever the status of its *author*. The author may be *dead* or alive, or the author might be a fictitious character. The perspective may be written in a journal, for instance, but it may turn out that the journal is little more than a literary creation of a fiction author. The author may be telling the *truth*, he or she might herself be *deceived* about his or her perceptions, or he or she might be deliberately *lying* – but whatever the circumstances of the author, living or dead, the expression 'I see now a particular person by the window' means the same thing, and is comprehensible, every single time it is employed. The same is true, Derrida says, of the 'I'. It means the same whether the author is living, dead or completely fictitious.

That the meaningful utterance or inscription of the 'I' *allows for* the non-intuition of the 'I' therefore *entails* the essential and structural *distinction* between the intuition of the 'I' and the functioning of the 'I' as a sign. The *life* or the *lived-experience* of the utterer is inconsequential to the operation of the 'I', which means that the *death* of the 'I' is, in fact, *already operating* in the 'I' every time it is used. This brings us back to the discussion of ideality that we undertook in our analysis of Chapter 4. There we said that whenever the subject employs signs *at all*, in order to establish his or her own relation to the *presence of the present*, he or she necessarily and essentially relates to idealities that *transcend* his or her own being. The very possibility of the sign, we said there, implies the death or the absence of the one using it. As Derrida says, '*I am* means therefore originarily *I am mortal. I am immortal* is an impossible proposition' (*VP*, pp. 46/54/60–1). Here in Chapter 7, Derrida takes this line of argumentation further. In Chapter 4, Derrida noted that the relation to the ideality that transcends the individual *implies* a relation to his or her own death, such that to utter *I am*, is to at the same time utter *I am mortal*, which is to say, *I will someday die*. Here, however, Derrida notes that not only does my use of idealities *imply* my death, the use of the 'I' structurally *requires* my death: 'My death is structurally necessary to pronouncing the "I"' (*VP*, p. 82/96/108). That is to say, the meaning of the 'I' must necessarily and structurally function the same way – *even in the absolute absence of the speaker*; the 'I' in the proposition '*I* am living' and the 'I' in the proposition '*I* am dead' *must mean the same thing*, and whether I am *in fact* dead or alive has no bearing upon the *meaning* of the propositions themselves: 'The statement "I am living" is accompanied by my being-dead and the statement's possibility requires the possibility that I be dead—and the reverse' (*VP*, pp. 82–3/96–7/108).

To complete this discussion of the essential distinction between intention and intuition, Derrida returns to the concept that he in Chapter 6 called 'archi-writing' (*VP*, p. 73/85/95), which he frequently refers to as simply 'writing'. Given everything we have said about the movement of signification, that language, to be *meaningful*, must be capable of functioning in the absence of the speaker and in the absence of the receiver, that it operates by way of repeatability, employing reiterable kernels of *meaning* from one empirical setting to the next, that it is the *trace*, the pure possibility of repetition, that makes the ideality of sense possible, and hence *re-presentation* that conditions and makes possible *presence*, Derrida claims, 'the freedom of language, "outspokenness," has its norm in writing and the relation to death' (*VP*, p. 83/97/108). While the voice has traditionally held the privileged position in philosophical perspectives on language, nevertheless even when the voice *speaks*, it can only do so by employing signs that point essentially to idealities possessing sustainable and reiterable kernels of signification; signs that, insofar as they are *ideal*, transcend the empirical being of the speaking subject employing them, and whose *meaningful operation* is itself the condition of the subject's *vocal use* of the signs. All of these characteristics are more closely emblematic of *written*, as opposed to *spoken*, signs. Spoken signs are considered the *most alive* because they are immediately connected to the animating intentions of the soul that utters them, but careful consideration reveals that these signs are also, for that very same reason, absolutely momentary, or even *most dead*. A *written* expression, once recorded, will continue to function indefinitely, long after the subject is gone. As Derrida says, 'This writing is not able to come to be added onto speech because as soon as speech awakens writing has doubled it by animating it' (*VP*, p. 83/97/108). As a *supplement*, therefore, *writing* precedes and conditions the operation of the voice.

If Husserl fails to articulate these same conclusions about the operation of discourse, or the *freedom of language*, it is because the *formalist* pole of his project (which demands the distinction between intention and intuition from which we *drew* those radical conclusions) is in tension with the *intuitionist* pole, which continues to govern, at an 'articulated distance' (*VP*, p. 76/89/100), Derrida says, the whole of Husserl's theory of language. Despite everything that Husserl has said about the structure of *meaningful* discourse, nevertheless, Husserl remains committed to the position that discourse, of its very nature, *aims at* the fulfilment of truth. Citing Husserl, Derrida writes:

'If the "possibility" or the "truth" happens to be lacking, the intention of the statement is obviously achieved only "symbolically"; it cannot derive the fullness which constitutes its epistemological value from intuition or from the categorial functions which must be exercised in its foundation. It then lacks, as one says, a "true", an "authentic" *Bedeutung*.' (*VP*, p. 83/97/109)[48]

Derrida goes on to say, 'In other words, the true and authentic meaning is the wanting to say-the-truth' (*VP*, p. 83/98/109). Here the French is particularly interesting, as the pairings of *vouloir-dire* ('meaning') are particularly contiguous. Derrida's words are, 'Autrement dit, le vrai et authentique vouloir-dire est le vouloir dire-vrai.' Another way to translate this would be, 'In other words, the true and authentic *wanting-to-say* [which, going all the way back to Chapter 1, is how Derrida understands this concept of the 'meaning' of a sign] is the *wanting to say-the-truth*.' What signs really *want to say*, according to Husserl, is, of their very nature, *the truth*. Insofar as it does not *fulfil* this task, discourse has *fallen short*, even if it is meaningfully structured. As Derrida says:

A discourse may have already conformed to its discursive essence when it was false, but it nevertheless attains its entelechy when it is true. One can well *speak* by saying 'the circle is square,' but one speaks *well* by saying that the circle is not square. There is already sense in the first proposition. But we would be wrong to infer from it that the sense *does not await* the truth. (*VP*, p. 84/98/109)

It is not *just* the case that discourse *aims at* truth and at knowledge, for Husserl, as though it were something that occurred after-the-fact as an add-on to meaningful discourse; rather, it is that knowledge is the *norm* that *opens up* the directedness-towards meaningfulness in the first place, 'the full presence of the sense to a consciousness that is itself present to itself in the fullness of life, in the fullness of its living present' (*VP*, p. 84/98/110).

What we must recognise, Derrida claims, is that even this so-called *formalist* component of Husserl's project, the emphasis on *pure logical grammar* from which we derived our radical conclusions above, is itself limited and perhaps even *shaped* and constituted by its intuitionist pole in Husserl's project. The *intuitionist* impetus, we recall, tends of its very nature towards knowledge and truth, and *demands* the fulfilled intuition, the full presence of the intended object to consciousness. We must bear in mind that even when we first discussed this formalism in Chapter 6, we spoke of it in terms of a 'pure *logical* grammar that is governed more or less immediately by the possibility of a relation to the object' (*VP*, p. 61/71/80). It is this *possibility*, Derrida now argues in Chapter 7, the possibility of a *fulfilled* intuition, that makes a discourse *meaningful* for Husserl. In other words, the *possibility of a fulfilled intuition* is what structures and shapes the so-called *a priori* laws of syntactical connection that *determine* the meaningfulness of a discourse for Husserl. The reason that 'the quadrilateral is round' is meaningful, while 'the hot is slowly' is not, is that the former, in virtue of its grammatical construction, at least *allows* the possibility of a relation to an object that *might possibly* attain fulfilment. As Derrida says, 'The difference between "the circle is square" and "green is or" or "abracadabra" [. . .] consists in the fact that the form of a relation to the object and of a unitary intuition appears only in the first example' (*VP*, pp. 84/98–9/110). Though the fulfilled intuition will always be frustrated in the case of 'the circle is square' or 'the quadrilateral is round', nevertheless, the sheer *possibility* of these expressions' *pointing* to an object – and this because of their conforming to Husserl's 'S is P' prescription for meaningful discourse – is what makes these propositions meaningful, for Husserl. A discourse is endowed with *sense* if it conforms to certain logical *laws*, and it conforms to such *laws* insofar as it is structured in such a way as to provide the possibility of the fulfilled intuition of the object. Hence, Derrida claims, Husserl has, 'according to the most traditional philosophical gesture, defined sense in general on the basis of truth as objectivity' (*VP*, p. 85/99/111). While there are no doubt countless modes of non-discursive signification, modes which express various depths and shades of *meaning* (such as sculpture, dance, painting, architecture, music, etc.), and while 'Husserl would not deny the signifying force of such formations', he would nevertheless refuse them the status of 'expressions endowed with *sense*, that is, the formal quality of logic as the relation to an *object*. Recognizing this is to recognize the initial limitation of sense to knowledge, of the *logos* to objectivity, of language to reason' (*VP*, p. 85/99/111). Hence Husserl repeats the traditional philosophical gesture, metaphysical in nature and teleological in scope, which dictates that *meaning* must conform with a *logic*, and this a *logic* pre-ordained by human reason, and driven of its very nature towards its own fulfilment – meaning *wants* to speak the truth, and to have that truth *realised*.

Nevertheless, as we have seen in this chapter, the particular uniqueness of the Husserlian project is precisely this internal constitutive contestation operating at the two poles of this tension. If the intuitionist pole of the phenomenological project provides the impetus for the *possible relation to the object* that structures the *pure logical grammar* of its formalist pole, at the same time, the formalist pole of this tension, thought through to its logical conclusion, entails the *freedom of language* and the *outspokenness of discourse*, the willingness to allow language to function in the radical absence of the subject and the intuition. Therefore we can see the way in which Husserl both *seems* and *does not seem* to belong to the metaphysics of presence; the *grip* that the metaphysics of presence holds on his thought, but at the same time, the radicality towards which his thought seems to point.

This concludes our discussion of Chapter 7, 'The Originative Supplement'. In what follows the three asterisks, Derrida takes stock of his discoveries in Husserl's text and formulates something of a 'Conclusion', in which he draws the entirety of the Husserl analysis into communication with the whole of the metaphysical tradition. Let us now turn to the 'Conclusion' of *Voice and Phenomenon*.

Conclusion

Derrida concludes *Voice and Phenomenon* by contrasting two modes of infinity: one thought within the framework of the Hegelian notion of 'Absolute Spirit' (as the *absolute wanting to hear itself speak*) and the other in the form of the différance, which Derrida has discovered within the Husserlian project, which entails the infinite deferral of presence; and he provokes this contrast by, in some senses, pushing Husserl's thought in the direction of a post-Hegelian Kantianism, employing the Kantian sense of the term 'Idea'. Thus, let us first define the Idea in the Kantian sense, and then embark upon our concluding discussion of *Voice and Phenomenon*. In the *Critique of Pure Reason*, Kant defines an Idea as 'a concept, made up of notions, which goes beyond the possibility of experience'.[49] For Derrida, this notion is inseparably tied to Husserl's concept of ideality; there is no concept of the ideal in Husserl without this Kantian concept of the Idea operating. As Derrida says, 'the ideal is always thought by Husserl in the form of the Idea in the Kantian sense' (*VP*, p. 86/100/112). Therefore, that it goes beyond the possibility of experience for Husserl entails that the ideal is *always, infinitely, to-come*; ideality, that is, can never be made fully present; it can never be fully given as an object of intuition. Hence once more we see that in a very important sense, Husserl's thought pushes him towards the *beyond* of the metaphysics of presence, but only in a sense.

Derrida begins this concluding section of *Voice and Phenomenon* with the following claim: 'We have put to the test the systematic solidarity of the concepts of sense, ideality, objectivity, truth, intuition, perception, and expression. Their common matrix is being as *presence*' (*VP*, p. 85/99/111). In French this reads: 'Nous avons éprouvé la solidarité systématique . . .'. His use of the word *éprouvé* here is quite interesting – it is the past participial form of the verb *éprouver*, which is another one of those motley terms whose polysemy Derrida exploits. In addition to the sense of *putting to the test*, or *experimentation*, it also has the sense of *experience*, as in *to experience*. There is a sense then in which Derrida's claim at the outset of this conclusion is that we have *experimented* with the systematic solidarity of these concepts rooted in presence, that is to say, we have *tested* this solidarity, because we have *tested the limits* of the solidarity of these concepts; and we have tested the limits because we have *experienced* these limits, and going along with the experience of these limits, we have begun to experience the passage *beyond* these limits as well. This is the experience of différance that Derrida is attempting to provoke, and it is the experience that would provoke thought beyond the metaphysics of presence, 'the thought of non-presence' (*VP*, p. 53/63/70).

Derrida once again reminds us of the senses of the notion of 'presence': 'the absolute proximity of self-identity; the being-in-front of the object in its availability for repetition; the maintaining of the temporal present, the ideal form of which is the self-presence of transcendental *life* whose ideal identity allows *idealiter* repetition to infinity' (*VP*, p. 85/99/111). Combining presence in both its *spatial* and its *temporal* senses, these three aspects of presence include, as we have seen above: the *presence* of the intentional acts to themselves, or the *absolute proximity of self-identity*; the presence of the object as an ideal object of intuition; finally, the self-presence of transcendental life in the temporal present, which allows for the constitution of the ideal sense. This is the structure of the *living present* which, as we saw in our analysis of Chapter 5, makes possible the iteration of ideality on the basis of the essential structure of *repetition* that lies at the core of the living present – it was only insofar as a sense is originarily *repeatable* that, we said, it could be *presented* in a primal impression. It is on the basis of this living present that the objectivity of the object, or the ideality of the ideal, is made possible as such. This is why Derrida says, 'The living-present, which is a concept that cannot be decomposed into a subject and an attribute, is therefore the founding concept of phenomenology as metaphysics' (*VP*, p. 85/99/111). It is not *decomposable*, because it is not something that, after-the-fact, happens *to* a subject or modifies a subject. It is, rather, the condition of the subject itself, *as such*.

But the living present is itself *ideal*, which is to say that, like the Kantian *Idea*, it can never itself be *given, as such*, in experience. The 'living-present is *in fact* really, factually, etc. deferred to infinity' (*VP*, p. 85/99/111). This infinite deferral, Derrida here says, is the différance, which is defined here as 'the difference between ideality and non-ideality' (*VP*, p. 85/99/112). With this claim, Derrida demonstrates the overall cohesiveness of *Voice and Phenomenon*. Above, we cited the following passage, stating there that Derrida makes one of the most important early claims of the book, important inasmuch as it lays out the stakes of the *project* of deconstruction:

> The whole analysis will move forward therefore in this hiatus between fact and right, existence and essence, reality and the intentional function. By indeed leaping over the mediations and by reversing the apparent order, we would be tempted to say that this hiatus, which defines the very space of phenomenology, does not preexist the question of language, and it is not inserted into phenomenology as within one domain or as one problem among others. It is opened up, on the contrary, only in and by the possibility of language. And its juridical value, the right to a distinction between fact and intentional right, depends entirely on language and, in language, on the validity of a radical distinction between indication and expression. Let us pursue our reading. (*VP*, p. 18/21/21)

In the 'Conclusion', Derrida now makes good on this promise – the *reading* that is *pursued* in Chapter 1 is now brought to its conclusion – having traversed the path through all the mediations which he here, in Chapter 1, claims to *leap over*, Derrida now, in the 'Conclusion', defines the différance as 'the difference between ideality and non-ideality' (*VP*, p. 85/99/112), which is for Husserl to say the difference between the *de jure* (or essential 'right') and the *de facto* (or the *in fact*). We must follow Derrida's steps here very closely.

The living present, the form of transcendental life, is the ideal structure of the givenness of subjectivity, but insofar as it is the ideal structure, and insofar as the ideal is *never* and can never *be* given, the *living present* itself, as such, is *never given* in the present. That is to say, the *living present* is **never** *present*; its *presence* is *always* deferred, infinitely. Yet, like all the other *essential distinctions* and *structures* upon which the phenomenological project is based, Husserl never relinquishes this ideality, which is never given in fact. Likewise, Husserl posits an *essential distinction* 'between objective expressions and expressions that are essentially subjective', demonstrating that 'absolute ideality can be only on the side of objective expressions' (*VP*, p. 85/100/112). As we have seen throughout, this is the problem guiding Husserl's thought during the entirety of his life, of the 'relationship, in particular, between the subjectivity of knowing and the objectivity of the content known',[50] the problem of the relation of the subjectivity of the subject to the objectivity of the object, and specifically within the domain of expressions that are essentially subjective, like the ones we discussed above as *essentially occasional*. Even in this domain, Husserl will argue that the *content* of the expressions themselves is ideal, and conclude on the basis of this point that the empirical fluctuation that accompanies the subject's meaning-intentions occurs only on the *subjective* side of the intention. Here, Husserl's passage, cited by Derrida, bears repeating, and we have highlighted in bold particularly noteworthy moments in the passage:

'The content that the subjective expression orienting its *Bedeutung* according to the situation aims at is an ideal unit of *Bedeutung* in precisely the same sense as the content of a fixed expression. This is shown by the fact that, **ideally speaking, each subjective expression is replaceable by an objective expression** which will preserve the identity of each momentary *Bedeutung*. ***Truly, we shall have to recognize that this substitution cannot be effectuated not only for reasons of practical necessity,*** *for example, because of its complexity,* ***but also that, to a large degree, it is not realizable in fact and even that it will remain always unrealizable.*** Clearly, in fact, to say that each subjective expression could be replaced by an objective expression is no more than to assert the *absence of limits [Schrankenlosigkeit] of objective reason.* Everything that is, can be known "in itself." Its being is a being definite in content, and documented in such and such "truths in themselves." . . . **But what is objectively quite definite, must permit** *objective* **determination, and what permits objective determination, must, ideally speaking, permit expression through wholly determinate word** *Bedeutungen* **. . .** ***But we are infinitely distant from this ideal . . . Strike out the essentially occasional expressions*** *from one's language,* ***try to describe any subjective experience in a univocal and objectively stable way: such an attempt of this kind is obviously vain.***' (*VP*, pp. 86/100–1/112–13)[51]

This passage itself provides us with a glimpse into the 'aporia'[52] of the Husserlian essential distinctions (*VP*, p. 86/101/113). First, the entirety of the phenomenological project *rests upon*, and so Husserl *must sustain*, the distinction between the *expressive* and the *indicative* modes of signification – even if the transcendental reduction has not yet been announced in the 1900–1 *Logical Investigations*, the impetus that will eventually *power* the reduction, the desire for *pure structures of meaning*, is indeed operative, and as Derrida will argue, everything that will come to be characterised beneath the banner of indication will be the same elements excluded in the mode of reduction: empiricity, exteriority and otherness. Hence the *essential distinction* between expression and indication (and going along with it, the distinctions between ideality and non-ideality, linguistic sign and non-linguistic sign, etc.) is indeed *essential* for Husserl. Second, the *de facto* use of signs, however, in communication, always involves a contamination by the *indicative* component of language. This is a point that we have explored from the beginning of the book. Thus, Husserl will be compelled to find a use of signs that is *not* communicative, which is to say, not indicative, and he finds such a use in the operation of the inner voice, the phenomenological voice, in the solitary life of the soul. Third, even leaving aside all the difficulties that we have encountered, involving the movement of temporalisation, etc., the interior monologue of the phenomenological voice, however, always employs signs of an *essentially occasional*, and hence, according to Husserl, essentially indicative nature – signs such as 'I', 'me', 'my', 'here', 'there', 'now', 'then', 'yesterday', 'today', 'tomorrow', etc. These signs, which are essentially indicative, are a constant accompaniment of the operation of the *inner voice*, which Husserl wants to maintain as purely expressive. Fourth, hence in order to maintain the pure expressivity of the inner voice, Husserl will be forced to conclude that the content of essentially subjective expressions is *ideally substitutable* with what would be purely objective (or ideal) content. The fluctuation of the empirical indeed operates on the side of the subject, but this is ultimately inconsequential for Husserl, because the content towards which the intention is directed is ideal and unchanging; and ultimately, *ideally*, it could replace the wavering empirical content of the subjective meaning-intention. Finally, the entirety of the sustainability of the expression/indication distinctions, however, rests wholly upon the ability to isolate a purely expressive mode of signification. If, even within the sphere of the inner voice, such a *purely expressive* function of signs is *in fact* elusive, then the very distinction upon which the *fact/ principle* distinction rests dissolves.

As Derrida says:

> Thereupon, these 'essential distinctions' are gripped by the following aporia: *in fact, realiter,* they are never respected, and Husserl recognises this. *In principle and idealiter,* they are erased since they only live as distinctions from the difference between principle and fact, ideality and reality. Their possibility is their impossibility. (*VP*, pp. 86–7/101/113)

Let us carefully dissect what this means. Put another way, *in fact,* the distinction between *fact* and *right* is never given. It is for this reason that, *in fact,* every single one of these essential distinctions, we have seen collapse upon itself through the course of our analysis – these distinctions are *never* sustainable, and Husserl says so explicitly, *in fact.* And *in principle,* the distinctions must ultimately cancel themselves, because the very difference between *fact* and *principle,* or *fact* and *essence,* would necessarily have to already be established *in advance* in order to sustain the distinctions in the first place. In order to have an *in-principle* distinction between, say, *expression* and *indication,* we would already require the establishment of the *essential distinction* between *fact* and *principle,* which is, we must remind ourselves, the very element that the *expression/indication* distinction would purport itself to provide. The expression/indication distinction, since it is never given *in fact* requires, in order to be sustained, the very thing (the radical distinction between fact and principle) to which it is ultimately designed to provide access. Husserl (against some of his other arguments and claims) will hold, in order to maintain the pure expressivity of the inner voice, that *all* of our expressions, even the essentially occasional ones, would ultimately be substitutable by an ideal, objective, content. *But,* this substitutability or this possibility itself is, Husserl says, *ideal:* 'ideally speaking,' he says, 'each subjective expression is replaceable by an objective expression which will preserve the identity of each momentary *Bedeutung.*' *Ideal,* that is to say, this substitutability is never given, *in fact.* In our reading of Chapter 4 above, we noted that any radical distinction between reality and representation can only arise through the use of the sign, whereby one domain or thing can be designated as 'real', and another as 'representation'. But once we acknowledge the nature of the sign as *essentially* representative, then this radical distinction, which only arises *with* the possibility of the sign, becomes unsustainable. Here in Chapter 7, Derrida makes a similar move. The *ideal,* for Husserl, can never be given *in fact,* nor can the *distinction* between the ideal and the *in fact* (which is itself ideal), and so it is only by way of a teleologically oriented *faith* that Husserl is able to sustain the distinction between *fact* and *ideal*: '*In its ideal value, the whole system of the "essential distinctions" is therefore a purely teleological structure*' (*VP*, p. 86/101/113).

This emphasis on the Kantian Idea in Husserl, Derrida says, which holds to the infinite deferral of ideality, should lead us to think that Husserl has never really believed in the teleological fullness of presence,

that he has never *derived* difference from the fullness of a *parousia*, from the full presence of a positive infinite, that he has never believed in the achievement of an 'absolute knowledge' as presence nearby to itself, in the *Logos*, in the achievement of an infinite concept. (*VP*, p. 87/101/114)

We recall that the founding gesture of the metaphysics of presence asserts the radical difference between reality and representation, holding that *presence* comes first, and then *representation* comes after. Our analyses of representation in Chapter 4, of the movement of temporalisation in Chapter 5 and of auto-affection in Chapter 6 demonstrated in each case that for Husserl, there is a constitutive, differential movement at work within the very constitution of sense and of the sign; this productivity would, it seems, severely undermine any absolute privileging of presence in Husserl's thinking. This suspicion would then be confirmed in Chapter 7, when we recognise the *infinite deferral of ideality* at work in Husserl's thought.

Yet, as Derrida also notes, this does not stop Husserl from positing a plethora of essential distinctions designed to do just that – to make presence primary and representation derivative: expression/indication, ideal/non-ideal, primal impression/retention, retention/reproduction, subject/object, intention/intuition, etc. Indeed these distinctions comprise the very heart of the phenomenological project; without them Husserl's project would not be what it is, perhaps would not *be* at all. As Derrida says, 'the entire phenomenological discourse is, as we have seen, gripped by the schema of a metaphysics of presence which relentlessly exhausts itself trying to make difference derivative' (*VP*, p. 87/101/114). The phenomenological project *exhausts itself* (or, 'runs itself out of breath', *s'essouffle*), for Derrida, precisely *because* Husserl does not believe in the 'full presence of a positive infinite', and yet, he constructs and continues to rigorously defend and reformulate an entire system of thought on the basis of the assumption that he *does*.

This discussion of the *positive infinite* brings us to Hegel, and to Derrida's assessment of the *closure* of the history of metaphysics. One might suspect that Derrida is attempting to champion Hegel *against* Husserl with the following quotation: 'Within this schema, Hegelianism seems more radical' (*VP*, p. 87/101/114), as though Derrida thinks that Hegel somehow got things *right*, and Husserl gets things *wrong*. But such a conclusion would be ill-advised. Let us look more closely at exactly what Derrida means. In the now-famous 'Preface' to *Phenomenology of Spirit*, Hegel makes the revolutionary claim that 'everything turns on grasping and expressing the True, not only as *Substance*, but equally as *Subject*'.[53] Hegel critiques Kant for leaving a vast domain of Being *unthinkable*,[54] and as Derrida says, Hegel 'brings to light that the positive infinite must be thought (which is possible only if it thinks *itself*) so that the indefiniteness of différance may appear *as such*' (*VP*, pp. 87/101–2/114). For Hegel, thought must reach all the way to the heart of being, but it can only do this by abolishing the distinction between thought and being (which is first radically posited by Descartes), and this abolition occurs by way of the development of Spirit, in what Hegel calls the 'Absolute' *thinking-itself*. The reader will hopefully by now detect the strong motivations of the metaphysics of presence within this concept, as well as the operation of auto-affection. This notion of the 'Absolute thinking itself' goes all the way back to Aristotle's *Metaphysics*, where Aristotle characterises the divine as *self-thinking thought* (*noesis noeseos*).[55] But in Aristotle, this thought occurs entirely without difference or mediation – the prime mover *thinks only* about what it means to be divine – and while it may act as the *organising principle* for the rest of the cosmos, in that it *attracts* the whole of being, the self-thinking thought of Aristotle's *divine* does not *permeate* the whole of being; rather, it is a self-contained self-thinking thought. In Hegel's system, however, it is only when the Absolute has posited itself as absolutely other, and then ultimately *overcome* that otherness, that the Absolute can truly be said to *think itself*. The Substance, as we noted in the quote from *Phenomenology*, must also become the Subject.

Hegel therefore *accomplishes* what Aristotle's thought merely *envisioned*; Hegel's thought *completes* the history of the metaphysics of presence, recognising an essential movement of *difference* or *mediation* as the condition of the self-thinking thought (or the auto-affection) of the Absolute. As Derrida says, '*The history of metaphysics is the absolute wanting-to-hear-itself speak*' (*VP*, p. 88/102/115). And it is in *this* sense, but only in *this* sense, that Hegel's thought, *from within the framework of the metaphysics of presence*, allows 'the indefiniteness of différance' to appear 'as such',[56] insofar as Hegel's thought requires an essential and constitutive movement of difference; and that therefore, *within the schema of the metaphysics of presence*, the comparison of Hegel with Husserl reveals that Hegel's thought is *more radical* than that of Husserl, because, *within the framework of the metaphysics of presence*, Husserl laboriously toils to *cancel* difference and to make it derivative. However, Derrida argues, this history of the metaphysics of presence is now closed. Hegel has accomplished what the metaphysics of presence set out to accomplish, and in so doing, he has cancelled the difference. That is, 'the achievement of absolute knowledge is the end of the infinite which can only be the unity of the concept, *logos*, and consciousness in a voice without différance' (*VP*, p. 88/102/115).

This unity, when accomplished, results in an *absolute life* which is at the same time an *absolute death*. As we have seen throughout, the metaphysics of presence considers the *voice* to be the primary mode of signification; the voice is most immediately connected to the *soul*, and hence it is immediately connected to the animating intention of the sign itself. The sign itself, strictly speaking, is like a *corpse*, a dead, inert *body* that requires the animating power of the *intention* (the expressive meaning-intention of a subject) in order to be *alive*. Hence the signs of the *voice* are most alive. However, as we have noted, the signs of the voice, *unlike* their written counterparts, fall dead the instant they are expressed. When one writes a letter, that letter might very well *live* well beyond the lifespan of the subject who wrote it, and may possibly live *forever*, unlike a spoken sign which, because it is most alive, is also most dead. We might even say (as Derrida does shortly) that the voice without writing is at once absolutely alive and absolutely dead.

How then does this connect back to Hegel? Hegel indeed *thinks* the infinite, but the infinite as the Absolute *thinking-itself*, without remainder or *outside*. Hegel thinks the Absolute operation of auto-affection; he thinks a structurally necessary *moment* of différance, a structurally essential relation of absolute self and absolute otherness; *but*, he does so only in order to ultimately *cancel* that difference. Spirit must posit itself as other only in order to ultimately recognise, fully and completely, the self *in* the other, at which point that opposition or that contradiction is overcome and hence the difference is *cancelled*, or, we might say, subsumed beneath a higher identity. But precisely *because* the difference is cancelled, there is no longer mediation, there is no longer movement, and thus there is no longer *life*. Hence absolute life, in the accomplished fullness of presence – a life without difference and mediation – is also *absolute death*. This is why Derrida says, '*The history of metaphysics is the absolute wanting-to-hear-itself speak*. This history is closed when this absolute infinity appears to itself as its own death. *A voice without différance, a voice without writing is at once absolutely alive and absolutely dead*' (*VP*, p. 88/102/115); and this is why the history of the metaphysics of presence is now, Derrida argues, closed.

But as Derrida argues, the infinite in Husserl, in the form of the Idea in the Kantian sense, functions differently than it does for Hegel. Here we must pay very close attention, for Derrida's moves are extremely quick. As we have just seen, for Hegel, the infinite is posited as a *telos* that must ultimately be *accomplished*. When it is accomplished, the difference that this thought posited as structurally necessary is ultimately cancelled, which we said, amounted to an absolute death. As Derrida claims, Hegel's 'appearing of the Ideal as infinite différance can only be produced in a relationship to death in general' (*VP*, p. 87/102/114). This Hegelian relationship to 'death in general' is *contrasted* straightaway with the Derridean relation to 'my-death': 'Only a relationship to my-death can make the infinite différance of presence appear' (*VP*, p. 87/102/114). In the constitution of 'transcendental life', the subject relates constantly to idealities that take him or her outside of him- or herself, in a necessary relation, not just to *any* outside, but to *my* outside, which is to say, to *my-death*. At the same time, and we might note, *against* Hegel, Husserl will attempt to marginalise this relation to my-death, which fits neatly within the scope of his project. 'Life', for Husserl, as we saw in the 'Introduction' to *Voice and Phenomenon*, is what unites the psychological life of the eidetic reduction, and the transcendental life of the transcendental reduction. 'Life', therefore, precedes and conditions the operation of the reductions, for Husserl, which is to say that life *escapes* the reduction, and death becomes an accidental, non-essential supplement to empirical life. This is what Derrida means when he then says that, 'By the same token, compared to the ideality of the positive infinite, this relation to my-death becomes an accident of finite empiricity' (*VP*, p. 87/102/114). Hegel, therefore, demands the passage through difference, only in order to cancel it, an absolute life that is also an absolute death; while Husserl, on the contrary, posits the fulfilled intuition as an unattainable ideal, constantly attempting therefore to make difference derivative, which means that the relation to my-death becomes a mere accident of empirical life. Each, therefore, misses something crucial about the relation between life and death, according to Derrida.

At the same time, the transcendental life, wherein is established the relationship of the subject to the ideality of the object, is itself constituted on the basis of a structure that is, essentially, infinitely deferring and deferred. What Derrida wants to show is that for Husserl, the infinite is indeed a *telos*, but it is a *telos* that is *essentially* unattainable; hence *finitude*, despite Husserl's best efforts, is a necessary and essential element of the structure. Presence, as the fulfilled object of intuition, is always, essentially, infinitely, *to-come*: '*The infinite différance is finite*' (*VP*, p. 87/102/114). But if 'life' is to be understood on the basis of this structure of infinite deferral, then life too is essentially (which is to say, not accidentally) finite; this discovery is key in *Voice and Phenomenon*. 'Life', as it has been revealed in the analyses of temporalisation and auto-affection, constantly differentiates itself on the basis of its *outside*, which is its death. To experience the différance is to experience the representation that is the condition of presentation (Chapter 4), the other that is the condition of the self (Chapter 5), the writing that is the condition of the voice (Chapter 6) and the absence that is the condition of presence, which is to say, the *death* that is the condition of *life*. But this is not the relation to an abstract, general or absolute notion of 'death' as found in Hegel. Rather, it is the relation to my-death, which now comes to characterise the différance: 'Différance, which is nothing outside of this relationship, thereupon becomes the finitude of life as the essential relation to itself as to its death' (*VP*, p. 87/102/114). This is why, despite Hegel's *appearing more radical* strictly *within* the schema of the metaphysics of presence, Husserl's thought nevertheless *points towards* the *outside* of the metaphysics of presence. It is the question of an infinite self-presence as opposed to an infinite deferral.

Husserl's thought, therefore, seems to be both committed and *not* committed to the metaphysics of presence. In his explicit commitments, as Derrida has tirelessly shown, Husserl remains ensnared within the structures of a metaphysics that makes presence (or ideality), first, and representation (empiricity, mediation, facticity, otherness), derivative. Nonetheless, as Derrida's analyses have *also* shown, Husserl's thought is ceaselessly pointing, in all of its movements, towards an *outside* of the tradition of the metaphysics of presence. So before concluding, we should say a few remarks about what that *outside* may look like: 'As for what "begins" then "beyond" absolute knowledge, *unheard-of* thoughts are required, thoughts that are sought across the memory of old signs' (*VP*, p. 88/102/115).

As we have attempted to show throughout the analysis, the push of thought towards this *outside* is a complicated endeavour. Deconstruction, we have said, is not something that Derrida perceives himself as having *created*, something that *he*, Jacques Derrida, *brings* to a text and imposes on it from outside the text. It is already operating, wherever *language itself* is operating. Therefore, deconstruction is already occurring within the texts of Plato, Aristotle, Kant, Hegel, Husserl, Heidegger, etc. But the entire history of the Western tradition is *constituted* by the founding gesture that would make *presence* first, and *difference* or *representation* (or language) second and derivative. Therefore, the entirety of the history of philosophical reflections on how *language* itself operates and *ought* to operate is also governed by these same presuppositions. *Thinking* beyond or outside this framework then, is very difficult. One cannot simply *revise old concepts*, as in so doing, these concepts then, like it or not, bring with them a measure of metaphysical *baggage*. At the same time, one cannot simply *create new concepts* either.[57] Whenever one creates *new concepts*, one is nevertheless working within the framework of metaphysics that *dictates* how concepts function. A *concept*, for instance, is synonymous with what Saussure called the *signified*, while the *word* would be analogous to the *signifier*. So to even speak of the creation of new *concepts* is, for Derrida, to already speak, in a sense, in the language of metaphysics. This is also why he famously says elsewhere that différance is 'literally neither a word nor a concept'.[58]

This is why the *thought of the outside* requires *unheard-of thoughts*, and Derrida is to be taken quite literally on this point, despite all of the paradoxical implications of this formulation – the necessity to *think thoughts that are unheard-of*. We have characterised différance as the *non-originary origin*, which is in some senses appropriate, but it is at the same time a risky formulation. For to speak of *origins* and of *originariness* is to already employ metaphysical language, as though we are seeking that which *comes first*; and as Derrida says, 'As long as différance remains a concept about which we ask ourselves whether it must be thought from presence or prior to it, it remains one of these old signs' (*VP*, p. 88/102/115). To genuinely *think* this différance requires a reformulation of *thought* itself, which is to say, it requires *unheard-of thoughts* provoked by 'an unheard-of question' (*VP*, p. 88/103/115). But it should be obvious by now that, by an *unheard-of question*, Derrida cannot simply mean 'a question that no one has ever thought to ask before', but rather, an entirely new *mode* of the question, with a completely different emphasis and purpose, one in which it is not supposed that there lies, on the other side of that question, a definitive *answer*, which is to say, a fulfilled intuition present for a consciousness. Therefore we must *hear* the concept of différance 'otherwise, that is, within the openness of an unheard-of question that opens itself neither onto knowledge nor onto a non-knowledge as knowledge to come. In the openness of this question, *we no longer know*' (*VP*, p. 88/103/115). This means neither the resignation of oneself to stupidity or ignorance, nor does it mean *non-knowledge* in the sense of *knowledge yet to be discovered*. It means rather that the *question itself is to become the model for thinking*. We often think of the *question* in the way that we were taught to think of it in school, as something that someone, who already *knows* the answer in advance, poses to someone who does *not* know it – the task of *thinking* then is to simply *arrive at the right answer*. But such a question cannot be considered a *genuine* question, precisely *because* the answer is already known. To say that the question is to become the model for thought is to relinquish the teleological faith in the *answer*. As Derrida says, 'Such a question will be legitimately heard as *wanting to say nothing*, as no longer belonging to the system of wanting-to-say' (*VP*, pp. 88/103/115–16). The question no longer wants-to-say, that is, it no longer wants to provide the *answer*. So to think this *thought of the outside* requires a reformulation of everything we mean by 'thought', 'concept', 'question', etc. 'In order to think this age, in order to "speak" of it, other names would be necessary than those of sign or re-presentation' (*VP*, p. 89/103/116).

This last point might well give us pause: has Derrida not himself argued, at great length in fact, in Chapter 4 (and have we not followed him in this argument throughout the remainder of the book), that *representation* must be thought as serving as the *condition* of presence? Is not the trace the pure possibility of repetition that makes the *present* possible? Husserl's example of the Dresden gallery can help us make sense of this. Derrida quotes an excerpted passage of Husserl:

'A name uttered in front of us makes us think of the Dresden gallery . . . . We wander through the rooms . . . . A picture by Teniers . . . represents a picture gallery . . . . The pictures in this gallery represent again pictures which for their part would make visible inscriptions that we are able to decipher, etc.' (*VP*, pp. 89/104/116–17)[59]

Husserl uses this example in *Ideas I* in order to explore the ways in which various *intentionalities* can be encased hierarchically within one another, as in a Matryoshka doll. In the example, a name is spoken, which inadvertently reminds the auditor of the Dresden gallery, and more specifically of the auditor's most recent visit. In the memory, the subject remembers walking the halls, and staring at a particular painting by Teniers[60] (here Husserl's choices of examples are quite interesting); this painting is itself a painting of an art gallery, which contains within it a multitude of other paintings. Husserl argues that, in the mode of *intending* this memory, the intention (the 'regard' or the 'look') can *remain*, it can be *sustained*, on any one of these various levels: there is the general level of the Dresden gallery itself; there is a secondary level of the experience of *walking* through the halls and looking at various paintings; there is perhaps a *tertiary* or even *quaternary* level of a memory of looking at a *specific* painting or at some *component* of that specific painting, etc.

Why do we say that Husserl's examples are *interesting*? They are interesting because he is attempting to articulate a structural *abiding presence of the gaze*, and yet he is already speaking of it in terms of a *memory* (which is a representation) and, *within this representation*, he speaks of a memory of an *artwork* (another representation), and more specifically, an artwork depicting other artworks (tertiary representation). We need only remind ourselves of the *role* of the artist going as far back as Plato. In Book X of the *Republic*,[61] Plato castigates the artist for producing merely a *copy* (a *pictorial representation*) of a *copy* (the particular 'thing' in the world). The empirical *thing* is a copy, albeit a fairly accurate one, of the *original*, which is the ideal Form. The work of art, therefore, merely reproduces a copy of an empirical thing, which is itself already a copy. Therefore, Husserl's example, while intended to *depict* the Matryoshka doll of possible abiding intentions, is itself such a nesting doll, presenting us with a remarkable *mise en abyme* of *representation*, culminating in a *memory* of a *painting* of *countless paintings*.

When Derrida says, 'Nothing has of course preceded this situation', and 'Nothing will suspend it with security' (*VP*, p. 89/104/117), he means that, strictly speaking, *there is no getting outside the gallery*. In other words, there is no *ground zero* of certitude or 'full light of presence' (*VP*, 89//104/117) which might serve as the backdrop against which we could ever distinguish *reality* from *representation*. To experience the finitude of infinite différance is to recognise that 'There has never been perception, and "presentation" is a representation of representation that desires within itself representation as its birth or death' (*VP*, p. 89/103/116). But to say as much is to demand a reformulation of the concepts of both 'presentation' and 'representation', because 'representation', strictly speaking, can *only* be thought as a *secondary repetition of primary presence*. That 'presentation' is always a representation of a representation means that 'the thing itself', the object of pursuit for the phenomenological project, 'always steals away' (*VP*, p. 89/104/117), because *the thing itself* is always, infinitely, deferred. Thus, the resolution of the conundrum, that representation is the condition of presence, and that 'other names would be necessary than those of sign or re-presentation' (*VP*, p. 89/103/116), is the realisation that, once *everything* is a representation of representation, 'the experience of the indefinite drift of signs as errancy and change of scenes (*Verwandlung*), linking the re-presentations (*Vergegenwärtigungen*) to one another, without beginning or end' (*VP*, p. 89/103/116), once there *is* no getting outside the *gallery*, the term 'representation', in the sense of a 're-presentation', is no longer sufficient. This is why, in a sense, the work of deconstruction, nearly ten years after Derrida's death, is in many senses just beginning. It requires nothing less than the responsibility of pushing the very activity of thought 'toward the unnameable' (*VP*, p. 66/77/86).

Final Thoughts

Having now completed our reading of *Voice and Phenomenon*, we would like to begin to transition into the next chapter of our book by noting two very important accomplishments of *Voice and Phenomenon*, accomplishments which will structure everything that Derrida does for the remainder of his life. These *accomplishments* are very firmly rooted in the *motivations* for the project of *Voice and Phenomenon* themselves. These points follow closely Lawlor's articulation of Derrida's motivations in his 'Translator's Introduction', and they are motivations regarding the reformulations of the concepts of 'truth' and of 'value'.

As Lawlor notes in his 'Translator's Introduction':

> there are two motivations for deconstruction, motivations which one might find surprising if one is familiar with the way Derrida's thought was appropriated and popularized during his own lifetime. Derrida's thought is motivated by the desire for truth and for the transformation of all values. (*VP*, p. xii)

As the reader may or may not be aware, Derrida's thought faced during his own lifetime, and still faces today, a great deal of *scorn*; likely Derrida faced more vitriolic acidity and ridicule than any other philosopher, certainly of his day and likely since as well, and much of this criticism was levelled specifically at Derrida's dealing with the concept of 'truth'.

Among the more famous of these is the very public textual rapprochement undertaken against Derrida by philosopher John Searle, which came to a conclusion with the publication of *Limited Inc.* in 1990. Though Searle refused to continue with the debate or to participate in the *Limited Inc.* volume, this nevertheless did not stop him from continuing to take jabs at Derrida in his later published works, as when he very poorly translates Derrida's famous line from *Of Grammatology*, '*Il n'y a pas de hors texte*'[62] as 'There exists nothing outside of texts',[63] a translation that, quite deliberately, avoids any serious engagement with the meaning, not to mention the most appropriate translation, of the quote. Another consistent attacker is Brian Leiter, who in a *philosophy bites* interview says of Derrida, 'philosophers generally think people like Derrida [. . .] are pretty bad philosophers and say a lot of silly and foolish things about truth, about meaning, about knowledge, and so on . . .'.[64] But perhaps the most vicious attack was the famous attempt, on the part of established philosophers (among them Willard Quine and David Armstrong) to prevent Derrida's being awarded an honorary degree from Cambridge University in 1992, citing his 'semi-intelligible attacks upon the values of reason, truth, and scholarship' ('*Honoris Causa*', pp. 420–1). There are certain academic circles wherein mocking Derrida, and precisely on the issue of *truth*, is readily acceptable. In fact, as the quote from Leiter demonstrates ('people like Derrida'), the name 'Derrida' becomes, in these circles, something of a reductive figurehead that represents *all* of what they deem to be 'bad philosophy'. With all this in mind, the declaration that Derrida's thought is concerned with the question of *truth* might perhaps come off as shocking or surprising.

But we must keep in mind, from the very first chapter of *Voice and Phenomenon*, Derrida, at the end of the chapter, is reflecting upon the notion that Husserl at times flirts with a concept of 'truth' as *production*, rather than as a *simple recording* of an ideality or *presence* that is already *out there* 'somewhere'. The analyses of representation in Chapter 4 and of temporalisation in Chapter 5 are driven in their entirety by the question of the *constitution* of truth. And when Derrida critiques the history of the metaphysics of presence, it is precisely in the name of 'truth': the metaphysics of presence holds a radical and fundamental distinction between 'reality' and 'representation', and claims that 'presence' is primary, while 'repetition' or 'representation' (language) are *secondary*, and as Derrida has attempted to argue throughout the entirety of *Voice and Phenomenon*, that claim itself is *not true*; it is *false*. But to undermine the metaphysics of presence – which, by the way, *defines* truth *as* presence – and precisely on the sense of the word 'truth', is to call into question everything we think we *know* about truth and knowledge and the relation between the two. It is *precisely* this task that Derrida undertakes in *Voice and Phenomenon*, and it is this task that Derrida, in the earlier essay 'Violence and Metaphysics: An Essay on the Thought of Emmanuel Levinas', argues that everyone who calls themselves by the name 'philosopher' must undertake for the foreseeable future. Hence one of the *accomplishments* of *Voice and Phenomenon* involves the preoccupation with and the attempt to reformulate the meaning of 'truth'.

The other motivation of *Voice and Phenomenon*, as Lawlor notes, is one of value, and of the *meaning* of 'value'. It is important to note that what Derrida has undertaken, through the deconstruction of presence, is the deconstruction of presence at precisely *its point of closest proximity*, the presence of *self-presence*. That is to say, Derrida has undertaken the deconstruction of the self-relation, and of our own presumptions as to the *immediacy* with which we relate to ourselves; 'deconstruction demonstrates that the self-knowledge of the "I am" is only apparent', as Lawlor says (*VP*, p. xxvii). In so doing, Derrida deprives *thought* of the *security* of its stable foundation. This provocation is a provocation to *think*, but to do so from within a position of instability, 'to exit the enclosure and experience the *insecurity* of the question' (*VP*, p. xxvii). This *insecurity* entails, as we have seen, that the *question*, as Derrida rethinks the notion, is not motivated by a teleological *faith* in the answer. The 'answer' would be a *present and fulfilled intuition* that would thereby close off the vitality of the question. Once an *answer* is given, the *question* would no longer be necessary; the matter would be settled. In Derrida's sense of the question, the matter is never settled, structurally, essentially and necessarily. This is a fundamental *insecurity*, precisely because it is unsettling, even terrifying perhaps, to think that there are no *answers* to the most important *questions* of our being; but this is the essential insecurity of life itself, and it is this insecurity that the deconstructive project opens up, that makes thinking possible, but thinking as *passage*, as opposed to thinking as *arrival*.

Finally, going along with these two, the presumed self-certainty of the 'I am' (a concept that Derrida will, in later texts, refer to as 'sovereignty') is the cornerstone of *much* of what informs our ethical and political concepts. Hence by deconstructing the notion of 'sovereignty' here in *Voice and Phenomenon* (even if that term does not itself appear even

once in the text), Derrida is provoking a reformulation of the question
of 'value' itself. In fact, we can safely say that *Voice and Phenomenon* is,
through and through, a reflection on the meaning of 'value' and of
'ethics' – it is a book of a profoundly *ethical* nature, even if ethical questions never emerge *as such*. The self-certainty of the 'I am' structures our
concepts of the 'will' and of 'freedom'. As we have seen, deconstructing
the metaphysics of presence is at the same time a deconstruction of the
voluntaristic metaphysics of the will and of domination and mastery.
In Chapter 1, we *chose* to 'be interested in this relation in which phenomenology belongs to classical ontology' (*VP*, p. 22/26/27), but on an
ongoing basis we discovered that this *choice* was ultimately unsustainable, as the fidelity to Husserl's thought constantly pointed us *beyond* this
belonging of Husserl to classical ontology. To deconstruct the notion of
'sovereignty' is therefore to deconstruct the *power* of the *will*. But to do
so then *demands* a rethinking of our treatment of *outsiders*: the madman,
the criminal, the traitor, etc., not to mention the poor and the broken.
The notion of 'sovereignty', the self-certainty of the 'I am', structurally
forbids the contamination by the other. It is this self-certainty that acts
as the guarantor for the concept of 'Natural Rights' that emerges in
the seventeenth and eighteenth centuries, which thereby serves also (in
Kant and elsewhere) as the theoretical basis of *democracy*. It is the notion
of 'sovereignty' that dictates that I *can*, or that I *can refuse to*, allow the
other into my world; that *we* may, *we have the right* (and the status of this
'we' is itself problematic), to close *our* borders and *keep out the others*; that
forgiveness is a *badge* that *I*, from a position of superiority, *can grant* or
can refuse to the other; that humans (some of them, at least), have *dignity*,
and non-human animals do *not*, etc. Therefore, the *deconstruction* of
sovereignty is tantamount to the *responsibility* to reformulate the very
question of 'value' itself, and of its basis. It is thus little surprise that
these are the very questions that will shape Derrida's later works; and
all of the analyses carried out in *Voice and Phenomenon* will inform those
later ethical and political concepts. Therefore, to conclude, and to echo
our earlier sentiments, *Voice and Phenomenon* provides us with the *germinal
structure of all of Derrida's thought*.

Notes

1. *Cartesian Meditations*, p. 139.
2. Aristotle, *De Interpretatione*, 16a.

3. This concept will play a hugely significant role in Derrida's understanding of the traditional definition of 'meaning'. In French, one of the primary ways of saying 'to mean' is by way of the phrase *vouloir-dire*, which literally means 'to-want-to-say'. There is thus an essential component of intention and will that underlies the traditional concept of meaning. This voluntarism will be central to the deconstruction that Derrida carries out, as we discussed above in the context of Heidegger.

4. Gottlob Frege, 'On *Sinn* and *Bedeutung*', trans. Max Black, in ed. Michael Beaney, *The Frege Reader* (Malden, MA: Blackwell Publishing, 1997), pp. 151–71.

5. See also Lawlor's note, *VP*, p. 97n1.

6. The Greek word *logos* is one with a very rich and complex history. It is the root of the suffix 'ology', upon which are based most of the sciences, 'psychology', 'biology', 'zoology', etc. But this colloquial sense of 'study of' is predicated upon an older sense of 'reason'. This can mean 'reason' in the sense of the *rational capacity* of the human animal, but it can also mean reason in an even broader sense of 'organisation of' or 'account for'. Since, for Aristotle, rationality was inherently connected to the animal's capacity for *language*, *logos* is also used to mean simply, 'language'. This is how Derrida uses it, as the Greek word for 'language', but given that Derrida is carrying out a deconstruction of Western metaphysics, it is important that we recognise that it is a word that possesses these other senses discussed here as well, as *logos* is indeed inseparable from them.

7. *Hic et nunc* is a Latin phrase meaning 'here and now', and more generally it refers to the empirical present, both spatial and temporal.

8. *Logical Investigations*, p. 185.

9. Aristotle, *De Interpretatione*, 16a.

10. *Telos* is a Greek word meaning 'goal', 'end', 'completion', 'perfection', etc.

11. *Geist* is the German word for 'spirit', and has a very long, rich and complicated history in the German language. Hegel's *magnum opus*, *Phänomenologie des Geistes* (*The Phenomenology of Spirit*), was published in 1807, and the notion of *Geist* plays a key role in Derrida's reading of Heidegger. See Jacques Derrida, *Of Spirit: Heidegger and the Question*, trans. Geoffrey Bennington and Rachel Bowlby (Chicago: The University of Chicago Press, 1989).

12. See Lawlor's Translator's Note 3, on p. xxix of *Voice and Phenomenon*. This passage in Husserl's text is found in the *Logical Investigations*, pp. 189–90.

13. *Logical Investigations*, p. 190.

14. *Logical Investigations*, p. 190.
15. In fact, the reader will note that when Derrida makes use of the distinction in Chapter 1 of *Voice and Phenomenon*, he explicitly says that it is a distinction that will come into play later, in §8 of the *Logical Investigations* (*VP*, p. 20/23/24).
16. *Ideas*, p. 160.
17. *Logical Investigations*, p. 1.
18. Lawlor's note on the French translations of these terms is particularly helpful in this regard: *VP*, pp. 101–2n2.
19. This strange formulation (*ontos on*) appears to originate with Plato. It combines the participial form of the Greek word *einai* (meaning 'to be') with the adverbial form of the participle. Hence it literally means something like *the beingly being*, or *the really real*, or the *most real* being, perhaps the *being of beings*, etc. See Anthony Preus, *Historical Dictionary of Ancient Greek Philosophy* (Lanham: Scarecrow Press, 2007), pp. 67–8.
20. This word, subtle and infrequent though it may be, is quite important, and occurs significantly in the very last sentence of the text. It occurs here for the first time in the text.
21. *Ideas*, p. 44.
22. Though Derrida does not here cite the Biblical passages at all, the precision of the formulation, and the tone of extremity (*we can go further*), suggest that Derrida is here alluding to the famous passage in Exodus, chapter 3, where Yahweh says to Moses, 'I AM THAT I AM.' See Exodus 3: 14. Derrida's French words in this passage are, 'Je **suis** celui qui **suis**.' In both instances, the tense of the verb *être* ('to be') is the first-person singular *suis*, or 'I am'.
23. The German word for 'moment' is *Augenblick*, which means, literally, 'the blink of an eye'.
24. Arguably, Husserl shares this designation with Henri Bergson.
25. *Consciousness of Internal Time*, p. 70.
26. *Ideas*, p. 195.
27. *Consciousness of Internal Time*, p. 43.
28. *Consciousness of Internal Time*, p. 41.
29. *Consciousness of Internal Time*, p. 42.
30. Recall that *Augenblick* ('the blink of an eye') is the German word for 'moment' or 'instant'.
31. The expression 'auto-affection' comes from Heidegger's characterisation of the structure of temporalisation in Kant. See Martin Heidegger, *Kant and the Problem of Metaphysics*, trans. Richard Taft (Bloomington:

Indiana University Press, 1990), §34, 132–6. Derrida adopts and expands upon this term, retaining in full its temporal dimension, but in order to characterise the way in which the self makes *contact* with the self in the self-relation. One could argue (and indeed the authors hold this position) that the entirety of *Voice and Phenomenon* is a meditation on the Western notion of 'auto-affection'.

32. *Logical Investigations*, p. 191.
33. *Phonē* is a Greek word meaning both 'sound' and 'voice'.
34. Martin Heidegger, *Being and Time*, trans. John Macquarrie and Edward Robinson (New York: Harper and Row, 1962), pp. 21–35.
35. These three words, *verbum*, *legein* and *logos*, mean respectively, 'word' (Latin), 'to speak' (Greek) and 'language' or 'reason' (Greek). See also note 6 to Chapter 2 of this book.
36. Aristotle, *De Interpretatione*, 16a.
37. In *Of Grammatology*, Derrida 'defines' différance as the 'unnameable movement of *difference-itself*'. See *Of Grammatology*, p. 93.
38. Aristotle's *first cause* in the *Metaphysics* is an *unmoved mover*.
39. René Descartes famously called for such a point in the second of his *Meditations on First Philosophy*.
40. *Consciousness of Internal Time*, p. 106.
41. *Consciousness of Internal Time*, p. 79.
42. In the 'Afterword' to *Limited Inc.*, this exact criticism is posed against Derrida by Gerald Graff on behalf of 'Some American critics . . .'. *Limited Inc.*, pp. 114–15.
43. *Logical Investigations*, pp. 191–2; my emphasis in bold.
44. *Logical Investigations*, p. 192; my emphasis in bold.
45. Derrida cites the following passage, from the *Logical Investigations*, in the footnote: '"In the statement of a perception, we distinguish, as for every statement, between *content* and *object*, and we do this in such a way that by content we understand the self-identical *Bedeutung* that the hearer can grasp even if he himself is not perceiving"' (*VP*, p. 79n/93n/103n2).
46. *Logical Investigations*, p. 218.
47. *Logical Investigations*, p. 219.
48. *Logical Investigations*, p. 196.
49. Immanuel Kant, *Critique of Pure Reason*, trans. Paul Guyer and Allen W. Wood (Cambridge: Cambridge University Press, 1998), A 320/B 377.
50. *Logical Investigations*, p. 2.
51. *Logical Investigations*, pp. 223–4.
52. As Lawlor notes, this term 'aporia' will eventually become a technical

term for Derrida, one that is distinguished from the 'problem'. See *VP*, p. 93n15. See also Chapter 3 of this book, 'Study Aids', specifically the section titled 'Aporias: Derrida's Later Concepts'.

53. G. W. F. Hegel, *Phenomenology of Spirit*, trans. A. V. Miller (Oxford: Oxford University Press, 1977), pp. 9–10.

54. Immanuel Kant is probably most famous for his establishment of the noumenon/phenomenon distinction. In an effort to resolve the epistemological *breach* of subject and object in the Modern period, Kant argues that the *noumenon*, or the *thing in itself*, is, *in itself*, unknowable; the rational subject can *think* the noumenon (hence the connection with the Greek word *nous*, or 'mind'), but it can never have *knowledge* of it. It can only have genuine knowledge of the *phenomena* of the thing, which are structured according to the pure categories of reason.

55. Aristotle, *Metaphysics*, Book XII, Ch. 9, in *Complete Works of Aristotle: The Revised Oxford Translation, Vol. 2*. Ed. Jonathan Barnes (Princeton: Princeton University Press, 1984), pp. 1698–9).

56. On numerous occasions, Derrida will explicitly say that différance first appears in Hegel, even though this claim is of course accompanied by many caveats. See 'Différance', p. 14. See also Leonard Lawlor, *Derrida and Husserl: The Basic Problem of Phenomenology* (Bloomington: Indiana University Press, 2002), p. 205.

57. This will, in some ways, separate Derrida from his contemporary, Gilles Deleuze.

58. 'Différance', p. 3.

59. *Ideas*, pp. 246–7.

60. David Teniers the Younger (1610–90) was a Flemish artist, employed by the Archduke Leopold Wilhelm, an avid art enthusiast, to catalogue the art collection he was amassing. Teniers did this, famously, by *painting*, in precise detail, the Archduke's collection, a number of times over a number of years. The detail is so meticulous as to include, not only *paintings* of the paintings, but also the inscriptions accompanying the paintings within the painting.

61. Plato, *Republic*, Book X, 598b–c, in *Complete Works*. Ed. John M. Cooper. Associate Ed. D.S. Hutchinson (Indianapolis: Hackett Publishing Company, 1997), pp. 1202–4.

62. Jacques Derrida, *De la grammatologie* (Paris: Éditions de Minuit, 1967), p. 227.

63. John Searle, *Mind, Language, and Society: Philosophy in the Real World* (New York: Basic Books, 1998), p. 19.

64. Brian Leiter, *Brian Leiter on Nietzsche Myths*, <http://philosophybites. com/2009/09/brian-leiter-on-nietzsche-myths.html> (last accessed 27 November 2013).

3. Study Aids

This chapter is designed to cover a couple of distinct but related bases. First, it is intended to function as a 'quick reference' for some of the more important concepts of both Derrida and Husserl – concepts that play a central role in *Voice and Phenomenon*. Second, I hope to offer the reader some positive strategies for taking the proverbial 'next steps' in engaging with and writing on Derrida's philosophy. This will take the form of a section containing recommended texts for 'Further Reading'. Finally, I hope to demonstrate the centrality of the analyses of *Voice and Phenomenon* for all the rest of Derrida's work, by offering a glossary titled 'Aporias: Derrida's Later Concepts', in which we shall offer concise descriptions of some of his ethical and political concepts from his later writings.

Glossary

This section is a 'glossary', but we must keep in mind that the terms that are employed in *Voice and Phenomenon* are not, strictly speaking, terms that can be *defined*, in any traditional sense.[1] To *de-fine* is to literally 'make finite', to set limits to and attempt to demarcate the *essence* of the concept to which the word one wishes to define *points*. By now it should be clear that such a characterisation cannot apply to Derrida's terms, for two primary reasons. First, they are concepts that are, as Derrida says, 'ultra-transcendental' (*VP*, p. 13/15/14). They are the *basis* of the transcendental, and are essentially fluid; hence one cannot assign *limits* to them, as they are precisely the structures that constitute and undo all notions of the 'limit'. Second, going along with this, Derrida's ultra-transcendental concepts bleed into one another. As we have seen, one cannot speak of 'différance' without at the same time invoking 'trace', 'archi-writing' and 'supplementarity'.

However, this section is designed to fulfil the role that a glossary would typically fulfil, providing concise descriptions of the central concepts of the book, in order to enable the convenience of quick reference on the part of the reader.

Archi-writing (writing)

This is one of those terms that only *explicitly* appears in *Voice and Phenomenon* one time (*VP*, p. 73/85/95), and it occurs more frequently in *Of Grammatology*. But all the same, it functions in *Voice and Phenomenon*, but usually just under the designation of 'writing'. This term is central in the destabilisation of the traditional privileging of the *voice* as the expressive medium closest to the soul. Going all the way back to Plato, and definitively in Aristotle, philosophers concerned with the question of the essence of language have held that what comes *first* in experience is the mental stratum, for which the *voice* (which is immediately connected to the soul) produces a spoken sign. Then, in order to ensure that the sign is communicable in the absence of the speaker, a *secondary* sign, the written sign, is produced, which transcribes the spoken sign. Archi-writing disrupts this traditional privileging of the voice. By archi-writing, Derrida means (along with **iterability**) the basic condition of the sign as such. One of the necessary conditions in order that the voice employ spoken signs at all is that the signs by which it speaks must already be *inscribed* in the language. That is to say, every time we speak any signs at all (even the sign 'I'), we are employing idealities that are permanent, stable, transferrable from one context to another and 'iterable'. They are signs that pre-exist me, and function with or without my presence. But these characteristics of permanence and stability are more properly characteristics of *written*, rather than *spoken*, signs. The voice is indeed immediately connected to the soul, but precisely on this account, the moment its signs are uttered they fall silent, while the ideal sense subsists. Even spoken signs, therefore, are 'inscribed' in the language. Without this inscription, spoken signs would not be possible.

Bedeutung

This German term is one that, along with **Sinn**, has a rich and complex history in German thought. In the *Logical Investigations* (and so in *Voice and Phenomenon*), it is basically synonymous with **Sinn**. Generally speaking, the word *Bedeutung* can be translated as 'meaning' (and this is how David Allison's 1973 translation renders it), though sometimes it is also translated as 'reference', in the sense of, that towards which a term or a name refers. For Husserl these two (the meaning and the reference, that towards which the term points) are basically the same thing anyway. Derrida, however, will want to give the term 'Bedeutung' a slightly more nuanced meaning. He notes in Chapter 1 of *Voice and Phenomenon* that Bedeutung for Husserl is always related to a concept of the 'will'. That is to say, the Bedeutung is what both the speaker and the sign *want to say* – the Bedeutung is the 'expressed' in the **expression**. Because of this, Derrida argues, the traditional French translation of *Bedeutung* as 'signification' is insufficient, and he employs instead another French expression for 'meaning', namely, *vouloir-dire*, which translates literally as 'to-want-to-say'.

Deconstruction

We risk blurring this concept irrevocably if we treat it as though it were a 'methodology' that were 'created' and applied by Jacques Derrida. It is not a strategy of literary criticism, nor is it relativism, subjectivism or nihilism, nor is it an 'ism' at all (as in 'deconstructionism'). In Chapter 4 of *Voice and Phenomenon*, Derrida begins working out what he means by this strange term, 'deconstruction'. It has to do with the disruption of the **metaphysics of presence**; and as he says in Chapter 4, the **metaphysics of presence** is constituted on the basis of a decision regarding the meaning of the sign. More specifically, it argues that presence is primary, while representation (the use of signs) is secondary and supplemental. We can see this in the form/matter distinction, which is one of the central distinctions in the tradition. This distinction privileges the 'form', which remains ever 'present' and unchanging, while the 'matter', which would come and fill out the form, is ever-changing. (Husserl employs his own version of this form/matter distinction in the concept of the **living present**.) Thus, all of its conceptual decisions of the **metaphysics of presence** will operate in accordance with a binary logic that privileges presence and attempts to suppress or repress absence. But in order to argue thus, the tradition of the **metaphysics of presence** must *employ* the very signs that it believes to be secondary and supplemental. The tradition must therefore erase the true nature of the sign by wilfully forgetting its representative character in the very moment that it uses it, and this erasure lies in the background of every moment of the philosophical tradition. This is where deconstruction gets underway, and this is why it is not something done *to* a text *by* a subject; rather, the very language of the text itself undermines itself, thereby undermining the would-be intentions of the given author (whether Plato, Aristotle, Hegel, Husserl, etc.). It is also important to note that, for Derrida, this metaphysical decision, the one that privileges presence, is unavoidable; presence is and always has been the founding value of the philosophical tradition, so to begin to challenge this is to already shift our thinking somewhere beyond philosophy, but to a place that is not really non-philosophical either. In other words, Derrida does not believe that we can just cast aside the problems that the philosophical tradition has left us with. We cannot simply *change* our concepts, because no matter how hard we try, those concepts will always bring with them some contamination of content. But neither can we just create *new* concepts either, because the laws and the logic that govern the creation of concepts operate in accordance with the very same foundational privilege of presence; hence the importance of deconstruction. If we cannot just cast aside the tradition and start anew (because to do so will always carry with it conceptual metaphysical baggage that will tie us more deeply to the tradition), we can nevertheless explore the ways in which the system of metaphysics undermines itself, by attempting to disrupt the system in its operation. In *Positions*, Derrida describes this in two moments. The first is a moment of reversal, wherein the governing binary of the text is overturned (representation over presence, writing over voice, etc.), while the second points beyond the binary itself (and hence beyond the system itself), towards the ultra-transcendental structure that made the binary possible in the first place. Therefore it points to an 'outside' of the system of metaphysics, attempting to constantly reformulate the question of what it means to think. Far from a nihilism, deconstruction is fundamentally utopian.

Différance

Of all of Derrida's terms, this one is likely the most difficult to 'define', and it is really one of the earliest, and longest-lasting, names that Derrida gives to this impossible but necessary structure that he attempts to identify in Husserl's writings (and elsewhere throughout the entire tradition). It is important to note, moreover, that of all of his terms, différance is one that is a completely Derridean creation (unlike many of his other terms, which are pulled out of the relevant texts and disseminated within the text itself). Différance is a participial modification of the French word *différer*, which is itself a bivalent term. On the one hand, *différer* means 'to differ' as in 'to not be identical with', while on the other hand, it also means 'to defer', as in 'to put off', 'to delay', 'to postpone', etc. Différance is therefore a contaminative structure, which both constitutes and unsettles the conditions of *presence*, in both a temporal and a spatial sense. Spatially it creates differences, gaps, etc.; temporally it delays or puts off the attainment, fulfilment or completion of presence. Différance is *discovered* in the analysis of the movement of temporalisation in Chapter 5. Inasmuch as the primal impression itself is always stamped by a sense that is already reiterable whenever it is impressed, this possibility of repetition is the condition of the primal impression itself. In other words, in the 'first' occurrence of the moment of present experience, there is already operating repetition and repeatability, a relation to what is outside of that moment of present experience. Repetition is not something that comes along after-the-fact and secondarily reproduces the presence of experience. Rather, the possibility of repetition (which he calls the **trace**) is a condition of the so called 'first'. Hence this relationality is *productive*; it constitutes the presence of the present moment. But inasmuch as the nature of time is that it opens onto what is *other* to it, it cannot forbid the *spatial* element either (however hard it may try). At the heart of transcendental consciousness, time bleeds into space, and space into time. This is what Derrida means when he says of différance that it is the 'becoming-time of space and the becoming-space of time'. In a similar manner (to the time/space distinction), this productive relationality is the condition of *all* of the cherished binaries of the Western tradition. But insofar as the relationality is vital and active, différance at the same time forbids the attainment of absolute presence. It conditions meaning, but insofar as this conditioning is active and unceasing, it does not allow the meaning to completely 'stabilise', which would disallow passage between a meaning and its opposite. Différance will entail that the interiority of any one term or meaning is always contaminated by what is other to it. So différance is the condition of possibility, but also the condition of impossibility.

Epochē

This ancient Greek word was a favourite of the early sceptical philosophers, and it means 'suspension', as in to suspend one's assertion, to withhold one's assent to this or that proposition. For Husserl, the epochē is the strategy of withholding assent to what he calls the **natural attitude**, which is the uncritical, non-reflective way we have of just 'accepting' as fact the 'real' existence of the external world. The epochē, we should note, is *similar* in some ways to Descartes' method of radical doubt, but the existence of the external world is not *negated* or *denied* by the epochē; rather, the belief in it is methodologically suspended. By suspending this 'faith', and keeping our analyses set on the structures of conscious intention and the possibilities of meaning, we can limit ourselves to a domain of knowledge that is absolutely indubitable. The epochē is very closely related to the **reduction**.

Expression
This is the English translation of the German word *Ausdruck*, and it is one of the two types of signs that Husserl identifies in the early pages of the *Logical Investigations*. While an 'indication' is a sign that points somewhere else, an expression is a sign that is itself meaningful, which is to say, that it is a direct manifestation of a linguistic, conceptual *meaning*. When Husserl sets about attempting to identify and isolate the structures of the pure possibility of meaning, it will be signs in their *expressive* form that he will be after. See also **indication**.

Indication
The English translation of the German word *Anzeichen*, this is the other of the two types of signs that Husserl articulates in the *Logical Investigations*. The indicative sign is a sign that in some sense *points* the recipient to something or somewhere else. A fever *indicates* an illness or infection in the body, but a fever does not *mean* illness or infection; animal tracks in one's yard *indicate* the presence of animal life, but they do not *mean* animal life. It is important to note, as Husserl does, that any time we use signs in communication with someone else, our signs, though expressions (insofar as they are linguistic, conceptual signs), are also indications, insofar as they point the listener to something else, whether an empirical object in the world or a psychological state on the part of the speaker. See also **expression.**

Iterability
This term only appears one time in *Voice and Phenomenon* (*VP*, p. 64/75/84) – 'reiterable' – but it is a term that plays a significant role, implicitly throughout *Voice and Phenomenon*, and explicitly in many of Derrida's later works. By 'iterability', Derrida means that a sign must be repeatable, as a condition of its being a sign. In order for a sign to function as a sign, at the bare minimum there must be some transferable 'content' that carries

from one empirical context to another, and is recognisable by others and across the span of time. See also Chapter 4 of *Voice and Phenomenon*, but especially (*VP*, pp. 42–3/50/55).

Living Present

This is the term Husserl uses to characterise, in a way that is phenomenologically rich, the structure of what he calls the 'consciousness of internal time'. It consists of the core of the primal impression, surrounded by a halo of retention and protention. The primal impression is the ever renewed *now-point* of each present perception, at each moment constantly filled out with new content. As each impression gives way to a new one, the sense of that experience is, Husserl says, *retained* over the next several moments, until it finally shades off and slips out of conscious view. This type of memory, in which that sense is retained, is what Husserl calls 'retention'. Each primal impression is accompanied by a retention of the just-past. In addition, Husserl says, accompanying the primal impression is also a directedness towards the future, filled out with certain implicit expectations. This directedness towards the future is what Husserl calls 'protention'. See also **primal impression**, **protention** and **retention**.

Metaphysics of Presence

This is another of those very Derridean terms that is nearly as difficult to pin down as it is ubiquitous in his writings. But it is in fact not as complicated as it may seem. The metaphysics of presence is basically synonymous with the history of Western religious and philosophical thinking. The metaphysics of presence operates on the basis of a decision, namely, that *presence* comes 'first', and then *representation* or *the use of signs* comes after-the-fact in order to attempt (deficiently or insufficiently, we should note) to reproduce the presence which has now in whatever sense been lost. The tradition valorises presence in both its spatial and temporal senses (see also **différance** for the ways in which Derrida attempts to disrupt this dual sense of presence); spatially, it valorises the presence of an intuitional act and its object to consciousness. This is why Husserl's phenomenological principle suspends the 'faith' in the real existence of the external world, precisely because it is *external* to consciousness, and hence it is contaminable by outside interferences; it is not 'present' enough to the soul. Temporally, the metaphysics of presence champions the present moment as the guarantor of certitude – the future is unknowable, and memory is, again, contaminable; the present is all of time that really *is*, and the phenomena of consciousness in the present moment are, as phenomena, indubitable. Whether the external world exists or corresponds to my perceptions of it, it is nevertheless the case that *I see what I think I see in the moment that I think I see it*. So the metaphysics of presence consists of a decision – presence is first, and representation second. On the basis of this decision, it posits binary distinctions in order to carve up the world as it needs to. The paradigmatic distinction for Derrida in *Voice and Phenomenon* is the form/matter distinction. Whenever this operates, the nature of any given thing is said to consist of a combination of form and matter – its form is its *essence*, which never changes, while the *matter* is the 'stuff' that fills the form out in all its empirical manifestations. The form is considered to be *most real*, while the matter is secondary, deficient and non-essential. As we can see, the privilege of the 'form' is that it maintains constancy through each new *present* moment. From present to present to present, the 'matter' is reconfigured ceaselessly, while the form stays the same. All the rest of the binaries of the metaphysical tradition operate in a similar manner. The term in the binary signifying that which is closest to or shares the most affinities with the soul, or that which is unchanging throughout all time, is the *present* term, making it the privileged term, while that which is fleeting, transient, secondary, etc., is considered the term of 'absence', deficient, flawed, even 'fallen'. We can also see, if we think about it, that this 'decision' that we said constitutes the tradition of the metaphysics of presence, the decision that presence is primary, in a certain sense forestalls thinking, because one already knows when one departs on the path of thinking where one's thought will end up. Thus, in attempting to **deconstruct** that tradition, Derrida is attempting nothing less than the reactivation of thinking.

Natural Attitude

The natural attitude is the non-thematic subjective attitude that takes for granted the real existence of a world external to consciousness. In this mode, the subject finds him- or herself in a world of objects, which subsist in pre-established systems of arrangement and value. The world *just is* as it *is*, and the objects in it *just are* as they *are*; this, with or without my knowledge of them, and with or without *any* knowledge of them. The subject also finds him- or herself at the same time a thinking thing – sometimes active, sometimes passive – an embodied soul or mind that looks out on this world of objects. The natural attitude is what is put into suspension in the enactment of the **epochē**.

Primal Impression

This is the term that Husserl uses to characterise the core of the living present. It is the constantly renewed now-point of each present perception. Each new 'now' is filled out with new content, and this content is 'impressed', Husserl claims, in the mode of primary impression. As it is the ultimate origin of what will come to be retained in the mode of retention, the primal impression is what Husserl calls the 'source-point' of perception. See also **living present**.

Protention

This term can also be thought as 'primary expectation', as Husserl calls it. Analogous to the role that retention serves with respect to memory, protention is a non-representational form of expectation. It is distinct, in other words, from the standard way in which we speak of 'expectation', as when we are awaiting this or that friend, or this or that event. Each moment of our conscious lives, Husserl claims, is accompanied by a basic, non-thematic structure of openness to the future. We sit in a chair without first checking its soundness because we *expect* that it will hold us; we lead with our head and shoulders through a closed door because we *expect* that the door is unlocked and will open unchallenged when we tap the handle. Most of the time, these primary expectations go entirely unnoticed, except when there is a breach of some kind – the chair breaks, or the door is locked. When this happens, our shock is an indication that we had previously expected a different outcome, even if this expectation was not completely obvious. This primary expectation is what Husserl means by 'protention'. See also **living present**.

Reduction

As we said when discussing the **epochē**, these two terms (**epochē** and reduction) are very closely related; so closely related, in fact, as to be almost, for our purposes at least, indistinguishable. As we said above, **epochē** means for Husserl the suspension of the natural attitude. This suspension is carried out in the mode of reduction. Over the course of his life, Husserl will revise a number of times the relations between the **epochē** and the reduction(s), also making more precise the senses in which the reductions function. In its more developed forms, there are

two modes of the reduction. The first is what is called the 'eidetic reduction' (this will later be almost completely synonymous with the **epoché**).
Eidos is an ancient Greek word that means 'form', and it is, in fact,
Plato's designated word for the forms (*eidē*). Under the eidetic reduction,
the phenomenologist brackets the real existence of the external world,
studying the objects of experience and intentional structures of consciousness. By way of a strategy called 'eidetic variation', the phenomenologist may examine the objects of consciousness and determine what
is and is not essential to their constitution. In so doing, he or she comes
to possess *eidetic* knowledge. However, this leaves a residue of the world,
namely, the psyché, untouched. When Husserl begins to radicalise the
phenomenological project, the psyché or the Ego will be bracketed, too,
and this will be the second mode of reduction, the transcendental reduction. This neutralises the whole of the world, including my own soul,
reducing it strictly to its status as sense. The mode of transcendental
consciousness is the condition of possibility for anything like a world,
according to Husserl.

Retention
Another way to think of this term is, as Husserl calls it, 'primary
memory'. Retention is a kind of memory, but essentially different,
Husserl says, from reproductive or representational memory. With
reproductive memory, we attempt to bring *back* before the conscious
gaze an experience that *was* present at one time, but has since slipped
out of consciousness. Retention, however, is still vitally connected to the
moment of the present. In other words, retention is a memory that has
never left consciousness. It is a contextualising memory that makes possible the experience of the present as such. Whenever you, for instance,
read a sentence in a book, you need to have kept in your consciousness
the previous several words that you have just read, in order to contextualise and hence understand what you are reading right now. See also
living present.

Sinn
Above, with regard to **Bedeutung**, we noted that these terms are
synonymous for Husserl in the *Logical Investigations*, and so for Derrida in
Voice and Phenomenon (since it is almost exclusively focused on the *Logical
Investigations*). Strictly speaking, *Sinn* is likely best translated as 'sense',
which in a broader sense, can also be rendered as 'meaning'. As Derrida

notes, Gottlob Frege (a contemporary of Husserl), published a famous paper, 'On *Sinn* and *Bedeutung*' (1892), in which he drew a sharp distinction between these two concepts. But in the *Logical Investigations*, Husserl treats the two as synonymous. When he finally does come to draw a distinction between the two terms (in *Ideas I* – 1913), it is not the radical distinction that Frege had imposed, but rather, **Bedeutung** is reserved for the sphere of specifically linguistic meanings, while Sinn covers the entire stratum of inner experience, including that stratum of pure presence that precedes language, the stratum that Derrida, following Husserl, refers to as the *pre-expressive stratum of sense*.

Supplementarity

This is another one of the fundamental terms of early deconstruction, and Derrida will gesture that it is synonymous (although to be sure this can never be a pure exchangeability) with **différance**, **trace** and **archi-writing**. The logic of the supplement, as Derrida attempts to think it, is that the supplement precedes and conditions that for which it is supposed to have been the supplement. This is not as complicated as it may seem. Looking to the entry on the **metaphysics of presence**, we see that the tradition is constituted on the basis of a decision – presence is first and representation second. That is to say, representation comes along after-the-fact in order to try to *hold onto* or to reproduce a moment of primary presence. Representation is a supplement. But as Derrida notes, the fact that presence *needs* a supplement at all is an indication that there is already, in the 'first' moment of presence, a fundamental, structural lack that will have *required*, in advance, the supplement to come and substitute for presence or to take its place. This means that even in its 'first' moment, presence is not 'full'; it is constituted by and with an originary absence.

Trace

This term is in a qualified sense synonymous with **différance**, and perhaps even closer to what Derrida calls **archi-writing**, given that 'trace' is a term of inscription. He defines the trace as the pure possibility of repetition (which would also put it in close connection with **iterability**). Yet another way to think of the trace is as the mark of otherness within the sphere of the same. Let us examine how this works. In Chapter 5 of *Voice and Phenomenon*, Derrida will say that the trace inserts the movement of différance into the pure presence of the now.

A necessary condition of any given sense being impressed in the primal impression of present experience is that it be, originarily, repeatable. There is no such thing, for Husserl, as a sense that could be rendered only once, in one moment, for one subject. That it is repeatable entails that it is retain-able, in the mode of **retention**. But **retention**, we have seen, is a mode of primary memory. This means that in a certain sense, a kind of originary memory is a precondition of the 'original' moment of presentation. This entails that the primal impression is always already in relation with, giving way to and giving itself over to, the mode of retention. This is why Derrida will argue that the trace *inserts* **différance**, which is productive relationality, into the self-presence of the now. The trace is the pure possibility of repetition (of sense); this entails a relation of the self-containment of sense to its own otherness; this is a condition of the givenness of primal impression; the primal impression conditions retention; thus the essential relationality of the trace constitutes the active production of the primal impression and the retention, in mutual commerce and self-differentiation.

Further Reading

Broad Overviews

The texts listed here are meant to be understood as providing general overviews of Derrida's thinking, should one wish to engage more deeply with Derrida's work. They are brief introductions, designed for accessibility, and both of them not only explicate the theoretical side of Derrida's work, but they then trace these theoretical elements into the later Derrida, after the so-called 'turn' in his thinking, towards the ethical and religious spheres.

Penelope Deutscher, *How to Read Derrida* (New York: Norton, 2006).

This volume is really nice for the Derrida beginner, in that each 'chapter' provides a very brief excerpt (usually no more than a paragraph) by Derrida himself, coupled with several pages of commentary by Deutscher. The reader is therefore given key passages, most of which are notoriously difficult, and then walked through strategies for reading such passages. In this sense it is almost like a philosophical and literary 'apprenticeship'. Deutscher's book is also helpful in that it provides some brief readings concerning some of Derrida's later concepts, such as 'gift' and 'forgiveness'.

Simon Glendinning, *Derrida: A Very Short Introduction* (Oxford: Oxford University Press, 2011).

Glendinning's book manages to pull off, in less than 150 pages, a general expositional overview of the major points and terms across the course of Derrida's development. It provides very short, digestible chapters each dedicated to a specific topic, term, or theme. The theoretical as well as the political and ethical are all covered in a clear but very concise manner that makes this an invaluable resource for those looking to further familiarise herself with the basics of Derrida's thinking.

Next Steps

By 'next steps', I mean texts that will deepen one's grasp of *Voice and Phenomenon*. This section is designed to point the reader in the direction of helpful primary and secondary material (including from the phenomenological tradition itself), relevant to *Voice and Phenomenon*. The body of secondary literature on Derrida is vast, and since this present volume deals with *Voice and Phenomenon*, which is an analysis of Husserl, I have listed here materials that either help one become more familiar with the phenomenological tradition itself, or that explore the relations primarily between Derrida and Husserl, but more generally between Derrida and the phenomenological tradition. However, I should offer a word of caution. The texts listed here are offered as 'next-step' sorts of texts, by which I mean that they are not to be taken lightly. With the exception of the specifically phenomenological materials, these volumes engage deeply with the question of Derrida's relation to the phenomenological tradition, and as such they presuppose a certain depth of knowledge of other figures (such as Heidegger and Levinas) from the tradition of phenomenology. Nonetheless, they are the best place to begin deepening one's knowledge of Derrida and his relation to the phenomenological tradition.

Dermot Moran and Tim Mooney (eds), *The Phenomenology Reader* (London: Routledge, 2002).

In order to truly enrich one's reading of *Voice and Phenomenon*, a bit more of an in-depth engagement with the phenomenological tradition is a must. Moran and Mooney's volume is not exhaustive by any means; but that is more a result of the massiveness and diversity of the phenomenological tradition itself than anything else. This is the only volume of *primary* materials I have listed in this section; and this is because it is simply an excellent anthology for familiarising oneself with excerpts from some of the major moments of the phenomenological tradition, *including* a fairly sizable bit of Franz Brentano (Husserl's mentor). Besides substantive excerpts from Husserl and Heidegger, one will also find excerpts from many of the other thinkers discussed in Chapter 1 of this book: Sartre, Merleau-Ponty and Levinas.

Dermot Moran, *Introduction to Phenomenology* (London: Routledge, 2000).

Though this book is only a little over a decade old, it is quite literally a classic. It is the perfect 'companion' piece to the Moran and Mooney anthology, and it may even be the case that, though both (primaries and secondaries) are crucial, given the necessarily limited selections included in the anthology, and the scholarly depth in *this* volume, Moran's secondary volume might have a slight edge. It is truly an accessible and clear work of exposition, and one that, in under 500 pages (of actual text), manages to cover with tremendous depth the most significant elements of the phenomenological tradition. Moran is primarily a Husserl scholar, and it shows; the work on Husserl in this volume is profoundly helpful. But it parallels the anthology in that it also includes chapters on Sartre, Merleau-Ponty and Levinas. This book, in combination with the Moran and Mooney *Reader*, would be an excellent way for one to flesh out his or her knowledge of the phenomenological tradition.

Leonard Lawlor, 'Translator's Introduction: The Germinal Structure of Derrida's Thought', in Jacques Derrida, *Voice and Phenomenon: Introduction to the Problem of the Sign in Husserl's Phenomenology*, trans. Leonard Lawlor (Evanston: Northwestern University Press, 2011), pp. xi–xxviii.

Leonard Lawlor is one of the foremost Derrida scholars, certainly in the United States and arguably in the world, and this is reflected in his 'Translator's Introduction' to the 2011 translation of *Voice and Phenomenon*. It is remarkably brief, given the clarity and density of its exposition; and it does an excellent job of quickly laying out the stakes and the progression of the argument of *Voice and Phenomenon*.

Leonard Lawlor, *Derrida and Husserl: The Basic Problem of Phenomenology* (Bloomington: Indiana University Press, 2002).

After over a decade, this book remains one of the best overall introductions to Derrida's thinking, but this requires some qualification, because it is not an 'introductory' text by any estimation. It explores thoroughly Derrida's engagements with and appropriations of Husserl's thinking, providing close, rigorous readings of nearly all of Derrida's major writings on Husserl's thought (including *Voice and Phenomenon*). Moreover, it follows the thread into Derrida's later, political writings as well, offering a close reading of *Specters of Marx*. Since it is so detailed in its discussion of Derrida's engagement with Husserl, and since it is during this formative period in Derrida's life that he 'becomes' Derrida, this volume analyses in admirable depth the formations of the concepts that would later come to mark the entirety of Derrida's thought. This is what is meant when we say that it is one of the best overall introductions to Derrida's thinking.

Paola Marrati, *Genesis and Trace: Derrida Reading Husserl and Heidegger*, trans. Simon Sparks (Stanford: Stanford University Press, 2005).

This book deals with the concepts of time, genesis, origin and trace in Derrida's interaction with the thought of Husserl and Heidegger. These are all concepts that have been explored extensively in the reading of *Voice and Phenomenon*. So, that said, assuming that the reader is willing to obtain some familiarisation with the thought of Martin Heidegger, Marrati's volume provides a deep and thoughtful immersion into a broader conversation regarding Derrida's understanding of finitude, ideality and the transcendental. This is a very good text to pick up after working carefully through *Voice and Phenomenon* and after having become familiar with some of the major elements in Heidegger's thought.

Joshua Kates, *Essential History: Jacques Derrida and the Development of Deconstruction* (Evanston: Northwestern University Press, 2005).

There is a sense in which this text sets out to be broader in scope than the other two major secondary texts listed here. Kates sets out with very specific questions in mind, having to do with the nature of deconstruction itself, Derrida's motivations, the question of Derrida's preoccupation with language and representation, and whether or not this commits Derrida to a form of scepticism. In trying to work out the answers to these questions, Kates turns primarily (though not exclusively) to Derrida's formative years in the phenomenological tradition. Along the way he provides reflections, some critical, on the other two texts (Lawlor's and Marrati's) mentioned in this section.

Aporias: Derrida's Later Concepts[2]

This final section is designed to provide an introductory foray into some of Derrida's later concepts. It is a 'glossary', similar to the one that begins the present chapter, but it is unique in that the terms found herein are not found in *Voice and Phenomenon* or, for that matter, any of Derrida's other late-1960s texts. This section is offered for two reasons. First, it is offered in order to provide a basic introduction to some of the questions and concerns that drive Derrida in his later thinking, so that one can leave this volume, not only with an in-depth understanding of *Voice and Phenomenon*, but also with a general introduction to the whole of Derrida's thinking. Second, it is also provided in order to demonstrate the continuity of Derrida's thinking, the fact that these later ethical, religious and political concepts emerge, not from nowhere, but rather from out of the very motivations and analyses that we find in *Voice and Phenomenon*. The two fundamental elements that will continue to play a significant role in Derrida's later thinking, and we will see these crop up in one form or another in each of these later concepts, are: (1) the deconstruction of the notion of 'sovereignty'; (2) the infinite deferral of presence.

Animality

Over the course of Derrida's career, and especially with the more extensive engagement with the thinking of Heidegger, the question of 'the animal' became increasingly pressing. It is not difficult to see why. Let us look for a moment at the notion of what he calls 'sovereignty'. This is the human perception of self-consciousness, that we seem to have direct, unmediated access to the fullness of experience regarding ourselves; we seem to be absolutely transparent to ourselves. This unmediated self-presence becomes, in the seventeenth century with Descartes, synonymous with reason itself, and then with Locke, it becomes the guarantor or the basis of what we call human 'rights'. These rights are absolute and unassailable, even by the monarch. There is an essential connection in the Western tradition between the concepts of 'rationality', 'sovereignty' and 'rights'. We can see this tendency at multiple points throughout the philosophical tradition. Descartes, for instance, divides the whole of reality into thinking substances (souls) and extended substances (or bodies). Once this either/or is established, and everything is *either* body *or* mind, and once 'thinking' is defined in the precisely anthropocentric way that Descartes defines it, identifying it as the essential activity of the soul, it follows, based upon the way that Descartes has organised his system, that animals have no souls, which is to say that animals do not *think*, and hence strictly speaking, cannot *feel* (insofar as sensation is a mode of thinking). For Kant (who is at least a little bit kinder to non-human animals in his writings than Descartes), only that which is capable of morality has dignity, and since only rationality houses morality, it follows that only human beings can have dignity. And while Kant will nevertheless say that we ought not to be wantonly *cruel* to animals, it has nothing to do with the animal itself, but rather, because *any* exercise of cruelty is an assault on *human* dignity. Heidegger, again, is much 'kinder' than Descartes, but he will nevertheless argue that animals 'are poor in world', which is to say, they indeed relate to the world, but not to the world *as such*. For example, a squirrel, to be sure, relates itself to the tree, but not to the tree *as* a tree, but rather, to the tree as 'a place to build my nest and hide my food', and this on the basis of the fact that a squirrel is not Dasein (not a being who concerns itself with the meaning of its being). The philosophical tradition has a long history of attempting to articulate what the *human animal* is, often on the basis of reason or language, and then once this criterion is posited, it lumps together all non-human animals under the designation '*the* animal', as though all non-human animals are, at bottom, really all the same.

When we attempt to formulate an ontological criterion of distinction between human and non-human animals, we are led to embrace a metaphysical separationism, in which all non-human animals are simply a *different kind of thing* than humans, and depending upon how we understand this separation, we might be led further to think that humans, being the dominant ones, can treat the non-humans however it suits us. This perception has become increasingly cruel and brutal of late. We no longer simply eat animals that happen to be already present here on earth, as our ancestors did. We now *manufacture* them in massive quantities. We falsify their procreative mechanisms by artificially inseminating them, instantly kill babies who do not meet certain criteria, we manipulate their genetic structures, feed them the lowest possible grade of food, and confine them in unbearably tight spaces for the brief duration of their lives, before savagely killing them in the most cost-effective ways possible. Moreover, we do what we can to avoid thinking about it, because the imagery of the savagery and barbarity of which humans are capable cannot *but* evoke our sympathy for the suffering creature. We therefore take great pains in order to wilfully blind ourselves to suffering. Derrida cites the utilitarian philosopher, Jeremy Bentham, who claims that the relevant question in how we treat our non-human counterparts is not the question as to whether or not they can reason or use language, but rather, whether or not they can *suffer*. This is significant, for Derrida, because *suffering* is another one of those traits that (along with reason, shame, language, self-awareness, love, etc.) has been traditionally deprived by man of the non-human animal, and limited only to the domain of human experience. Only humans, as Descartes attempted to argue, can truly *suffer*. But 'suffering' connotes *incapacity*. In the Greek, *pathos* (from whence the word 'suffering' is derived) is opposed to *ethos*; and ethos is concerned with what one *does* whereas pathos has to do with what happens *to* one. (The word 'passion' for instance comes from pathos, and we use it in the way we do because the passions are what *overtake* us – we do not choose them.) To say that only humans *can* suffer, therefore, is to say that only humans have the power to be powerless. But this in itself challenges our accepted notion of 'sovereignty', infusing it with a *weakness*. Here, Derrida will employ elements of his argument from *Voice and Phenomenon*, in order to demonstrate that our perceived access to our own consciousness is not as immediate as we might think.

Conversely, Derrida says, those of us who do *not* wish to go the route of metaphysical separationism might think that the only alternative is to embrace a biologistic continuism, where life is organised hierarchically, with rationality at the top, but without any precise ontological breach between a species and that species immediately beneath it. This strategy, though well-intended, Derrida thinks, is still quite problematic for a number of reasons. First, there is still a hierarchy in play, where the limits and the differences between various species are organised sequentially, which does not respect the many differences and relations between all varieties of animal life. Second, rationality is still the benchmark against which the other animals are 'measured', so when we extend 'rights' to other animals, it often tends to be on the basis of the extent to which they are perceived to be *like us*. Again, the deconstruction of sovereignty will operate here in such a way as to undermine the perceived absolute authority of rationality. Moreover, Derrida will argue that an ethics based upon categories of 'identity' (respect the ones who are 'like us') is not truly an ethics at all. Finally, following on the previous note, depending upon where one draws the line of 'rationality' (and depending on how one understands the measure of responsibility to non-rationality), having this 'continuum' in play can provide (and has done so in the past) a measure of 'scientific justification' for all manner of cruelty and murder against even our fellow *humans*. Derrida will propose instead what he calls 'limitrophy', which means a broadening and intensification and dissemination of the limit. Rather than attempting to 'cancel' differences or limits, it multiplies them. This abolishes the hierarchy, because 'rationality' (which has already been problematised through the deconstruction of 'sovereignty') becomes simply one difference among others; but in abolishing the hierarchy, this limitrophy re-establishes the many variations that obtain between different species of life.

For further reading, see *The Animal that therefore I Am*; *The Beast and the Sovereign, Volume I*; *The Beast and the Sovereign, Volume II*.

Aporia

This is a Greek term that literally means 'no way out' or 'impasse', combining the alpha privative with the root *poros* meaning 'passage'. As Derrida's questions and concerns begin to shift more explicitly into the domains of the political, religious and ethical (although, to be clear, these questions were always operating in Derrida's work, and he says so explicitly), he begins to characterise the work of deconstruction in the terms of 'aporia'. In the 1989 essay 'Force of Law: The "Mystical Foundation of Authority"', he defines this as 'an experience of the impossible' (p. 243). Indeed, many of the terms discussed in this section (**forgiveness**, **gift**, **hospitality**, **justice** and **responsibility**) fall explicitly under the banner of the aporetic in Derrida's later writings. For

Derrida, the aporia is essentially connected with the moment of 'decision'. The decision is always, essentially, fundamentally 'undecidable'. To put this in very basic terms, we need only consider what happens in cases where a 'decision' must be made. We characterise a moment as a moment of 'decision' precisely because, while there may seem to be, as we say, 'pros and cons' that pull us into opposing directions, there is, on either side of the decision, nothing definitive that would delineate a clear path for us. The word 'decision' is etymologically connected to words that mean 'cut' (like 'scissors', 'incision', etc.). To make a 'decision' is to make a cut in the fabric of things – a cut that was not previously there, and there is nothing that could clearly mark out for us, prior to that decision, the path that must be chosen. This is precisely what we mean by 'decision'. Derrida will argue in *The Gift of Death* that the decision is always something akin to a Kierkegaardian 'leap of faith', and always a kind of 'madness', in that it defies reason. Reason cannot dictate (and if it could, the moment would not, properly speaking, be a moment of decision). To experience the aporia is to experience that one *must* decide and cannot *avoid* deciding, but that the decision will ultimately be made in the face of undecidability. To experience the aporia is to be drawn into the experience of the necessity of impossibility. This point is paramount; in describing these aporetic structures, Derrida does not want to suggest that they are absolutely impossible. For instance, the **gift**, Derrida says, is not absolutely impossible. The point of the aporia is that the aporetic concept *becomes* possible *as* the experience of the impossible.

For further reading, see *Aporias*; 'The Force of Law: The "Mystical Foundation of Authority"'; *The Gift of Death Second Edition & Literature in Secret*.

Democracy to Come

The concept of 'democracy to come', which employs the structure of infinite deferral that we have seen in *Voice and Phenomenon*, is first hinted at in 'The Force of Law', officially introduced in *Specters of Marx*, addressed in *The Politics of Friendship* and articulated more thoroughly in *Rogues*. As in the cases of all his other aporetic concepts, Derrida wants to radically distinguish what he calls 'democracy to come' or a pure democracy from democracy as it is and has been in fact instituted in historical and political constitutions. In *Rogues*, he writes that 'Democracy has always been suicidal, and if there is a to-come for it, it is only on the condition of thinking life otherwise, life and the force of life' (*Rogues*, p. 33). Here we must recall that this reformulation of the concept of life was one of the central tasks of *Voice and Phenomenon*. The concept of life against which this reformulation takes place is one of absolute and unmediated self-presence which, we concluded in the end, once obtained, is at the same time absolutely alive and absolutely dead. In *Rogues*, Derrida suggests that democracy suffers from an autoimmunitary logic. Here Derrida is lifting a term from the domain of biology; 'autoimmunity' describes any number of diseases whereby the body of the organism begins to recognise its own constituent parts as foreign and hostile to it, and therefore begins to attack itself.

That democracy suffers from an autoimmunity which is, Derrida says, 'constitutive' (*Rogues*, p. 63), entails that it destroys itself by means of and in the name of the very thing that gives it its impetus in the first place. In the name of democracy, democracy destroys itself. Let us look to how it is constitutive; democracy, Derrida says, is the inheritance of a promise, the promise of freedom and equality, for instance. This promise, however, can only be brought to fruition in a system of rule; in order for 'democracy' to be, in order for it to genuinely be a 'rule' of the 'people', it must set conditions for what counts in order that one be one of the 'people'. It must make decisions about who is, and who is not, a friend to 'democracy', as well as how to treat those who are outside the system, and this is absolutely imperative; for if the wrong sorts of participants are allowed entry into the 'demos', then the democracy itself and all that it stands for, is threatened. The democratic values of freedom and equality would be in peril if the wrong elements were permitted entry into the borders, or into the political life, of the democracy. If we push this logic to its limit, we see that in attempting to constitute itself as a 'people', the democracy thereby attempts to homogenise the diversity that gave it its purity. In attempting to be most fully 'alive' democratically, by securing its own identity, it thereby becomes absolutely suicidal. As Derrida notes, the most horrendous totalitarian regimes ascended to power through democratic mechanisms.

'Democracy to come' functions similarly to **justice**. Indeed, Derrida notes that there is an inextricable and essential relation between the two terms. Democracy to come is not to be thought of in the sense of a Kantian Idea. The Idea in the Kantian sense, even if infinitely deferred, Derrida says, is at least in principle (and here Derrida does assert that he is speaking of contemporary applications of Kant, as opposed to a strictly Kantian interpretation) an ideal 'possibility'. Democracy to come, however, is not to be thought of as a possibility, even an infinitely deferred possibility, which might lie at some ideal horizon of the end of history. Democracy to come is an **aporia** that is, of its very nature, impossible. This is what distinguishes the to-come (the *à venir*) from the 'future', for Derrida, the 'future' being conceived as a time that will at some point be 'present', while the to-come remains forever to-come. But as is the structure of the **aporia**, the possibility of this promise of democracy is experienced precisely as the experience of its impossibility.

Moreover (and as is the case with **justice**), democracy to come is not something for which we can wait. Rather, the demand for democracy to come is here and now. It therefore calls for 'a militant and interminable political critique' (*Rogues*, p. 86). So long as the so-called 'democracies' of the world tolerate unnecessary suffering, starvation, oppression, international or interreligious hostility, preventable disease, poverty, and so on, whether within their own borders or elsewhere, these democracies are insufficient, and stand in need of provocation and critique. But this brings us to another type of democratic autoimmunity, one perhaps predicated on an altogether different understanding of the concept of life. This 'expression of autoimmunity' (*Rogues*, p. 87) is the right to interminable self-critique. Fundamental to the concept of democracy is the 'right' to publicly criticise any and all aspects of the system. This 'right' is autoimmunitary in the sense that it is both the fulfilment of the promise and the threat of death to democracy. It is on the basis of this right to interminable critique that democracy understands itself as infinitely perfectible; at the same time, however, the allowance of this unconditional criticism opens democracy to the threat of its own undoing, in that nothing in principle is protected from this right to criticism, including the constitutions and the laws of the system, and even the founding principles of democracy itself. See also **aporia** and **justice**.

For further reading, see *Who's Afraid of Philosophy?*; *Eyes of the University*; *Rogues*; 'The Force of Law'; *Specters of Marx*.

Forgiveness

Derrida's analysis of 'forgiveness' employs both the deconstruction of sovereignty, and the structure of the **aporia**. 'Forgiveness', he claims, is an ethical concept rooted in the Abrahamic tradition, and as such it requires a bit of reformulation from the way in which we typically think of forgiveness. That it is an 'ethical' concept entails that it has essentially to do with the face-to-face relation, and specifically between the offender and the offended, the guilty and the victim; no *state* and no *third party*, in other words, would have the *right* to grant forgiveness – only human beings can. In addition, that 'forgiveness' is an ethical concept entails that it is *not* an 'economic' concept. By 'economic', we mean that 'forgiveness' must not be bound up with the notion of 'exchange', as it very often is. 'Forgiveness' is often understood as a balancing of the scales, as when we might say that a person who has served time in jail has now been 'forgiven' by society; he has *paid* his debt, and so is now *worthy* of a second chance. But if his *crime* has resulted in a *debt* which he has now *paid*, this is not an 'ethical' event at all, but rather, an economic one – the scales were thrown out of balance and now he, through his incarceration, has righted them. Likewise, we might demand, as a condition of our 'forgiveness', the repentance of the other. This too is an economic notion, a *quid pro quo* that distorts the 'pure' notion of 'forgiveness'. It is to say, *if* you will change, *then* I will 'grant' you forgiveness. Moreover, inasmuch as it demands that the person *become* something *other* than the person who committed the transgression, the forgiver is not forgiving the transgression (or the transgressor) at all. Pure forgiveness, therefore, must be unconditional (because any condition establishes an economy of exchange).

But furthermore, this 'non-exchangeability' factor must be completely 'pure' itself in order for forgiveness to be pure. If the act itself is understood to be essentially 'forgivable' in the first place, then it is believed to be the sort of thing that can be rectified. If it is 'forgivable', it can be made *right* somehow – the balance of justice can be re-established; but this again institutes at least the structure of an economic concept, because if it contains the possibility of being made *right*, it does not require forgiveness in the first place. Therefore, if the act is forgivable, 'forgiveness' does not apply. The only cases in which forgiveness, strictly speaking, applies are cases in which the act is 'unforgivable'. But of course, if the act is unforgivable, it cannot be forgiven.

Moreover, let us come back for a moment to the notion of 'third-party forgiveness', which as we saw, Derrida claims is impossible. Only the violated individual has the right to grant forgiveness to the offender. Yet this implies also that a 'survivor', strictly speaking, cannot grant forgiveness to the offender, if the person whom the offender wronged is now dead. The 'victim', strictly speaking, cannot engage in the face-to-face in order to grant the forgiveness. But then, if we follow this logic a bit further, any time a human being has been the victim of an unforgivable act, even if his or her *body* survives, there is a very real sense in which that person, the person who was violated, is now *dead*. His or her body may still exist, but the person him- or herself, who underwent the trauma, is now gone, and a different person is in his or her place. Hence there is a very real sense in which, though forgiveness cannot be granted by a third party, it must *always* be granted by a third party; *only* a third party can forgive.

Finally, the concept of forgiveness is often conceived in terms of 'power', as though it were a 'token' or a coin that a human sovereign (the victim) has the 'right' to give. This is rooted in a traditional understanding of the concept of 'sovereignty' as the right of exception. The 'force of law' resides precisely in the fact that the sovereign can, at *will*, suspend the law; this power lies in the fact that he can grant clemency to whomever he chooses under any circumstances whatsoever. The sovereign, in other words, has the 'power' over the 'guilty' party, such that it is in his or her 'power' to, if he or she *wills*, grant clemency to the condemned. This right exists in virtually all juridical structures. The sovereign's right to grant clemency is rooted in his or her own power over the condemned. Hence while it is an act of 'forgiveness', it is a forgiveness that is structurally violent. It first 'asserts' the power that it holds over the other, and then, by an act of 'will', relinquishes this power. A very similar thing happens in many cases where what we call 'forgiveness' is at work. Our act of forgiveness, rooted in a concept of sovereignty transferred from the state to the individual, is in fact an expression of our 'power'. We believe that we have power over the other, that they are now at our mercy, and through our own 'power' and 'will' we grant them clemency. Forgiveness, as it is often misconstrued in other words, rests upon a *human possibility*, an 'I can' rooted in the self-sovereignty of the individual. Derrida, however, claims that pure forgiveness cannot rest upon a violence of this sort. It must be an unconditional forgiveness, rooted not in the notion of 'sovereignty', not in the form of a top-down 'power' that one exercises over another, but rather upon a fundamental experience of weakness or powerlessness. This kind of forgiveness, pure forgiveness, Derrida argues is both necessary and impossible. See also **aporia**.

For further reading, see *On Cosmopolitanism and Forgiveness*.

Gift

The **aporia** of the gift operates very similarly to that of **forgiveness**, employing in like manner the deconstruction of sovereignty. In order to truly be a 'gift', the gift cannot be part of an economic or self-motivated strategy, which is to say, it cannot involve calculability or exchange. In a very basic sense and on the most fundamental levels, we *know* this to be the case. For instance, even in the most mundane form, when a giver gives a gift only in order to procure some benefit for him- or herself, we recognise without hesitation that the giving of this gift, and hence the gift itself, is impure insofar as it is bound up inextricably with whatever it was that the giver sought to obtain *for him- or herself*. But when we push this logic to its limit, as Derrida does, it becomes evident that the pure gift, as such, is a structural impossibility.

For instance, we have said that in order for the gift to be pure, it must be given with no expectation on the part of the giver for anything in return. But this constraint would apply in addition to any desired sign of gratitude on the part of the recipient. Something as simple as a 'thank you' would be a return on the part of the recipient that would contaminate the purity of the gift. This is especially the case if the giver were to give the gift *so that* he or she would get a 'thank you'. But on an even deeper structural level, in order for the gift to be pure, the recipient must not be or feel in any sense 'provoked' to return the favour. In other words, if the giving of the gift creates in any sense in the recipient the desire to 'pay it back', then it has called the recipient into an economic relation, which distorts the purity of the gift. Yet the recognition of having received a gift cannot *but* inspire the desire to show one's gratitude. Therefore, in order for the gift to be pure, the recipient must not know that the gift has been given. The gift must be given *in secret*.

This secrecy, however, must extend also to the giver, and not just on the part of the recipient, but on the part of the giver him- or herself as well. In other words, the act of giving must also be kept secret from the giver; the giver cannot recognise that he or she has given a gift. If there is recognition on the part of the giver of having given a gift, of having done something good, then this recognition itself becomes a 'benefit gained', and the gift as such is cancelled. In St Matthew's gospel, Jesus says to the crowd, 'When you give to the poor, do not let your left hand know what your right hand is doing, so that your giving will be in secret.'[3] This is very close to the sense that Derrida intends.

The pure gift, therefore, the gift as such, is one that is not recognised as having been received on the part of the recipient, or as having been given on the part of the giver. But this makes the pure gift a structural impossibility. However, in keeping with the structure of the aporia, the gift is possible in and as the experience of the impossibility of the gift. See also **aporia**.

For further reading, see also *The Gift of Death Second Edition & Literature in Secret*; *Given Time: I. Counterfeit Money*; *Mémoires: for Paul de Man*; Caputo and Scanlon, *God, the Gift, and Postmodernism*.

Hospitality

Hospitality is perhaps one of the most significant ethical concepts from Derrida's later works. It is interesting because it not only involves the structure of **aporia**, but it also includes elements of both infinite deferral and the deconstruction of sovereignty. Hospitality, in a very broad sense, is an ethical concept that means the welcoming of the other into what is *mine*. But, Derrida claims, hospitality is *not* just 'one' ethical concept among others. Echoing Heidegger's 'Letter on Humanism', Derrida will point to the etymological note that the Greek word *ethos* (from whence we derive the word 'ethics') is connected with the concept of 'home' or 'familiar place of dwelling'. In other words, to speak of 'ethics' at all, Derrida claims, is to speak of one's welcoming of the other into one's own familiar place of dwelling. Ethics, in other words, *is* hospitality. Moreover, hospitality is a value with very deep roots throughout the entirety of Western culture. The Judeo-Christian story of Lot and his family is mirrored in the story of Baucis and Philemon in the Greco-Roman canon. As Derrida says, 'Hospitality is culture itself and not simply one ethic amongst others' (*On Cosmopolitanism and Forgiveness*, p. 16). Let us therefore analyse this concept a bit further.

To exercise hospitality, I must welcome the other into my home (in whatever sense I understand this term 'home'). This welcoming is something that I as host must 'grant' to the other, in order that he or she may be permitted to enter into my home. But note, the foreigner is entering into *my* home; that is to say, the home remains *mine*. It is my 'property', and I am its master. And in order to exercise hospitality, I must remain the master of the house, because if I do not remain master of the house, I can no longer demonstrate hospitality, since the house is no longer mine. I must therefore decide who can enter, and when, and under what conditions.

But, as we said, hospitality is the welcoming of the other into what is mine. And in order for this hospitality to be pure, it must be unconditional. To say, *I will welcome you if* . . . is to place limits on the hospitality, in two senses. First, it places *a priori* limits on the *otherness* of the other. That is to say, it allows the other in, so long as he or she is not *drastically* other, so long as there is sufficient identity and conformity of the other to my 'expectations'. It is therefore not the 'otherness' of the other, but rather, the 'sameness' of the other, that would be welcomed on this view. Second, insofar as this otherness is limited, the welcoming itself is also limited. It says, *I can only welcome so much, and no more.* True hospitality, therefore, must operate in the absence of any and all horizon of expectations; pure hospitality would be an infinite openness (here we might even say, 'deferral') to that which is *to-come* (the *à venir*), whatever, whoever, and in whatever circumstances it may come.

We can therefore already anticipate the next step in the analysis. Above, we said that the home must remain 'mine', my 'property'. But it is precisely for this reason that the welcoming and the otherness in our 'impure' hospitality were limited as they were. We place limits on what we will tolerate into our home, precisely so that we can maintain power over our home, and in order to maintain power over our home, we must maintain power over the other who is *in* our home. To relinquish this power therefore (as we have just suggested is necessary for hospitality as such), is to also relinquish the power of one's own sovereignty, which is to say, one's own mastery over what is his or her 'property'. This pure notion of 'hospitality' therefore would be one without an operative notion of 'sovereignty'. Hospitality would not, that is, derive from the 'I can' of a sovereign, as in 'I can grant you . . .'. It would be wholly unconditional, welcoming to the other, and first and foremost, to the other whose coming cannot be foreseen. We can therefore see that pure hospitality would carry with it a tremendous degree of risk. Indeed, Derrida will note that the *de facto* institution of a pure form of hospitality would be 'irresponsible'. He writes:

It is a question of knowing how to transform and improve the law, and of knowing if this improvement is possible within a historical space which takes place *between* the Law of an unconditional hospitality, offered *a priori* to every other, to all newcomers, *whoever they may be*, and *the* conditional laws of a right to hospitality, without which *The* unconditional law of hospitality would be in danger of remaining a pious and irresponsible desire, without form and without potency, and of even being perverted at any moment. (*On Cosmopolitanism and Forgiveness*, p. 23)

As with the other modes of **aporia**, the concept of hospitality must operate in the experience of the impossibility of pure hospitality. In other words, it *must* establish laws and limits, but it should always do so with an eye towards a pure form of hospitality. *Because* hospitality is impossible, it must be pursued. The moment we think that we have established hospitality, we have by definition lost it. This is how the **aporia** operates. See also **aporia.**

For further reading, see *On Cosmopolitanism and Forgiveness*; *Of Hospitality*; 'Hostipitality'.

Justice
Justice is a concept that, with the 1989 essay, 'The Force of Law: The "Mystical Foundation of Authority"', begins to take centre stage in Derrida's thinking. The establishment of the law, Derrida argues, any law or system of laws, takes place upon a fundamental groundlessness. That is to say, insofar as it is the founding moment or foundational, institutive act, the establishment of the system of law cannot itself be preceded by anything that would ultimately justify its foundation. The establishment of the law always takes place, and necessarily so, beyond the law. Law, therefore, is always a 'construction', which means that law is always 'deconstructible'. But as Derrida notes, this is not a bad thing at all. The fact that the law is always deconstructible entails that we can always continue to pursue political and juridical progress. As a matter of fact, that the law is infinitely deconstructible demands that we must do so. This pursuit, now cast in Derrida's writings as the very operation of deconstruction itself, is required in the name of justice, which, Derrida notes, is not itself deconstructible. Deconstruction is now to be enacted in the name of a justice that is not itself deconstructible. This reveals something quite interesting about the aporetic structure generally, inasmuch as this same logic would apply to all the other aporetic concepts that we have discussed herein (**gift**, **hospitality**, **forgiveness** and **responsibility**). These aporetic concepts themselves now serve in Derrida's thinking as the possibility or the condition of deconstruction itself. They themselves are not deconstructible, but every decision ever made in their name will always be deconstructible. There is a sense in which, therefore, just as Derrida says, *'Deconstruction is justice'* ('*The*

Force of Law', p. 243), we can just as easily echo, 'deconstruction is the gift', 'deconstruction is hospitality', 'deconstruction is forgiveness' and 'deconstruction is responsibility'. Whenever and wherever a decision is made in the name of hospitality, for instance, deconstruction must inter-vene, knowing that hospitality 'as such' is not possible, and must always be relentlessly pursued. This aporetic, structural impossibility therefore becomes the condition of deconstruction. This is what Derrida means when he says that 'Deconstruction is possible as an experience of the impossible' (*'The Force of Law'*, p. 243).

Derrida organises the analysis of justice around three **aporias**, which seem to follow logically from one another. The first is the '*Epochē* of the Rule'. This **aporia** functions similarly to that of **responsibility**. In order for a decision to be 'just', we think, it must conform to a 'rule' or to a 'law'. But if this is all that the decision does, that is, if it merely follows a prescribed law, then this decision may be 'legal' inasmuch as it accords with the law, but it is not 'just', which is to say it is not a decision based upon or in pursuit of justice. History has given us no shortage of laws or systems of law that were later deemed fundamentally unjust, so the according with the law is not itself an indication of justice, and the mere thoughtless application of the law would in fact abnegate the moment of decision. Moreover, it would not be possible, strictly speaking, to merely apply the law in a way that would truly be just; laws are of their very nature general and universal, while each case is unique and singular. A judge, for instance, does not and must not merely 'apply' the law; yet the judge must no doubt refer to the law, as no one would consider a judge to be 'just' who did not at least in some sense calculate his or her decision with reference to the law. The judge must therefore interpret the various singular elements of the case and on their basis, make a decision. But in making a decision, the judge reinstitutes the law in each application. But to reinstitute the law requires that we first suspend it; hence this reinstitu-tion will always be a repetition of the foundational act of violence that gave rise to the system of law in the first place.

The second **aporia** is what he calls the 'Haunting of the Undecidable'. The decision of justice begins, as Derrida notes, in the attempt to read, interpret, understand and even to calculate the meaning of the law. But this 'decision' itself, which would render calculation necessary to the execution of the law, would not itself be calculable; and in order to be a true 'decision', it must recognise this fact. Every decision must pass through the experience of undecidability, in the awareness that there is nothing calculable or predictable which would in advance necessitate this or that particular decision, inasmuch as the universality and generality of the law does not and cannot perfectly 'fit' the particulars of this singular case. Undecidability, Derrida claims, is not merely an oscillation between two would-be decisions, but rather the experience of the impossible decision, which is to say the incalculability of the decision itself, coupled with the necessary duty to make a decision, and one that takes into account the law. But once this decision has been 'made' and executed, then a rule has been applied. But as we have noted, a decision that follows from the application of a rule is not strictly speaking a decision, and is hence certainly not strictly speaking 'just'. The undecidability that conditioned the decision continues to haunt the decision itself like a ghost, such that there is no point in time at which we can truly say, 'this decision was just'. To echo here the language of *Voice and Phenomenon*, the presence of justice is infinitely deferred. But this brings us to the next point, because Derrida will want to keep the notion of 'justice' disentangled from the 'Idea' in the Kantian sense, which would function as a 'regulative Idea'. This brings us to the third **aporia** of justice.

Derrida titles the third **aporia** the 'Urgency that Obstructs the Horizon of Knowledge'. It is important to note the meaning of this term 'horizon'. A horizon would be, Derrida claims, the opening and the limit against which one's progress would be defined. It is the opening in the sense that it orients the direction in which the pursuer would move; and it is the limit in that it is believed that one will at last arrive at the horizon. So on the one hand, the passage towards the horizon would be one that would resign itself to the realisation that the horizon is not and cannot be, perhaps even must not be, here, now. On the other hand, the presupposition is that one will finally make it to the horizon, at which point the horizon would be fully present in the time and space of the subject. Justice, for Derrida, can never function in this way. On the one hand, even if the 'presence' of justice is, as we have said, infinitely deferred; nevertheless, the demand for justice, the call to justice, is always immediately present; hence the 'urgency'. We cannot 'wait' for justice because the demand for justice itself does not wait. On the other hand, even if we had all the time in the world, even if we were given the full 'presence' of all the knowledge of the law and its conditions, it would nevertheless remain the case that this particular moment and this particular decision stands outside the generality of those conditions and those laws; and hence when the decision would be made, it would be an application which would be deconstructible, essentially and necessarily. Therefore, justice, unlike the horizon, can never be 'present'. See also **aporia**, **responsibility** and **democracy to come**.

For further reading, see 'The Force of Law: The "Mystical Foundation of Authority"'; *Specters of Marx*.

Responsibility

The **aporia** of responsibility derives from the fact that the concept of 'responsibility' contains two irreconcilable demands: (1) the demand for the dissolution of the individual into the ethical community; (2) the demand for the absolute singularity of the individual. This opposition emerges in the course of Derrida's engagement with Kierkegaard's interpretation of the story of Abraham's sacrifice. More specifically, according to the story, as Abraham and Isaac approach the site where the sacrifice is to take place, Isaac questions Abraham as to the whereabouts of the sacrificial lamb, to which Abraham replies, 'God will provide a lamb for the burnt offering.'[4] This, Derrida says, is tantamount to Abraham's *not speaking*. Abraham responds by not responding. Insofar as he does not disclose to Isaac the secret between him and God, Abraham does not speak. Nor has he communicated his intentions to his wife Sarah. He bears in an absolutely solitary manner the burden of his own responsibility. Let us look at this further.

When we say, 'be responsible', what we often mean is that there are certain accepted societal or cultural norms or mores, accepted ethical codes, that the individual object of our scorn is defying, and which, as a member of that ethical community, he or she ought not to defy. By saying, 'be responsible', therefore, what we are saying is that the individual to whom we speak needs to reflect seriously as to what those norms and mores *are*, and then make every effort to follow them to the letter. This is one sense in which we speak of 'responsibility', the admonition to conform to the ethical community. Now, if Abraham had answered Isaac with the truth that was in his heart (though, to be sure, Abraham does not *lie* to Isaac either), if he attempted to *explain* the nature of his responsibility, it would be in order ultimately to attempt to persuade Isaac – who in this case *is* the ethical community, as he and Abraham are the only two parties around – of the rightness of Abraham's actions. It would be, in other words, to attempt to win Isaac over to the realisation that Abraham *must* do what he is about to do, thereby reconciling Abraham back into the ethical community. But to the extent that Abraham would speak in this manner, he would thereby divest himself of the full burden of his decision. In this sense, the effort to be 'responsible' in fact collapses into irresponsibility. By attempting to 'be responsible' in dissolving ourselves into the ethical community, we in fact *relinquish* the responsibility for our decisions.

Conversely, when we say, 'be responsible', we sometimes also mean, 'stand by your decisions, as your own'. In other words, and against the previous understanding of responsibility, to say, 'be responsible', also entails that one *not* be reassimilated back into the generality of the ethical community, that one be absolutely unique and singular. This will be the model of 'pure' responsibility for Derrida, pure in that it bears absolutely the weight of its own decisions, and makes no effort to ameliorate its gravity by attempting to 'justify' itself to the demands of the general. In the face of the 'reason' of the ethical community, responsibility of this sort, insofar as it does not seek reassimilation, can appear only as a madness. See also **aporia**.

For further reading, see *The Gift of Death Second Edition & Literature in Secret*; *Aporias*; 'The Force of Law: The "Mystical Foundation of Authority"'.

Notes

1. Arthur Bradley makes a very similar point to the one I am here making. See Arthur Bradley, *Derrida's* Of Grammatology: *An Edinburgh Philosophical Guide* (Edinburgh: Edinburgh University Press, 2008), p. 145.
2. In writing this section, the following sources have been consulted: Leonard Lawlor, 'Jacques Derrida', *The Stanford Encyclopedia of Philosophy*, Fall 2011 edn, Edward N. Zalta (ed.), <http://plato.stanford.edu/archives/fall2011/entries/derrida/> (last accessed 27 November 2013); Jack Reynolds, 'Jacques Derrida', *Internet Encyclopedia of Philosophy*, James Fieser and Bradley Dowden (eds), <http://www.iep.utm.edu/derrida/> (last accessed 27 November 2013).
3. Matthew 6: 3.
4. Genesis 22: 8.

Bibliography

Works by Derrida

Derrida, Jacques. *Acts of Religion*. Ed. Gil Anidjar. New York: Routledge, 2002.

—. *The Animal that therefore I Am*. Ed. Marie-Louise Mallet. Trans. David Wills. New York: Fordham University Press, 2008.

—. *Aporias*. Ed. Werner Hamacher and David E. Wellbery. Trans. Thomas Dutoit. Stanford: Stanford University Press, 1993.

—. *The Beast and the Sovereign, Volume I (The Seminars of Jacques Derrida)*. Trans. Geoffrey Bennington. Chicago: The University of Chicago Press, 2009.

—. *The Beast and the Sovereign, Volume II (The Seminars of Jacques Derrida)*. Trans. Geoffrey Bennington. Chicago: The University of Chicago Press, 2011.

—. 'Différance'. In *Margins of Philosophy*.

—. *Dissemination*. Trans. Barbara Johnson. Chicago: The University of Chicago Press, 1981.

—. *Edmund Husserl's Origin of Geometry: An Introduction*. Lincoln, NE: University of Nebraska Press, 1989.

—. *Eyes of the University: Right to Philosophy 2*. Trans. Jan Plug and Others. Stanford: Stanford University Press, 2004.

—. 'The Force of Law: The "Mystical Foundation of Authority" '. Trans. Mary Quaintance. In ed. Gil Anidjar. *Acts of Religion*.

—. *The Gift of Death Second Edition & Literature in Secret*. Trans. David Wills. Chicago: The University of Chicago Press, 2007.

—. *Given Time: I. Counterfeit Money*. Trans. Peggy Kamuf. Chicago: The University of Chicago Press, 1994.

—. *Glas*. Trans. John P. Leavey, Jr. and Richard Rand. Lincoln, NE: University of Nebraska Press, 1986.

—. *De la Grammatologie*. Paris: Éditions de Minuit, 1967.

—. '*Honoris Causa*: This Is Also Extremely Funny'. In ed. Elisabeth Weber. *Points: Interviews 1974–1994*.

—. 'Hostipitality'. In ed. Gil Anidjar. *Acts of Religion.*

—. *Limited Inc.* Trans. Samuel Weber. Evanston: Northwestern University Press, 1988.

—. *Margins of Philosophy.* Trans. Alan Bass. Chicago: The University of Chicago Press, 1982.

—. *Mémoires: for Paul de Man.* Trans. Cecile Lindsay, Jonathan Culler, and Eduardo Cadava. New York: Columbia University Press, 1986.

—. *Of Grammatology.* Trans. Gayatri Chakravorty Spivak. Baltimore and London: The Johns Hopkins University Press, 1974.

—. *Of Hospitality: Anne Dufourmantelle Invites Jacques Derrida to Respond.* Trans. Rachel Bowlby. Stanford: Stanford University Press, 2000.

—. *Of Spirit: Heidegger and the Question.* Trans. Geoffrey Bennington and Rachel Bowlby. Chicago: The University of Chicago Press, 1989.

—. *On Cosmopolitanism and Forgiveness.* Trans. Mark Dooley and Michael Hughes. London and New York: Routledge, 2001.

—. 'La phenomenology et la clôture de la métaphysique'. *ΕΠΟΧΕΣ*. Athens. February 1966.

—. *Points: Interviews 1974–1994.* Ed. Elisabeth Weber. Trans. Peggy Kamuf and Others. Stanford: Stanford University Press, 1995.

—. *The Politics of Friendship.* Trans. George Collins. New York: Verso, 2006.

—. *Positions.* Trans. Alan Bass. Chicago: The University of Chicago Press, 1981.

—. *The Post Card from Socrates to Freud and Beyond.* Trans. Alan Bass. Chicago: The University of Chicago Press, 1987.

—. *The Problem of Genesis in Husserl's Philosophy.* Trans. Marian Hobson. Chicago: The University of Chicago Press, 2003.

—. *Psyche: Inventions of the Other, Volume II.* Ed. Peggy Kamuf and Elizabeth Rottenberg. Stanford: Stanford University Press, 2008.

—. *Rogues: Two Essays on Reason.* Trans. Pascale-Anne Brault and Michael Naas. Stanford: Stanford University Press, 2005.

—. *Specters of Marx: The State of the Debt, the Work of Mourning, and the New International.* Trans. Peggy Kamuf. London: Routledge, 1994.

—. *Speech and Phenomena, and Other Essays on Husserl's Theory of Signs.* Trans. David B. Allison. Evanston: Northwestern University Press, 1973.

—. *Voice and Phenomenon.* Trans. Leonard Lawlor. Evanston: Northwestern University Press, 2011.

—. *La Voix et le phénomène.* Paris: Presses Universitaires de France, 2003 [1967].

—. *The Work of Mourning.* Ed. Pascale-Anne Brault and Michael Naas. Chicago: The University of Chicago Press, 2001.

240   Derrida's *Voice and Phenomenon*

—. *Who's Afraid of Philosophy?: Right to Philosophy 1.* Trans. Jan Plug. Stanford:
Stanford University Press, 2002.
—. *Writing and Difference.* Trans. Alan Bass. Chicago: The University of Chicago
Press, 1978.

Works by Husserl

Husserl, Edmund. *Cartesian Meditations: An Introduction to Phenomenology.* Trans.
Dorion Cairns. Dordrecht, Boston and London: Kluwer Academic
Publishers, 1999.
—. *The Crisis of European Sciences and Transcendental Phenomenology: An Introduction
to Phenomenological Philosophy.* Trans. David Carr. Evanston: Northwestern
University Press, 1970.
—. *Ideas Pertaining to a Pure Phenomenology and to a Phenomenological Philosophy, First
Book.* Trans. F. Kersten. Dordrecht, Boston and London: Kluwer Academic
Publishers, 1998.
—. *Logical Investigations, Volume I.* Trans. J. N. Findlay. With a new preface by
Michael Dummet, and edited with a new introduction by Dermot Moran.
London: Routledge Taylor and Francis, 2001.
—. *On the Phenomenology of the Consciousness of Internal Time (1893–1917).* Trans.
John Barnett Brough. Dordrecht, Boston and London: Kluwer Academic
Publishers, 1991.
—. *Phenomenology and the Crisis of Philosophy.* Trans. Quentin Lauer. New York:
Harper and Row, 1965.
—. *Philosophy of Arithmetic: Psychological and Logical Investigations with Supplementary
Texts from 1887–1901.* Trans. Dallas Willard. Dordrecht: Kluwer Academic
Publishers, 2003.

Other Works Cited

Aristotle. *Complete Works of Aristotle: The Revised Oxford Translation, Vol. 1.* Ed.
Jonathan Barnes. Princeton: Princeton University Press, 1984.
—. *Complete Works of Aristotle: The Revised Oxford Translation, Vol. 2.* Ed. Jonathan
Barnes. Princeton: Princeton University Press, 1984.
Boyer, Carl B., Rev. Merzbach, Uta C.. *A History of Mathematics,* 2nd edn. New
York: John Wiley and Sons, 1991.
Bradley, Arthur. *Derrida's* Of Grammatology: *An Edinburgh Philosophical Guide.*
Edinburgh: Edinburgh University Press, 2008.
Caputo, John D. *The Prayers and Tears of Jacques Derrida: Religion Without*

Religion. Bloomington and Indianapolis: Indiana University Press, 1997.

Caputo, John D., and Michael J. Scanlon, eds. *God, the Gift, and Postmodernism*. Bloomington: Indiana University Press, 1999.

de Beauvoir, Simone. *The Prime of Life*. Trans. Peter Green. New York: World Publishing, 1962.

Descombes, Vincent. *Modern French Philosophy*. Trans. L. Scott-Fox and J. M. Harding. Cambridge: Cambridge University Press, 1980.

Deutscher, Penelope. *How to Read Derrida*. New York: Norton, 2006.

Eves, Howard. *Foundations and Fundamental Concepts of Mathematics*, 3rd edn. Mineola, NY: Dover Publications, 1990.

Foucault, Michel. 'Introduction'. In Georges Canguilhem. *The Normal and the Pathological*. New York: Zone Books, 1991.

Frege, Gottlob. *The Foundations of Arithmetic: A Logico-Mathematical Enquiry into the Concept of Number*. Trans. J. L. Austin, M.A. Evanston: Northwestern University Press, 1950.

—. 'On *Sinn* and *Bedeutung*'. Trans. Max Black. In ed. Michael Beaney. *The Frege Reader*. Malden, MA: Blackwell Publishing, 1997.

Glendinning, Simon. *Derrida: A Very Short Introduction*. Oxford: Oxford University Press, 2011.

Gutting, Gary. *French Philosophy in the Twentieth Century*. Cambridge: Cambridge University Press, 2001.

—. *Thinking the Impossible: French Philosophy Since 1960*. Oxford: Oxford University Press, 2011.

Hegel, G. W. F. *Phenomenology of Spirit*. Trans. A. V. Miller. Oxford: Oxford University Press, 1977.

Heidegger, Martin. *Being and Time*. Trans. John Macquarrie and Edward Robinson. New York: Harper and Row, Publishers, Inc., 1962.

—. *Kant and the Problem of Metaphysics*. Trans. Richard Taft. Bloomington and Indianapolis: Indiana University Press, 1990.

—. *Pathmarks*. Ed. William McNeill. Cambridge: Cambridge University Press, 1998.

Hill, Claire Ortiz, and Haddock, Guillermo E. Rosado. *Husserl or Frege?: Meaning, Objectivity, and Mathematics*. Chicago: Open Court, 2000.

Kant, Immanuel. *Critique of Pure Reason*. Trans. Paul Guyer and Allen W. Wood. Cambridge: Cambridge University Press, 1998.

Kates, Joshua. *Essential History: Jacques Derrida and the Development of Deconstruction*. Evanston: Northwestern University Press, 2005.

Kierkegaard, Søren. *The Concept of Anxiety*. Ed. and trans. Reidar Thomte in collaboration with Albert B. Anderson. *Kierkegaard's Writings, Vol. VIII.* Princeton: Princeton University Press, 1980.

—. *Fear and Trembling.* Ed. and trans. Howard V. Hong and Edna H. Hong. *Kierkegaard's Writings, Volume VI.* Princeton: Princeton University Press, 1983.

Lawlor, Leonard. *Derrida and Husserl: The Basic Problem of Phenomenology.* Bloomington and Indianapolis: Indiana University Press, 2002.

—. *Early Twentieth-Century Continental Philosophy.* Bloomington: Indiana University Press, 2012.

—. 'Jacques Derrida', *The Stanford Encyclopedia of Philosophy*, Fall 2011edn. Ed. Edward N. Zalta. <http://plato.stanford.edu/archives/fall2011/entries/derrida/> (last accessed 27 November 2013).

—. *Thinking Through French Philosophy: The Being of the Question.* Bloomington and Indianapolis: Indiana University Press, 2003.

—. 'Translator's Introduction: The Germinal Structure of Derrida's Thought', in Jacques Derrida. *Voice and Phenomenon.*

Leiter, Brian. *Brian Leiter on Nietzsche Myths.* <http://philosophybites.com/2009/09/brian-leiter-on-nietzsche-myths.html> (last accessed 27 November 2013).

Levinas, Emmanuel. 'Sur les "Ideen" de M. E. Husserl'. *Revue philosophique de la France et de l'étranger*, CVII (1929), 54th year, no. 3–4, March–April, pp. 230–65 .

—. 'Martin Heidegger et l'ontologie'. *Revue philosophique de la France et de l'étranger*, 113 (1932), pp. 395–431.

—. *Totality and Infinity: An Essay on Exteriority.* Pittsburgh: Duquesne University Press, 1969.

Lévi-Strauss, Claude. *The Savage Mind.* Chicago: The University of Chicago Press, 1966.

Macksey, Richard, and Eugenio Domato, eds. *The Structuralist Controversy: The Languages of Criticism and the Sciences of Man.* Baltimore: The Johns Hopkins University Press, 1970.

Marrati, Paola. *Genesis and Trace: Derrida Reading Husserl and Heidegger.* Stanford: Stanford University Press, 2005.

Moran, Dermot. *Introduction to Phenomenology.* London: Routledge, 2000.

Moran, Dermot, and Tim Mooney, eds. *The Phenomenology Reader.* London: Routledge, 2002.

Nietzsche, Friedrich. *Basic Writings of Nietzsche.* Ed. and trans. Walter Kaufmann. New York: Modern Library, 1966.

—. *The Gay Science, With a Prelude in Rhymes and an Appendix of Songs.* Trans. Walter Kaufmann. New York: Vintage, 1974.

—. *On the Genealogy of Morality*. Trans. Maudemarie Clark and Alan J. Swenson. Indianapolis and Cambridge: Hackett Publishing Company, Inc., 1998.

Peeters, Benoît. *Derrida*. Trans. Andrew Brown. Cambridge: Polity, 2012.

Plato. *Complete Works*. Ed. John M. Cooper. Associate Ed. D.S. Hutchinson. Indianapolis: Hackett Publishing Company, 1997.

Powell, Jason. *Jacques Derrida: A Biography*. London and New York: Continuum, 2006.

Preus, Anthony. *Historical Dictionary of Ancient Greek Philosophy*. Lanham: Scarecrow Press, 2007.

Reynolds, Jack. 'Jacques Derrida'. *Internet Encyclopedia of Philosophy*. Ed. James Fieser and Bradley Dowden. <http://www.iep.utm.edu/derrida/> (last accessed 27 November 2013).

Sartre, Jean-Paul. *Existentialism and Human Emotions*. Trans. Bernard Frechtman. New York: Philosophical Library, 1957.

Saussure, Ferdinand de. *Course in General Linguistics*. Ed. Charles Bally and Albert Sechehaye, with the collaboration of Albert Riedlinger, trans. Roy Harris. La Salle: Open Court Press, 1972.

Schrift, Alan D. *Twentieth-Century French Philosophy: Key Themes and Thinkers*. Malden, MA: Blackwell Publishing, 2006.

Searle, John. *Mind, Language, and Society: Philosophy in the Real World*. New York: Basic Books, 1998.

Sokolowski, Robert. *Introduction to Phenomenology*. Cambridge: Cambridge University Press, 2000.

Wilder, Raymond. *Introduction to the Foundations of Mathematics*. New York: John Wiley and Sons, 1952.

Willard, Dallas. 'Translator's Introduction'. In Edmund Husserl. *Philosophy of Arithmetic: Psychological and Logical Investigations with Supplementary Texts from 1887–1901*.

Zahavi, Dan. *Husserl's Phenomenology*. Stanford: Stanford University Press, 2003.

Index

Image, 23, 49–50, 104–5, 119–20, 148, 151, 168, 223
  Imagination, 29, 59, 103–5, 108, 118–21, 123
Immanence, 26, 53–4n
Immediate, 31, 37, 93–5, 98–9, 101, 117, 122, 125, 129, 153, 177, 223
Imperative, 226
Impossibility, 42, 110, 158, 164, 188, 210, 225, 227, 230–1, 233–4
Impression, 31–2, 62–3, 116, 124–5, 127, 129–30, 134–5, 157, 160, 169, 184, 189, 210, 212, 214, 217
Impurity, 100, 157
Incarnation, 156
Indefinite, 190, 197
Indication, 12, 26–9, 59, 72–9, 81–8, 91–6, 99–103, 105, 107–8, 111, 120, 122, 137–8, 140–6, 155, 158, 164–5, 169–70, 185, 187–9, 211, 214, 216, 234
Infinite, 8–9, 30, 33, 62, 69–71, 109, 174, 183, 185, 189–93, 196, 221, 225, 231–2
Infinity, 10, 52, 62, 70, 114, 183–5, 192
Insecurity, 46, 126, 199
Inside, 7, 39, 63, 77, 78, 89–90, 114, 116, 126, 164, 169
Instance, 27, 30
Instant, 107–8, 111, 122–3, 124–5, 129, 132, 144, 191, 202n
Institution, 7–8, 232
Intention, 2–3, 28, 38–9, 57, 77, 81, 87–8, 92, 94–5, 97–101, 105, 107, 114, 117, 142, 145–6, 150, 153, 155–6, 164, 166–7, 171–5, 178–80, 186–7, 189, 191, 196, 201n, 209, 211, 236
  Intentionality, 45, 51, 54, 77, 79–80, 95, 106
Interiority, 73, 77, 90, 100, 103–4, 106, 118, 120, 122, 130, 139–40, 150–3, 159, 163–4, 210
Interpretation, 68, 91–2, 94, 96, 113, 144, 155, 200n–1n, 203n, 226, 236
Intersubjectivity, 36, 63, 97
Interval, 163

Intuition, 21, 23, 35, 39, 44, 47, 60, 61, 63, 68–9, 71, 97–9, 103, 116, 122, 144, 146, 149, 154, 156, 165–6, 170–5, 178–84, 189, 192–4, 199, 212
  Intuitionism, 47, 69, 166, 170
Invisible, 49, 144
Iterability, 207, 211–12, 216
Iteration, 152, 157, 184

Justice, 8–10, 224, 226–8, 233–6

Kant, Immanuel, 25, 46, 53n, 63, 69, 106, 160, 183, 185, 189–90, 192, 194, 200, 202n–4n, 222, 226, 235
Keep, 139
Kierkegaard, Søren, 9, 14n, 16–17, 46, 225, 236
Knowledge, 3, 24–5, 27, 35, 44, 48, 52–3n, 57, 59–61, 63, 69, 83, 86, 101, 107, 115, 121–2, 144, 146, 154, 156–7, 165, 171, 178, 181–2, 189, 191, 193, 195, 198–9, 204n, 211, 213, 215, 218–19, 235

Lacan, Jacques, 51
Lack, 1, 63, 74, 87, 99, 165, 167–8, 180–1, 216
Language, 2, 6, 11, 27, 40, 43–4, 48–50, 56n, 59–61, 66–70, 72, 75–7, 79–80, 84, 86–7, 90–4, 100–1, 108–12, 114, 118, 121, 123, 130–1, 139, 141–2, 148, 154–5, 159, 161, 166, 170, 172, 174, 180, 182–3, 185–7, 194, 198, 201n, 203n–4n, 207–8, 216, 221–3, 235
Leibniz, Gottfried, 62, 113
Lévi-Strauss, Claude, 50–1, 56n
Levinas, Emmanuel, 3, 10, 37, 44–5, 52, 55n–6n, 199, 218–19
Life, 3–4, 6, 8–9, 11, 13n–14n, 17, 20, 26, 40–4, 46, 51, 54n–5n, 59, 63–5, 69–72, 77, 80, 86, 90–1, 93–5, 97–101, 103–5, 108–9, 116–18, 120–4, 129–30, 138, 140–4, 151, 153, 156, 164, 179, 181, 184–7, 191–3, 197, 199, 211, 214, 220, 223–7